LAUGH IF YOU LIKE, AIN'T A DAMN THING FUNNY

LAUGH IF YOU LIKE, AIN'T A DAMN THING FUNNY

Based on the Life Story of Ralph "Petey" Greene As told to Lurma Rackley

Lurma Rackley

To order additional copies of this book, contact:
Xlibris Corporation
1-888-795-4274
www.Xlibris.com
Orders@Xlibris.com
21767

CONTENTS

ACKNOWLEDGEMENTS

I'D LIKE TO think that Petey and A'nt Pig were watching over me, pushing me along to complete this book for Petey; so I thank them and other angels in their family and mine, in Spirit. My mother, Gloria Blackwell, a retired English professor, edited the book more than once and encouraged me by telling me she cried over the ending each time, even though she knew what was coming. Chuck Ramsey believed in me and provided pictures he took over the years of his good friend Petey Greene. Petey's nephew Clayton LeBoeuf looked for a patron so we could get his uncle's story told. And a host of other family and friends didn't let me forget this project, asking me annually, "When is that book coming out?" I want to acknowledge the role Xlibris played, offering an affordable way to publish. Finally, this book is dedicated to my son, Rumal, and other young men of his generation who need to know that no obstacle is too great to overcome. Success is yours, if you believe in it.

Lurma Rackley

PROLOGUE

LAUGH IF YOU Like . . . is based on the life story of Ralph "Petey" Greene, a young man born with extraordinary promise and natural comic genius who spent years "clowning around" and spiraling to life's lowest depths. Then he conned, rhymed, "speechified" and laughed his way to heights he hardly dared imagine.

Though based on the actual antics and characters in the life of Petey Greene, *Laugh If You Like* . . . offers a prototype of the early years of many black men of Petey's generation throughout the United States—men raised by Southern grandmothers during the 1930s when racial segregation and poverty set the tone for their lives. What makes this story remarkable is the way Petey employs the indomitable spirit and the coping mechanisms his grandmother, A'nt Pig, passed on to him. Her unconventional wisdom colors his outlandish responses to the racial and economic oppression that constantly threatened to lock him away from recognition and accomplishment.

Because *Laugh If You Like* . . . is set in Washington, D.C., this story treats the reader to a rare glimpse of life in the nation's capital in the mid-1930s, from the other side of the tracks. In young Petey's world, television was yet to enter American homes, but radio linked the country with news of the Depression and, at the end of the decade, World War II.

Boys carrying shoe-shine boxes jumped on and off trolley cars clanging down Pennsylvania Avenue past Franklin Delano Roosevelt's White House and along other main routes, on dollar-a-week passes.

Young hustlers styled and profiled in their Big Apple caps, white shirts, pleated pants and two handkerchiefs in the back

pocket, up and down Seventh and T streets near the legendary
Howard Theatre at Sixth and Wiltberger, in the heart of D.C.'s
mecca for black business and entertainment.

The National Zoo, Rock Creek Park, acres of woodland where
the Kennedy Center now stands, and nearby barges anchored on
the Potomac's shore were the playgrounds for young adventurers
in search of snakes and dare-devil thrills.

In Petey's childhood, much of what is Washington's
Georgetown neighborhood of today—with its chic, high-priced
specialty shops and exclusive boutiques, its million-dollar homes
and high-rent carriage houses, its international wheeler-dealers at
the posh Four Seasons Hotel, its six-figure waterfront office space—
was where the city's poorest blacks lived in "rinky-dink run down
houses" just blocks away from wealthy whites.

Kerosene lamps gave light to homes with no electricity, and in
winter, cherry-red-hot pot-bellied stoves warmed front rooms.
People carried heated bricks up rickety stairs to chase the chill off
bed covers, or lit small coal-oil stoves to fight the icy air blasting
in past defenseless windows. In some backyards, fires blazed
beneath outdoor pumps to thaw icicles, then children filled
wooden buckets and "toted" water inside for washing and cooking.

It is in this black Georgetown of pigs and chickens and outdoor
toilets with wooden seats, of washer women and day laborers, of
numbers runners and bootleggers, of church-goers and hard
workers, where Petey Greene's childhood escapades and everlasting
bond with his grandmother form the basis of *Laugh If You Like,
Ain't a Damn Thing Funny*. Against this backdrop, Petey's most
hilarious and poignant tales come vividly alive.

Before his death of cancer in 1984, at the age of 53, Petey
Greene told me his life story in a series of taped interviews. Aside
from his own raucous behavior, the stories he tells about his family
and friends are often stranger than fiction.

Stories of his father, a brilliant but profane and violent man
who spent more time in prison than he did at home, and who
was locked away in Alcatraz when Petey sailed past as a serviceman
on his way to Japan and Korea.

Stories of his mother, who once killed a woman in self-defense, and was, therefore, the subject of articles in the Afro-American newspaper when Petey was in grade school.

Stories of a dapper, church-going grandfather who wore nylon boxer shorts, but had huge calluses on his hands from carrying hods of bricks on his job, at a time when black men were not allowed to work as bricklayers; they could only do the hauling.

And most especially, stories of an illiterate grandmother with an arsenal of home remedies who once cleared warts off Petey's face by washing his face in his own urine, then lathering him daily in tar soap.

Underlying the tears and hilarity, the pain and glory in all his stories is the adoration that exudes through Petey's accounts of his grandmother, Maggie Floyd, known to everyone as A'nt Pig. Arriving in Washington during the years when droves of women known as "Freedom Bags" fled the south in search of a better life, Maggie Floyd dedicated herself to making money every way she could— most often in creatively illegal ways that she shared with Petey.

"My grandmother smoked a pipe, chewed tobacco, wore big ol' shoes and a rag 'round her head, and never went to school. But she was the smartest person I've ever known," Petey says, before rattling off a litany of schemes and philosophies, folk remedies and old wives tales rooted in A'nt Pig's South Carolina upbringing.

Laugh If You Like . . . undoubtedly gets to the heart and funny bone of black people of all classes and generations. But it goes much further: It is a classic American story of scrapping to phenomenal success from the bottom of the barrel; and it is a universal story of great pathos and humor that will intrigue people of all races and ages.

Anyone who's ever been or known a mischievous little boy will delight in the tale of Petey the Cowboy ruslin' cattle at night with a torch—a "herd" of stray dogs chased down a dirt alley into a horrified crowd of children playing under the corner lamppost.

Anyone who knows what a spanking feels like will cringe for Petey when A'nt Pig stops in the middle of baking biscuits to trudge to the neighborhood school to tan Petey's bare hide in front of the entire fourth grade class, after the teacher sends word that Petey is "running his mouth."

Anyone who's read "Tom Sawyer" will recognize the inspiration that strikes Petey on the playground of Stevens Elementary School when he relieves a boy of his scrumptious lunch. Or, years later, when he establishes a numbers-running operation of his own for his junior high classmates, patterned after the one A'nt Pig had operated at home ever since Petey could remember.

Through elementary and junior high school, to dropping out of high school to join the Army, Petey's life is filled with hysterical accounts of wrongdoing, of "cutting up." Soldiers will remember sergeants like the one Petey encounters in basic training who admonishes, "Drop everything you're doing and come when you hear the whistle." But they may not have seen a fellow private like Petey who plotted purposely to run out, buck naked and breathless when the whistle blew, panting, "I was just getting ready to take a shower, Sarge!"

Those interested in the entertainment business will relish the opportunity to read of Petey's experiences as an emcee and comedian at the historic Howard Theater in Washington, D.C., the Comedy Club in Baltimore, and the picnic grounds at Wilmer's Park, in Maryland. Petey knew them all, from Pigmeat Markham to Sam Cooke, from Moms Mabley to Walter Jackson, from the Impressions to Eddie "Cleanhead" Vinson—and they loved his routines as much as he loved theirs.

In the late 1960s and early 1970s, Petey took his comedy to other stages, including Georgetown's Cellar Door, then a premiere night spot for jazz performers. At the Cellar Door, Petey was the opening act for such luminaries as Thelonius Monk and Jimmy Smith.

Petey's interest in the entertainment business originated in his childhood in the 1930s and early 40s, when the Howard was in its heyday. Petey's father was among those who frequented the legendary strip where stars and patrons caroused and partied in and out of scores of successful clubs and restaurants, making

Washington, D.C. the hot spot of East Coast black entertainment. In later years, when Petey came home from the Army, he never missed the chance to "hang out" in many of the same late night spots.

People may see something of themselves or loved ones, too, in Petey's valiant and finally successful struggle to stop drinking alcohol—a struggle he waged long after years of nothingness as a "wine-head bum," and criminality as a thief; long after he "made something" of himself, but just after he found God.

Petey told me he was in prison when his beloved A'nt Pig died, and that she visited him on the night after her funeral. After she told him, "You're on your own now, Bo'," he made the decision to turn over a new leaf—though not all the way over: To get out of prison, he fell back on the con artistry he honed in the small house in Georgetown, at A'nt Pig's side.

Laugh If You Like . . . opens with A'nt Pig's ethereal visit to the jail and Petey's successful trick to win parole five years into a ten-year sentence for robbery. The account of this full-fledged con takes us through the first chapter, and reflects Petey's capricious, never-a-dull-moment style of "jailing" that is seen in ensuing chapters. Translation: He made himself seem cooperative and indispensable to guards while keeping his fellow inmates off-kilter with a series of bizarre schemes designed to ensure him special regard, privileges or money.

Petey's reflections on the lessons A'nt Pig taught him remain a constant focus of this book, from his boyhood days when "my name became well-known in Washington, D.C. because I could play the dozens better than anybody else in town," and "signify," get other people in trouble for the sake of a good joke. Beyond school, the stories move to Petey's years in the Army, in Annapolis, MD, and overseas in the Korean War; to the time when he held intermittent blue-collar jobs, hustled on weekends in small Southern and East Coast towns, and worked occasionally as a comedian, before he landed in prison.

Finally, we see how Petey earned his place in Washington history as a "tireless spokesman for the poor people he knew and loved best," as a *Washington Post* editorial described him at this death. Petey's often shocking sense of humor and his tributes to his grandmother remained his trademarks as Petey worked for an anti-poverty program, the United Planning Organization; created a support group for ex-convicts, EFEC (Efforts for Ex-Convicts); and devoted his popular radio and irreverent television talk shows to uplifting the downtrodden, "the little people," as he called them.

Petey Greene began his radio broadcasting career as a deejay and host spinning tunes over prison radio. He ended it delivering commentary in 60-second spots called "The Second Cup of Coffee," during the morning drive time on WYCB, a gospel station in Washington, D.C. From gospel station WUST, he also broadcast a show aimed at his "Twilight Family," hundreds of senior citizens who adored Petey Greene because he played their music, spoke their beliefs, and sponsored events explicitly for them. And from the same station, he organized a club of young people, his "ABC Family"—boys and girls who were attracted to Petey because of his message and his accomplishments.

During his television career, Petey won two EMMY awards for outstanding individual achievement, from the Washington, D.C. Chapter of the National Academy of Television Arts and Sciences; and numerous community service awards and honors. He used his half-hour, weekly television show to talk about anything and everybody, with brilliant bursts of insight and novel viewpoints and language that kept viewers tuning in again and again, for more than a decade.

The "man in the street" was not the only one who listened to or watched Petey Greene. At one point in his 16 years as a broadcaster, Petey's ardent admirers reached as far as the White House, when then Vice President Hubert Humphrey asked his press aide, Ofield Dukes, to introduce him to Petey Greene. Mr. Humphrey had heard Petey's broadcast on the car radio, over his chauffeur's favorite station. According to Mr. Dukes, the vice president remained a loyal listener, fan and friend of Petey Greene throughout Mr. Humphrey's years in the nation's capital and back home in Minnesota.

Senators and congressmen, mayors and city councilmembers, rich and poor, young and old, black and white, the well-known and seldom seen, were all moved by Petey Greene. A year and a half before he died, Petey was invited by the student council to be the keynote speaker at graduation ceremonies for Walt Whitman, a predominantly white high school in wealthy, suburban Montgomery County, MD. He considered the invitation one of his highest achievements. In turn, the young audience filling Constitution Hall gave Petey Greene rousing ovations before and after he delivered the commencement address, sharing the platform with Maryland Congressman Mike Barnes.

At the time of his death, Petey was developing a national following through his talk show, "Petey Greene's Washington," broadcast over a local station and on the Black Entertainment Television (BET) cable network. When his deep, gravelly voice would sign off with,

"I'll tell it to the hot, I'll tell it to the cold, I'll tell it to the young, I'll tell it to the old, I don't want no laughin', I don't want no cryin', and most of all, no signifyin' . . . ,"

BET's phone lines would light up with callers from around the country asking, "Who IS this man?"

Laugh If You Like . . . answers that question, and shares with the world two characters who will inspire laughter and capture hearts, just as the real-life Maggie Floyd and Ralph Waldo Greene Jr. did when they lived.

Author's note: The spelling of some names (especially of people Petey met in prison) may be altered, attributable to Petey's memory and pronunciation. Others are identified only by first name.

CHAPTER 1

Beginning as It Ends

"BOY, I KNOW your mouth is gone get you killed or get you rich one day. 'Cause you the talkingest damn boy I ever seen. Heish up now and go on up to bed."

From a corner behind him, Petey heard his grandmother, A'nt Pig, her deep, slow voice evoking her South Carolina roots. When she told him to "heish" his mouth, he always wanted to laugh, because A'nt Pig also ordered him to "Heish up the window," when she wanted it *opened*. Hush and heist sounded the same in A'nt Pig's dialect.

As usual, her rough scolding was laced with amusement and adoration. He whirled around at the sound of her voice, though he knew without a doubt A'nt Pig was not there. Closing his eyes, he could see her, tall and ebony with silvery-white hair, smiling down at him as she had done so often when he was a boy.

"What's the matter?" his friend Chinch asked, when Petey suddenly stopped talking in the middle of his running commentary on how some prisoners were too trifling to ever figure out a way to serve their time in Cell Block 3, and get to watch television in the day room late into the night as they and a few select others were now doing.

"What's the matter?" Chinch asked again. Petey turned slowly to face his friend he'd met more than 20 years ago. "Ain't nothing wrong. What? I gotta be talking to y'all hog-headed niggahs all the time? I'm just tired, that's all." Though he was older than Petey, Chinch accepted the explanation quietly. Petey had told him long ago, "You can't make me talk nor stop me once I'm on a roll."

Chinch had heard Ralph "Petey" Greene make that boast in 1941 when Petey was a skinny, rust-colored, 10-year-old kid—and already the rhyming, signifying, dozens-playing champion among his peers. In later years, Chinch had seen Petey, "drunk as a skunk," work the crowds with his comedy routine down at the picnics at Wilmer's Park on Sundays, after Petey got out of service. Chinch was not likely to start challenging Petey Greene in 1961 at the D.C. jail.

Petey decided not to tell Chinch he thought he heard A'nt Pig's voice. That sounded too eerie, and it probably just meant he was worried about her. "But I don't need to worry. I know she gone get better. Something like that cold they say she got can't stop her for long," he silently assured himself. "Even if her memory ain't sharp as it used to be, she'll come up with one of those remedies from Carolina she used on me all my life."

He thought back to a time when he was 12 years old, begging her to spare him the embarrassment of the cold-prevention routine she subjected him to until he turned 13. About mid-October each year, A'nt Pig would empty a small pouch of Union Leader tobacco into her corn-cob pipe, then wash out the pouch and fill it with foul-smelling asafetida. Petey would stand beside her, hanging his head and shifting from one foot to the other, watching her puff on her pipe while she looped the white cloth bag with draw string to tie around his neck.

Then she would rub his narrow chest with mutton tallow and wrap his torso in a strip of flannel torn from her long underwear.

"Keep this on through spring, you won't get the consumption," A'nt Pig would command, before lifting her 5'10" bulk from the worn arm chair and heading for the kitchen, where she always tallied the day's numbers game receipts—an illegal activity neighborhood police tacitly allowed.

"But none of the other children have to wear this. And they ain't got on these long drawers or long black stockings neither. I can't even take gym class. By the time I get all this stuff off, gym be over. The other kids laughing at me, with this ol' nasty stuff on," Petey pleaded.

"Humph! That's why half of them got consumption and T.B. and missing school. You going every day." Waving an end to the conversation, A'nt Pig settled at her kitchen table. There was no more need to talk about it. From the stories passed along by her mother and grandmother before her, A'nt Pig was convinced the pungent plant gum resin worked like a charm to ward off disease the way garlic held off vampires.

Petey had his own explanation of why it worked. On the dilapidated porch of their house on 23rd Street that October day in 1943, with his fresh bag around his neck, Petey complained to his best friend, Freddy Coles. "I know why I don't never catch no cold or nothing. It's because the other children won't sit by me when I'm wearing this thing. So if they got something, I shore won't catch it."

*　　*　　*

The next day, Petey swaggered toward a table in the jail's bleak rotunda to visit with his mother, a privilege accorded to Cell Block 3 prisoners. Inmates with no jobs that earned them special treatment visited through phones on a hard plastic panel in a separate part of the huge, five-story, red brick building.

The Bastille-like jail, built in 1872 occupied a neighborhood in Southeast D.C., not far from Capitol Hill. A double-wire fence around the perimeter and inch-thick steel window frames had been added in 1947 by then-Superintendent Donald Clemmer, following a widely publicized escape.

Jackie Greene nervously flicked her cigarette, rarely looking directly at her son. Instead, she concentrated mainly on the military scene painted on the jail rotunda's high ceiling. Then she shifted in the hard, metal chair and cleared her throat. "How you doing?" Jackie asked, finally focusing her eyes on Petey, minutes before she delivered the bad news.

Petey stared at his mother, a tall, dark-brown woman with high cheekbones like A'nt Pig's. Her obvious discomfort confused him. Certainly the restricted surroundings didn't make Jackie uneasy. She was no stranger to jails, having spent the last 20 years off and on visiting either his father or younger brother at the prison in Lorton, Va. She'd even seen the deep insides of the D.C. Women's Jail herself years ago. His mind raced through all the things that could be upsetting her. Maybe his father was in trouble with the law again. Maybe A'nt Pig's cold was worse.

"What's the matter with you? Everything all right at home? Y'all heard from Daddy? How's A'nt Pig?" Petey demanded, his head tight with an uncertainty that wavered toward dread.

"Petey, A'nt Pig is dead."

"What you say?" He tried to calmly refuse understanding.

"She dead, Baby. She wandered off. They say she was looking for you, trying to get back to the old house, in Georgetown. Her mind wasn't sharp no more, you know. She got too cold, by the time they found her. We took her to . . ."

Petey leaped from his chair raising his arms and screaming "No No Noooooo" heavenward, begging God to hear his anguished assertion and turn back time. As the pain and helplessness on his face gave way to anger, he grabbed the falling chair and threw it across the aisle into the dull gray wall of the large hallway, yelling out his denials and pounding the air with his grief. He spun around wildly, as though looking for something to attack.

Jail guards were stunned. They knew Petey well, as a comical drunk who had been in and out of jail for years before finally being nailed on the robbery charge he was now serving. Even as they rushed over to roughly subdue him, they knew this behavior didn't fit; there must be a reasonable explanation. "What's going on?"

"It's his grandmother," Jackie sobbed, yanking at the first guard's arm. "She's dead; she raised him. Don't hurt him." But there was no need to beg. The guards had heard Petey boast about his A'nt Pig, and they understood. On those many occasions when the woman who introduced herself as Maggie Floyd paid Petey's bail following his arrest for public drunkenness, Petey had bragged. "I been my grandmother's heart since I was two weeks old. She lets everybody know I am her favorite grandchild." He had even told them the old story of more than 30 years ago when his mother, a scared 16-year-old, handed him to A'nt Pig two weeks after his birth.

"You said if the first one was a boy, you wanted him. Well, here he is," Jackie had said, thrusting her curly-haired baby to his 50-year-old grandmother. A'nt Pig had placed her pipe on the window ledge, and cradled the baby expertly against her ample bosom. "I ain't gone keep this boy from the cradle to the crutch. When he get some size, you gotta come get this boy."

Her home had been his ever since, and relatives always said, "A'nt Pig has no intention of ever letting that boy go."

While guards looked on, Petey's rage gave way to a vacant stare. His angular shoulders slumped as he willingly turned toward his cell in an apparent stupor. "We'll take care of him," Sergeant Crauly assured Jackie, patting her forearm. "Let us know when the funeral is so he can get the papers to come."

*   *   *

Petey sat on the edge of the single bed in the small cell he occupied alone, one of the perks accorded to prisoners who held jobs such as his in the jail dentist's office. Getting the job had taken trickery and weeks of kissing up to the two white prisoners who worked for Dr. Gerald Steinberg. When he convinced Jack Carter and Tim Moreland to recommend him, Petey became the first black prisoner to win the cushy assignment as dental assistant.

He took no notice of the tiny table, transistor radio, reading lamp, or small throw rug he'd been privileged to add to his coveted space. Instead, he leaned back and stared at the peeling plaster in a corner of the cell's ceiling, until darkness and quiet engulfed the floor. A'nt Pig had been buried that day. But Petey had not left D.C. Jail.

Earlier that evening, two of his fellow inmates from the old neighborhood had found out about Petey's absence from the funeral. They angrily berated him, accusing him of not being grateful for all his grandmother's sacrifices throughout his life. But their scathing condemnation had fallen on deaf ears.

"Hey, Bo', you got to straighten up now, you know." A'nt Pig was sitting at the foot of his bed. She was not the A'nt Pig whose strength and memory had begun to fade just before Petey entered prison a year ago. This was the A'nt Pig of his childhood, big-boned and with near-black skin, and thick, white hair mostly covered by a bandanna. As in those days, the hem of her full, heavy skirt brushed across the tops of thick, black, lace-up shoes.

Petey's mind was so heavily shrouded with grief, the shock and fear that raced up from his gut saw no entry. Through a veil of inner tears, he calmly viewed A'nt Pig as a figment of his imagination, invited by his guilt over not accepting a pass to her funeral. Then she placed her long, strong fingers on Petey's leg, patting him gently. His heart racing, Petey realized this A'nt Pig was more than a wishful dream.

Without pause, he babbled out his emotions the way he had done since childhood when something went wrong, knowing she would listen to his side before taking any action. "A'nt Pig, I couldn't come to your funeral. I knew if I saw you in that casket, I'd try to climb in there with you." For the first time since his mother gave him the news four days before, tears streamed down Petey's face unchecked and uncontrollable.

"It's okay, Rabbit. You know I know why you didn't come. But I don't want you to pretend I'm not dead, just 'cause you didn't see them put me in the ground. I'm really gone, and you on your own. I won't be there for you, can't help you like I done before," A'nt Pig said, reminding Petey of her 31-year role as his loving safety net.

"I think this here will be the last time you'll see me, but I'll be watching you. I know you gone make it, 'cause you the smartest boy I ever seen. You just gotta shape up, Bo."

Petey, still sobbing, called after her, his arms stretched toward the empty space where she no longer sat.

*   *   *

In a matter of months, Petey was transferred to the Central facility of Lorton Prison, a 50-building complex 20 miles away, where prisoners with long sentences like his 10 years normally served out their time. When he stepped off the bus and into the processing area, he ran straight into his father's reputation.

"*Ralph Greene?* Ralph Greene is your father," the guard asked. The senior Ralph Greene—who once served time at Alcatraz—had wreaked havoc at Lorton. This Ralph didn't look much like the short, wavy-haired tyrant who had been in and out of Lorton when he and the guard were both just beyond boyhood some 25 years before.

"If my name is Ralph W. Greene Jr., what you think my father's name is?" Petey's flippant remark and his father's legacy landed him in solitary confinement for a few days, until his reputation for comedy quickly earned him a spot hosting a prison show, and thereafter, the choice jobs he finagled during the remaining years of his term.

*   *   *

"Hey, Thad, I'm going to take over Lorton. It's just a matter of time," Petey said to his brother one day on the courtyard's diamond, a few weeks after Petey's arrival. "I organized that baseball team up at the D.C. Jail; I'll organize one down here, too. I had the best job in CB-3; I'm not doing no manual labor down here, neither."

Thad Greene, confined in Lorton for safe-cracking, didn't doubt for a minute his brother would make good his prediction. He'd seen Petey con his way to victory time and again during their childhood. He thought about a story Petey entertained him with one day last week, after they came together in the prison's chapel to share a letter from their brother Clayton.

"I can remember me and Clayton was sitting on the playground of Stevens Elementary, eating our lunch. Clayton was 'bout 6, I was 'bout 7. We had some biscuits, cause you know we didn't get none of that fresh bread. We had biscuits. We was eating biscuits with peanut butter between 'em," Petey reminisced. He thought about the all-black, four-story, neighborhood elementary school on 21st Street, six blocks from the White House. Petey entered kindergarten at Stevens during the second term in February, following the January he turned 5 years old.

"You a lot younger than us, Thad, so you might not remember that in them days, if you ate peanut butter, you was going to have to drink some liquid behind it. I mean water or soda or something, because peanut butter was not none of that bullshit peanut butter like you got now. If you left the top off the peanut butter at night, it was all over. You had to take a ax to break that stuff.

"I used to get even with Clayton when I was mad with him. I'd leave the top off the peanut butter on his ass." Petey's gap-toothed smile was the same one Thad remembered from the mischievous days so many years ago at the Georgetown house where Petey was king. A'nt Pig's other grandchildren were just peasants passing through, Thad laughed to himself.

Petey's continuing tale cut into Thad's wandering thoughts. "So we sitting there eating our little peanut butter. A little ol' boy named Saxfield came and sat down near us. He had a neat little lunch box. Saxfield liked us. He was a nice, middle-class boy.

"He said: 'Hey Clayton. Hey Ralph.' We watched him open his little box up. I looked over there and said to myself, 'Damn, look at this sucker.' Sandwich is cut nice. Got a boiled egg. Got a piece of fruit in that box.

"Now this is back in them days when it wasn't no tin foil paper. It was wax paper, you understand. I say: 'Man . . . ' to the side where Clayton is. 'Look at that cabbage on that sandwich.' Clayton say: 'That ain't no cabbage, that's lettuce.'

"The sandwich had ham and cheese. I say to Clayton: 'Why is he got stuff like that, and look at ours?' He say: 'Cause he is rich and we is poor.' My mind started working. I say: 'Man, just freeze. We gone get that sandwich. We ain't gone take it. You just do what I tell you. Make out we fighting over this sandwich.'

"Clayton yelled: 'Well give me your jelly!' 'No, you gimme that peanut butter!'

"We arguing and Saxfield is looking. He's getting real interested in what we talking about. 'Could I have . . . ?'

"I said: 'Just get on away from us. This is ours.' We still talking: 'Man give me that jelly, I'll give you the peanut butter.'

"Saxfield said: 'Please could I have . . .'

"'Get on way from here, boy. We don't want you 'round us anyway cause you think you better than we are 'cause of where you live.' I was into the act now.

"Poor little Saxfield held out his food: 'I'll give you one of these sandwiches.'"

"I hollered: 'Don't nobody want none of that damn sandwich!'

"Clayton whispered: 'Don't press it.'

"So we traded him all our stuff and got his sandwich. I said: 'Let's go.' Now, we on the other side of the playground. To show you how the teachers was, we on the other side of the playground, eating. Good-ass sandwich. I know we ain't gone get no more like this for years.

"The teacher is walking the playground, watching the children. As she get 'round by Saxfield, she look down and saw that boy with them biscuits. She know this is not this boy's lunch, you understand what I mean.

"I said: 'Oh oh, she see him.' She was talking to him 'bout these biscuits. She know goddamn well he ain't supposed to have this hard tack shit here.

"I say: 'Here she come. Eat fast!' We eating fast as we can. Eating. Eating. She come over.

"'Ralph. Clayton. Come here.'

"'Yes Ma'am.'

"'What are you doing taking this boy's sandwiches?'

"'We didn't take them. He gave them to us.'

"He piped up: 'Yes. I did. I gave them to 'em, because I like peanut butter and jelly.'

"She said: 'Boy, just shut up,' and turned to us. 'If I see y'all eating this boy's sandwiches tomorrow . . .'"

Petey's wide mouthed-grin mirrored Thad's, both men glad for the time to forget the present and revel in the innocent fun of a past that seemed like another lifetime.

*   *   *

Two years passed at Lorton before Petey came up for parole. Though he had originated daring ways to run contraband, and ingratiated himself to prison guards who let him break rules, he had not been formally charged with any wrong doing. For the record, Petey had been a model, at times even self-effacing prisoner.

He was confident officials had no inkling of his recently opened "tourist home"—confessional booths where inmates could have sex with their wives and girlfriends when they came to "pray" in the prison chapel, where Petey worked as a trustee or usher in charge of supervising Sunday visits. Likewise, he knew officials were unaware of the "canteen" he operated for select prisoners. Through Petey, the "in crowd" could order fully-dressed hamburgers from the mess hall mid-afternoon, in exchange for cartons of cigarettes—the unofficial currency among inmates.

Glad to have Chinch finally down at Lorton with him, Petey pulled his old buddy to the side the night before his parole interview, saying, "They don't have nothing on me. I know I'm gone make parole."

Even still, they both knew there was reason to be nervous about going before the board. The two of them had just seen a fellow prisoner with a clean record kill himself after being denied parole. Ironically, his last name was also Greene. "Eatum-up Greene," had an 18-year sentence but had truly served six of them as a model prisoner when he went before the board. The following day, the usually gregarious, jolly "Eatum-up," sat silently in the mess hall.

"What happened?" Petey asked. "They denied me." Less than an hour later, his body was found hanging by his belt from the railings of the second tier in dormitory 20.

When Petey entered the small, drab, hearing room, three members of the five-man parole board watched intently—Major Frank Ershler, Rev. Albion Ferrell, and George Jefferson. The full pages of Petey's record rested on the table.

"We see where you've never been in trouble since you've been incarcerated," Rev. Ferrell said, looking at Petey's record from his year and a half at D.C. Jail, and two years at Lorton. Rev. Ferrell smiled pleasantly, seemingly inclined to grant parole. But Major Ershler, a short, white, retired army officer, took a different tone. "We aren't going to let you out."

"Why, Sir?" Petey asked, forcing his voice to remain steady and polite, clenching his long, thin fingers into tight fists.

"You know why we don't have any trouble in these records of yours? Because you are jail-wise. You are not going to convince me that you've been here all this time and haven't done anything wrong. And I see here where you are a drunk. If we let you out in the street, and you get another drink in your hand, a pistol might be the next thing you hold. You might kill somebody.

"The fact that you have faked a clean record doesn't mean a hill of beans to me." Looking at the crestfallen faces of his colleagues, both black, who had been impressed by Petey's record, Major Ershler added, "But we'll think about it. We'll let you know tomorrow morning."

Petey's stomach pitched and heaved like a kayak in a storm on open seas, as he walked toward the dorm looking for Chinch.

"Chinch, man, I wanted to hit Major Ers'la' on his jaw, but I know he was waiting for me to play into his hands. So I played it cool. I didn't give 'em no reason to keep me in here. Man, I'm so sick of grinning at these crackers and living with these niggahs! Shit! I don't think I'm gone be able to sleep tonight!"

The next morning, in the quiet administrative office, Petey cautiously opened the paper that held his fate. The word "Denied," blocked everything else from his line of vision, and anger roiled up from his tight stomach. Heading back to Dormitory 20, he glanced up at the overcast sky that threatened a storm.

Torrents of rain pelted the prison grounds that evening as Petey spat his venom out to the men who clustered around him inside, between the cells and the railing of their floor. "Well, boy, they ain't seen nothing yet. They think I ain't got in trouble. I'm gone be wide open now. You talking 'bout bringing some dope in here! And running that tourist home in the chapel when these wives and girlfriends come down? I'm doubling my game!"

But Chinch, who always said he never understood how a man with Petey's comic genius wound up in jail, spoke up. "Look man, don't pay that parole board no mind. So they denied you. All you got to do is keep stepping. You got everything in the penitentiary going for you. The warden's wife like you, the warden like you, everybody like you.

"So you got denied parole. If you go out here and act like the rest of these damn fools you see 'round here, you ain't doing nothing but taking yourself back. Already, you run all the shows, you got the whole freedom of the penitentiary, just be ready for 'em when they call you next time."

Petey pretended to ignore Chinch, and walked toward his cell. On the way, he could swear he smelled the heavy odor of Union Leader tobacco and heard A'nt Pig admonish, "You listen at what Chinch is saying to you, boy."

*   *   *

The next month, sitting at his administrative job in the jail's single-story school building—once again, the first black to get such a choice assignment—Petey put his feet on his desk and daydreamed he was talking to A'nt Pig about parole. "I gotta have me a trump card, don't I, A'nt Pig," he mused. Gazing out the window across the barren grounds as another winter storm brewed, Petey's eyes fell on the water tower looming in the distance, and he laughed aloud when the idea came to him.

That evening, in the crowded mess hall, Petey called to one of the inmates who lived in his dorm, Jim Wagess, whose nickname was Baldy. "Hey Baldy, come over here and eat with me." Baldy was glad for the opportunity to take his mind off his parole hearing due that summer. If anyone could make him laugh, Petey could.

"Hey, Petey, I hear you and Sgt. Shirley are tight over at that school. He's been driving everybody else crazy. How you get a racist guard like that to get his foot off your neck and his behind in your pocket?"

Petey put his arm around Baldy's thin shoulder, and emphasized each word of his explanation. "Because I am a story teller and I'm good, you understand? I could hold a boa constrictor's attention." As the two men walked back to the dorm, clutching their denim jackets tightly to their chests, Petey entertained his friend with tales of exploits at the school. Then he turned to the subject he really had in mind.

"Hey, Baldy, I know how we can both get out of this joint. See that water tank over there? Well, man, you know what you oughta do? Climb up on there one day like you gone jump off and then stay up there. Then they'll start to tell you to come down. Don't do it. They'll send for me. Then we'll get to talking and you make out you listening, then come on down. They'll feel sorry for you and be grateful to me, and we can both make parole."

Glaring at Petey as though he were a rat in an alley, Baldy answered, "Get the hell out my face, you damn fool! I'm not going up on that thing. It's too cold out here, and the thing might fall over! Besides, that don't make sense. You crazy?"

For the next few months, each night Petey would break away from the gang squatting around talking about prostitutes, pimping, and assorted street hustles, to pull Baldy aside. "Hey, Water Tower Slim, think about what I told you."

"Get the hell away from me, man," was the younger inmate's stock answer.

One day that spring, on their way from the dining hall—the center building of a U-shaped area with 10 dormitories on either side—Petey said to Baldy, "Let's walk over by the infirmary and just look at that tower, man. It ain't gone fall, you damn fool."

Meandering toward the tower in the pleasant 70 degree breeze, Petey thought about how good it would feel to be free again. He could almost taste the joy of not being at the mercy of guards who arbitrarily gave and took away privileges for their own obscure reasons. When they reached the tower, Baldy leaned his head back and squinted toward the far-distant top.

"How you know they coming to get *you* if I don't come down?"

Petey took the exasperated tone used by teachers who are explaining a homework assignment for the tenth time. "I know these crackers, and these niggahs. Who runs this joint? Me, right? I *know* they coming to get me, niggah! And when you come down, they'll feel sorry for you. When your parole hearing come up, they gone let you out early!"

Baldy straightened his shoulders, leveled his voice, and, started walking away, shooting back at Petey, "You think so? Well, I tell you what. *You* go up there, and then *you* stay up there 'til . . . ."

Petey cut him off. "Aw, man, you don't want to get out the penitentiary. I'm gone get out, with or without you. You don't want to get out."

One steamy summer afternoon the following month, Baldy could hardly hold back the tears that threatened to drop on his "Denied" slip from the parole board. He had never been in any trouble at Lorton; had hardly talked to anyone but Petey, and only then because they had both grown up in Georgetown. Boys and men who grew up in that section of D.C., whether in Georgetown proper or the adjacent neighborhood known as Foggy Bottom, all stuck together as Georgetowners. And besides, Petey could always cheer him up. That night, Baldy nudged Petey's side. "I'm going on that tower in the morning. I got nothin' to lose."

"Aw, you bullshittin'. You ain't going nowhere, niggah!"

At 10:30 the next morning, the black desk phone rang in the school building. "Petey, get over here quick! It's a man up on the tower! They asking for you."

Though Petey had planned the escapade, he had not really believed it would happen. His heart raced like a motor generating a speed boat, and his hands dripped with sweat when three guards burst through the office door.

"All right, Petey. Let's go."

"Go where?"

"They want you over at the water tower. Inmate Wagess is up there and now everybody is hollering for you."

Frantically looking for a way to stall for time, so he could flesh out his plan, Petey told the guards, "You don't need to drive me over there, I can walk."

As fate would have it, or as Petey would later think, his guardian angel of a grandmother planned it, Donald Clemmer, the long-time chief of the Corrections Department, was on Lorton's grounds that day. When Petey arrived, he could hardly believe what he saw.

There was Baldy, up on the tower all right. Peering up together were Superintendent Kermit Wheatley, Mr. Clemmer, a cluster of guards and inmates—all work had stopped in the excitement over the inmate on the tower. An inmate named Strickland was hollering: "Hey Wagess, come on down. They ain't gone do nothing to you."

Approaching humbly in the blazing sun and heavy, sweltering temperatures, drying his hands on his grey prison khakis, Petey first addressed the warden. "Mr. Wheatley, you send for me?"

"Hello, Petey. Mr. Clemmer sent for you."

Mr. Clemmer shook Petey's hand, explaining, "Petey, that boy is up on that tower, and we have tried the chaplain, the warden, everybody to get him down, with no success. Your name keeps popping up. They keep saying if anybody can talk him down, it's you."

Still trembling inside, Petey asked politely, diffidently, "Can I say something right now? I don't want no part of this. If I get to talking to this boy and he jump, uh uh, I don't want the blame."

Loosening his tie, Mr. Clemmer thought for a minute. He ran one hand across his thinning, straight black hair, then answered. "Petey, we don't think he is going to jump. He's mad with the parole board, not us. The parole board denied him, and you know we don't have any influence over the parole board. Just try to explain it to him, Petey."

While talking to the officials, Petey kept an eye on the prisoners in the background, betting cartons of cigarettes on whether the man would jump; and stole short peeps up at Baldy on top of the tower. Petey could hardly resist the temptation to say, "You dumb motherfuckers! You see he's standing in the shade! He ain't hardly serious."

Baldy played his role to the hilt, moaning loudly and sobbing, "I want to see my mama. I want my children. I want my wife. I'm going to jump if I can't go home."

Petey decided they shouldn't push their luck. Addressing Donald Clemmer, whose face and neck flushed red in the merciless blaze, Petey agreed to help. "Okay. I'll do it, but you have to let me talk to him my way. I won't be talking 'bout whose fault it is he still in the penitentiary."

"Petey, you can do anything you want. Just get him down off of that tower before the newspapers find out about this." Donald Clemmer had had his share of scrutiny from the newspapers and Congress during his decades as jail superintendent, and later, head of the D.C. prison system.

One of the guards handed Petey a megaphone. "Jim Baldy!"

"Who is that? Is that you, Petey? Man, I want to go see my mother and my children."

Turning to Mr. Clemmer, Petey said, "You heard what he said."

"Well, tell him we'll take him up there to see his mother and his children." Sweat formed in the crease of Mr. Clemmer's frown.

After Petey passed along the concession, Baldy hollered down again, "I want to go to the mayor's office."

Petey blared through the megaphone, "You can go there, too. Now come on down man. They gone take you to see your family."

"Naw they won't. They gone put me in the hole if I come down."

Dropping the megaphone to his side, Petey looked Mr. Wheatley directly in the eyes. "Y'all gone put him in the hole?"

"Petey, I swear we aren't going to put him in the hole. We're going to take him on uptown to see his folks." Mr. Wheatley shaded his eyes with a large hand, squinting from Petey up to Baldy.

"Y'all wouldn't cross me, now, would you?"

"Petey, get him down. It's not on us, it's on the parole board."

A steady hum of activity radiated from the inmates who were slapping hands and trading bets, happy for the break in their monotonous routines. Realizing that the officials might soon lose patience, Petey went into his serious act.

"All right, Baldy, let me tell you something. If you jump and kill yourself, motherfucker, you ain't gone see no goddamn body."

A guard nervously walked toward Petey. "Don't talk like that!"

Dramatically, Petey thrust the megaphone toward the guard. "Here, you do it, then. . . . Mr. Clemmer, if he's gone tell me how to talk . . . ."

"Give Petey that horn and take your ass on back over by the inmates," Mr. Clemmer erupted in anger and frustration. "Matter of fact, all of you move back! Back up! Go ahead, Petey." The crowd reluctantly pushed backwards several feet.

"Look, man. Come the fuck on down. They ain't gone put you in no hole. They gone take you uptown, and to see the mayor, just like you asked," Petey yelled into the loud speaker, rivulets of sweat rolling down his neck and back.

"Ask 'em if you can go with me?"

Mr. Clemmer said simply, "Petey, what size suit do you wear?"

In one final shout on the megaphone, Petey told Baldy, "They say I can go with you."

"Well, I'm coming down."

Mustering all his authority, Petey commanded to the crowd that had inched close again, "Everybody back up. Back up, Mr. Clemmer, everybody. He's coming down. We don't want to make him nervous. I'll go meet him at the bottom."

Baldy slowly climbed down the 200 tower steps while the crowd stood 75 feet away watching anxiously. At the bottom step, Baldy fell into Petey's arms, bawling like a baby. In his ear, Petey whispered in feigned anger, "Why you stay in the shade, fool?"

Ignoring the question and the uncomfortable feel of his sweat-drenched prison uniform, Baldy leaned further into Petey's shoulder to conceal his glee. "We got em, didn't we? Did I get em good?"

Inside the mayor-commissioner's office late that afternoon, a freshly suited Baldy and his family sat uncomfortably in the somber wood-paneled conference room. They quietly listened to Mr. Clemmer explain the circumstances to city officials, black and white, who were gathered there; and heard him thank Petey.

"It might have been a catastrophe without Petey Greene," he beamed over at Petey. "We tried the chaplain, the warden, other inmates. Nothing was working for nearly two hours. Then when we called Petey, it only took him 19 minutes to talk this inmate down."

Petey nodded humbly, then looked heavenward and silently told A'nt Pig. "What they don't know is it took me six months to talk that niggah up there." With an impish grin, he added, "Think I got a good chance of making parole this time, don't you?"

Then Donald Clemmer, still smiling broadly, addressed Petey directly. "Well, Petey, we are so pleased with what you've done, we want to give you a year off your sentence."

Petey's mind churned wildly. He had to decide on his game plan instantly. He had served a little over 4 years of a 10-year sentence and was coming up for parole again in about 90 days. In a matter of seconds, he reviewed all the possible outcomes and scenarios. Then taking a deep breath, he settled on a course and stated firmly, "No sir. I don't want you to give me *nothing*. I don't want no compensation."

Mr. Clemmer, Superintendent Wheatley, Corrections Department deputy director Kenneth Hardy, the mayor's representative, Baldy, and the Wagess family were all stunned. "What?" Mr. Clemmer said, as though he had not heard Petey clearly.

Petey explained solemnly. "I don't want to be compensated. This man's a fellow inmate. He's my friend. It could have been me up on that tower. Then to take a year of compensation for helping, uh uh, no, I couldn't do that."

Everyone stared in amazement, the silent question hanging in the air: "Three hundred sixty-five days? You're turning down a whole year? Why?"

His mind filling in the details of his fictional rationale as he spoke, Petey continued piously, "I'm just glad God gave me strength to do that, to help."

He had not been back at the Lorton complex for a full hour before everyone had heard the news. "You dumb motherfucker, you turned down a year?" one of his dormitory mates roared.

"Hey man, look, I was glad to do it." Petey answered quietly, staying in character so completely, he almost convinced himself of his altruism . . . until he ran into Chinch.

"Boy, I been hearing them talk about you turning down that year. Saying you must be a sissy or in love with one and don't want to get out. Other people say you done got religion. But you ain't got to try to fool me. I'm yo' friend. When they told me what you had done, I said to myself, 'Goddamn if that nigger ain't a chip off the old block,'" Chinch said, his eyes glistening with pride and amusement.

Petey took a cigarette from his older friend's pocket and relaxed his pretense for the first time in nine hours. "Yeah man, I wouldn't talk about this with anybody but you. You know I figured if I'da took that year, the parole board woulda just had a excuse to turn me down when I'm up. They'd say, 'Well, he'll be out shortly, so the parole board don't need to get involved in this.'

"This way, if they still deny me parole, I know how fair Ken Hardy and Donald Clemmer is. I know I got that year hanging on the gate. I know that year is automatic. I figured it's worth the gamble, man."

Three months later, on a clear early winter day in 1964, Petey sat across from the same members of the parole board who denied him before. Major Ershler spoke first. "Well, we see here that you talked an inmate down from the water tower."

Cloaked in a somber mood and holding his hands together on the table top, Petey said softly, "Yes sir."

"And we also see that you refused a year's reduction in your sentence . . ."

Petey revived the utterly sincere tone he had used that hot summer day in the mayor's office. Looking from Major Ershler to Rev. Ferrell to Mr. Jefferson, and occasionally down at his own clasped hands, Petey delivered his speech.

"Let me say this to all of you here, sir. I'll tell you like I told Mr. Hardy and Mr. Clemmer. I'm glad I was able to get Mr. Wagess down. And if I had to get a reduction in sentence by doing that, then I really wouldn't want it. Maybe one day I'll be in a predicament and Mr. Wagess might have to help me. Or somebody might have to help me. So I don't think the year mattered that much. It was that God gave me the strength to be able to help."

Each face in the room held a respectful gaze as Major Ershler said, "We'll let you know something tomorrow."

Back at the dorm, his friends crowding around him with questions of "How did it go? You think you made it?" Petey clenched his fist in victory. "I *know* I made it, I made that motherfucker, boy! I ain't even worried."

When he was called to the administrative office to receive his slip the next day, Petey was not surprised to see the typed word, "Granted." Yet he was not ready to give up the game. Turning to the guard in charge of the office, he asked gently, "Sir, you don't mind if I pray, do you? I just want to pray."

"Go right ahead."

Dropping slowly to the floor, lifting his closed eyes toward the ceiling, Petey said aloud, "Thank you, Father. I'll never be back. Thank you."

On his way out of the door, Petey heard the guard solemnly predict to the office secretary, "That boy will never be back here." Petey could hardly suppress the urge to whirl around and brag loudly and confidently, "You better believe it. You are definitely right!"

The only thing left was to find a job, a prerequisite for release. "I'm gone find the *right* job. And it ain't gone be no manual labor," he vowed silently, then added, "I already got my plan of action, A'nt Pig."

*   *   *

Petey couldn't think of a time when he'd been more optimistic about the future, unless it was that day when he was 10 years old and A'nt Pig hit the number for nearly $5,000. She had been "robbing Peter to pay Paul," ever since his grandfather died the year before, leaving them in dire financial straits. The house needed repairs, Petey wore tattered clothes and nearly soleless shoes, and weeks went by when school lunch was Petey's only square meal. A'nt Pig was deeper in debt than ever before when the number changed her luck.

Although it was a chilly, Saturday afternoon in early April, the atmosphere inside the old house at 1152 23rd Street felt like Christmas morning. A'nt Pig stirred the embers of the living room's pot-bellied stove, then called outside to Petey, who had just returned from an exploring expedition in the thick woods and streams of Rock Creek Park with his best friends, Freddy Coles and Junior Lee. His one-eyed, mangy dog trudged behind him.

Earlier in the day, Petey and the other two boys had borrowed a trolley pass from Freddy's mother. With one pass, the three of them could take the Number 10 street car to Suburban Gardens, at the end of the line. There, they rode the ferris wheel and plotted the rest of their weekend. After stopping by their houses, they intended to walk to the nearby Potomac River to play a game of dare—testing bravery and soaring ability over seemingly vast reaches between barges anchored along the shore.

As Petey came up the crumbling steps of his house, he passed Eddie, the dark-haired Jewish man who tallied up the neighborhood numbers take on an adding machine in A'nt Pig's kitchen each weekend. A'nt Pig once explained to Petey, "Every time I write a dollar worth of numbers, the white man get 70 cents, I get 30 cents. If somebody on my list hit for a dollar, they get $540, I take $60 and put it in my pocket. You hear what I'm saying?"

In less than three years, Petey would be running his own successful numbers operation for students and a few teachers at Francis Junior High School, a few blocks away.

When Petey got inside the house that day, A'nt Pig was praising the Lord for letting her know to put money on that winning number. She had already decided where she would hide what she did not spend right away. She had no faith in financial institutions since losing thousands of dollars in a bank during the Depression.

She motioned for Petey to sit on the couch beside her. "Let me tell you something, Rabbit. We ain't gone let on we got this money. I'm gone pay the bills, save some to buy a house, fix up this house a little bit, and we gone get you some new clothes. But I don't want the rest of them chaps to know 'bout this money. They'll bleed us dry, if we let 'em."

Petey loved the way A'nt Pig talked to him as if he were an adult, and it was the two of them against the world. Ever since that cold day she buried her husband, Allen Floyd, she had taken to coming to Petey's bedroom at night to check his kerosene heater. "This coal oil stove keeping your room warm?" she'd ask. Then she would sit at the end of his narrow bed passing on information she thought he needed to know, until he fell asleep.

Sometimes she'd be in a comical mood, and give him advice that made him laugh. "Let me tell you, Rabbit. You don't never study a white man. At no time. You handle a white man. You have a category where you put a cracker, so you can handle him. On the other hand, you *study* a niggah, 'cause you got to be with him 70 hours out a day," she would start.

She would push an old ragged towel tighter against the crack in the window frame, where it fought a losing battle against the fierce wind, then continue: "Study a niggah's head. If he get to arguing with you, and you see a vein come up and his nostrils get to spreading, bust him in the face, 'cause he ain't up to no good."

Sometimes their chats would follow an argument A'nt Pig had with her youngest daughter, Jackie, who piled into A'nt Pig's house with her other children whenever she found herself out on the street after a fight with a boyfriend or for not paying rent. A'nt Pig berated her daughter for being "so triflin'," but always opened her door in those emergencies.

When Jackie arrived, A'nt Pig's small dining room converted to a bedroom with roll-away cots for the children; and the pull-out sofa in the living room became Jackie's bed. The crowded quarters, and the financial burden of feeding so many extra mouths, often led to flareups between A'nt Pig and Jackie. On those nights,

A'nt Pig would climb the rickety stairs to one of the two upstairs bedrooms for a serious talk with Petey.

"Boy, don't never hurt nobody's feelings. It's the worst thing in the world to have your feelings hurt, because your feelings control your heart and your heart hook up to your mind, and make you just do simple things when your feelings hurt. If you don't want your feelings hurt, then don't hurt nobody's feelings."

Memories of A'nt Pig sharing her philosophies returned to Petey during his years in service, afterwards as he spiraled down toward a life of nothingness with "winehead bums," as he called them, during his time in jail, and on to the years when he finally was living the way he wanted to live. Through it all, he never set out to hurt anyone; he preferred to make people laugh.

CHAPTER 2

Grandmothers Worlds Apart

BY THE TIME he was almost 4 years old, Petey knew he was good at making people laugh. That was the year, too, when he learned how to use profanity like a seasoned sailor—the year he learned his father didn't value a good laugh like A'nt Pig did. No, Ralph Greene Sr. valued cussin' and fighting.

Ralph Sr. was a caramel colored pretty boy with a Napoleonic complex. Though he was a voracious reader, an accomplished guitarist, and an expert chess player, he spent most of his time running with a gang, involved in criminal activity. Or fighting for any reason. "My daddy would fight a rock," Petey would later tell his best buddy in the army.

When Ralph was out of jail in those early days, he wanted to spend time with his children; he was intensely proud of them, but he had a bizarre way of showing his love. "Come here, you little cocksucker. You want yo' ball back? Stop that whining and *take* it back! If you want something, *fight* for it, you little motherfucker." In this manner, Ralph Sr. taught his sons what he thought they should know about getting along in the world.

"A'nt Pig, wash Butch off and put some nice clothes on him. I'm going to take him and Sugar Boy uptown so I can show them off," Ralph said one Friday evening, back when Clayton was called "Sugar Boy" and some people were still calling Ralph Jr. "Butch"—just a few weeks before A'nt Pig moved from 11th Street to the Georgetown neighborhood, where her grandson's newest moniker, "Petey," would take and stick with him throughout his life.

Ralph's parents kept his younger son, Sugar Boy. By their respective grandmothers, the boys were scrubbed twice, dressed in clean knickers and white shirts, and had their curly hair combed flat on their heads. Ralph Sr.—just barely 20 years old—wore pleated, cuffed pants with two handkerchiefs in the back pocket, a Big Apple cap cocked at a jaunty angle, and a white shirt, in the manner of his fashionable, hustler friends.

Holding the hands of almost 4-year-old Ralph Jr. and nearly 3-year-old Clayton, Ralph strutted up Seventh Street N.W., toward the corner of T, to shoot the breeze with his cohorts. Because he was brash and popular, Ralph had earned the right to join the congregation at Seventh and T—*the* corner amid Washington, D.C.'s bustling, prosperous corridors of business and entertainment activity—legal and illegal—for "colored" people.

While activity brimmed along U Street, on 14th Street, and even in a few scattered sites in other quadrants of the city, the *in* crowd locked up the square block at Seventh and T. From Duck Jackson's place to Herb Saunders Stage Door Canteen, from Chicken Charlie's to the Lincoln Colonade, from the best eating places to the hottest clubs and busiest rooming houses, the black elite and the hustlers spent their time and their money along the strip.

When Ralph and his sons arrived, crowds of young men with their hair conked and greased leaned against shiny cars parked along the curb in front of the hub of activity—Tim's Confectionery, better known to everyone as Tim's Hot Dog Stand. The pungent aroma of broiling meat wafted out to mix with the smoke from cigarettes dangling from the corners of young men's mouths.

Two of Ralph's friends whistled at women wearing the pompadour hairstyle, who had just left Waxie Maxie's record shop, where 10 speakers blared at once, each playing a different tune. "Hey, I'll see you at Duck Jackson's place after the show at the Howard tonight," someone yelled to a friend on his way around the corner to buy tickets at the Howard Theatre. The Howard, built in 1910, closed for a while after the Great Depression started in 1929, but had reopened in 1931, with Duke Ellington performing.

"Hey Ralph. These your sons? You got some cute children here, man." A tall, lean teenager wearing sharp black and white oxford shoes and leaning on a polished 1934 Chrysler, smiled, patting the children on their heads. Ralph threw his head back, chuckled, then made an instant decision to show his friends just how much his sons took after their daddy.

At first the boys thought their father was kidding when he leaned down to them and said, "Tell that man to kiss your motherfucking ass." But he was not smiling, so Sugar Boy's baby voice rang out, "Kiss my ass." The men hollered, slapping each other's palms, saying, "OooWhee, Ralph, you ain't shit, man."

Ralph did not join in the hilarity rippling through the group of young slicksters. Instead, he turned to his namesake and demanded, "Butch, I said tell that man to kiss your goddamn ass."

"That's not nice, Daddy, I'm not gone say that." Little Ralph Jr., his eyes dark and wide, with long, thick lashes like his father's, started to cry.

Ralph Greene Sr., with a temper legendary among his peers, exploded so violently, even his friends were shocked. "You little bitch motherfucker! You ain't nothing but a sissy. Can't fight. Can't cuss. Get the fuck on away from me. TAXI! I'm sending your yellow ass on back home. Cocksucking bastard!"

When he climbed out of the Diamond cab just blocks away on 11th Street, tears still coursing down his small face, Petey had just about made up his mind to be the best cusser in Washington, D.C.

"What happened, Rabbit?" A'nt Pig asked from the porch as her grandson kicked dirt on his way toward her. "Daddy wanted me to cuss, and I didn't do it." A'nt Pig loved Ralph Sr., admired his tenacity and his respect for the dollar. She did not want to speak ill of him in front of his child. Putting aside the sewing on her lap, she reached for this little boy who owned her heart. All she said was, "I don't know why Ralph *do* that. He know I don't allow no cussin' in this house."

Silently, she wondered why Ralph had so much anger inside him. He'd been raised by middle-class parents, in a home just five blocks away, on Sixth Street. "Such a fine looking boy, with such potential. If Jackie just give this boy half the support he need," she thought, shaking her head over her daughter's desire to constantly run the streets looking for a party.

Then she remembered how Petey carried on so about his visit to the Greenes' home last week. She decided maybe Ralph felt stifled by his own mother's ways, and took an early escape. "That woman has always had too much time on her hands," A'nt Pig decided, her full body shaking with laughter at the thought of Petey last week.

It started with Francine Greene coming up the walkway holding Sugar Boy's hand.

*   *   *

A dog walked across A'nt Pig's yard toward the house next door. Petey threw a lump of dirt at him, then looked up to see a neat, well-dressed woman coming toward them, holding the hand of his brother who would turn 3 in three months, as Petey turned 4. In every way, the woman was the opposite of A'nt Pig.

"Here come Grandma Greene and Sugar Boy," Petey yelled excitedly to A'nt Pig, who sat in a chair on the porch, sewing a button on her husband's dress shirt. Francine Greene, who stood no taller than 5 feet in her heels, wore a three-piece boucle suit and bark grained suede shoes.

"Humph," is what A'nt Pig had to say about it, tamping tobacco from her small white pouch into her pipe. She leaned back in her chair, exposing her battered, high-topped shoes. Her heavy cotton skirt brushed across the frayed shoe laces.

"Hello, Butch," Grandma Greene cooed. Petey ran up on the porch beside A'nt Pig, who snapped: "We don't call him Butch no more. His nickname is Petey now. You know how he cain't call that man Petely's name right? That's where it come from."

Francine Greene politely accepted the correction. "Oh, well, come here *Petey*. Let me kiss you."

"Don't kiss that boy! You'll put ringworms in his face," A'nt Pig declared, thrusting her arm between the boy and his paternal grandmother. Petey and Sugar Boy grinned into hands cupped over their mouths. Francine smiled weakly, then sat on the porch beside A'nt Pig on a wooden milk crate standing on its end.

"You know, Maggie, you really should think of becoming an Eastern Star, at our church." Francine fanned herself with the Evening Star newspaper she brought with her. The dateline read Thursday, October 11, 1934. "Warm for this time of year, isn't it?"

"Humph," A'nt Pig snorted, puffing on her pipe.

"I read in the paper Mrs. Roosevelt is celebrating her birthday today," Francine said, searching for something Maggie Floyd might want to talk about. "Fine woman, Mrs. Roosevelt," A'nt Pig said, not looking up from her sewing.

Francine glanced at the headlines above the fold on the front page, to see if something there might spark a conversation. One of the headlines read, "Liquor Board Acts to Check Drinking at Football Games," and another, "Boy Is Proclaimed Yugoslavian King in Solemn Rites." She had heard rumors that Maggie Floyd sold bootleg liquor, so that topic was off limits; and she was sure this woman would not be interested in the goings on of royalty in Yugoslavia.

After a short time of watching the boys play in the yard, and having no luck finding a topic she and Maggie Floyd could discuss, Francine rose to leave. "Come on, Sugar Boy."

Petey jumped up eagerly and ran to A'nt Pig. "Can I go round there and spend the weekend with Sugar Boy?"

"Yeah, you can go round there wit' 'em."

Francine Greene, surprised and happy for the chance to have her first grandchild for a few days, left the newspaper on the crate. In her most sincere tone, Francine turned to A'nt Pig, assuring, "We'll take good care of him." Maggie still did not look at her, saying with disinterest:

"Humph. Keep him."

The sun set as the children walked down the street with their father's mother. Sugar Boy wore neat, clean play clothes. Petey skipped along in a ragged T-shirt and pants cuffs rolled up over a pair of large, scuffed black high-top shoes.

The next day, the sun beamed a pleasant 83 degrees on the Greenes' house, a large, detached home surrounded by a white fence. Flowers lined the walkway. Inside, a piano abutted one living room wall. Eggshell white, frilly lace draped across the arms of the massive chairs and couch, upholstered in dark print. Matching lace doilies perched in the centers of the coffee tables and end tables.

Upstairs, after glancing to see if his brother had awakened, Petey jumped out of bed and ran to the window when he heard the noise of a truck rumbling outside. A faint breeze fluttered the lacy curtains of the room's large window. Hours later, at high noon, Sugar Boy and Petey tore up and down the block with several children whose clothes were more like Petey's ragged outfit than Sugar Boy's matching shirt and pants.

Francine stood in the doorway, feeling a deep sadness over the direction Ralph's life had taken. Barely 20 years old, he'd had two sons already and three stints in jail for crimes ranging from disturbing the peace to gambling to petty theft. She untied her apron and called the boys in.

Inside, Petey gawked at the table set neatly and offering piping hot bowls of soup along with sandwiches cut into sharp squares on small plates.

"Go wash up, boys." The children bounded off and returned with the same energy. Petey ate noisily until his Grandma Greene chided, "Slow down. We are quiet and polite at mealtime." Hurriedly wolfing down his last bite of sandwich, Petey jumped up and headed for the door. Just as he reached the screen, Francine grabbed his small arm. "No, Butch! You boys are going to get a bath now."

"Huh?"

Upstairs in a spotlessly clean bathroom, a large tub stood on four legs with feet that looked like paws to Petey. Confusion did a dance with anger in Petey's mind, but all he could do was pout.

Francine had left him no choice but to get in the tub. He spent a while watching Sugar Boy play and splash happily, then reluctantly joined in.

After their Grandma Greene dried the boys off carefully, Petey reached for his ragged play clothes. "No Butch, you boys are going to take a nap now."

"A what?" Petey dropped his mouth and scrunched his small face up at his Grandma Greene in total confusion. Looking down at his sincere, wide eyes, Francine felt a tug at her heart. It reminded her of Ralph Sr., as a 3-year-old, when he came to live with them after his mother, her baby sister, died. Ralph had slowly adjusted to the ways of the Greene household, and forgotten he was not her natural-born son.

"You're going to bed for a while," Francine said with a patient smile. Petey did not give up.

"Ain't this the middle of the day? Ain't this Friday?"

"Come on, now," Francine said, firmly leading him to Sugar Boy's bedroom, and dressing him in bell pajamas she had bought for $1. Then she stretched out in her own room and blocked out the memories by staring at the high bed posts and frilly covering until she fell asleep. Sugar Boy promptly dozed off in one of the small beds in his room, but Petey fought sleep by tiptoeing to the window every few minutes to steal envious looks at children outside.

When Francine came in to tell the boys they could get up, she brought two knicker suits, shorts and jackets, and two white shirts. "Put these on." Incredulity struck Petey again, but he was afraid to argue. When they got downstairs, he ran out the door and toward the street to play before Francine could catch him.

"Come back, Butch. You boys must play on the porch now. Come back," Francine yelled after him without going outside, assuming that her instruction would be obeyed.

On the porch, Sugar Boy opened up a can of pick-up sticks and called to Petey. "You better come on." Petey, seething with anger, hovered by the newly painted fence talking with two little boys through the gate. When Francine came onto the porch with her knitting needles and the beginnings of a sweater, she assumed a commanding tone. "Butch, come back on the porch, dear."

Petey's grandfather, a government worker returning from his job, came up the sidewalk behind him. "Hi, boys. You enjoying yourself, Butch?" He cupped his grandson's small, curly head and steered him toward the porch. He knew full well what his wife expected, but part of him felt sorry for this one. "His daddy wanted to run all the time, too," Bernard Greene remembered.

"Yes sir," Petey lied, hanging his head and staring longingly at the two boys who ran on down the street. He listlessly drew a circle on the wooden floor of the porch with a wooden stick from Sugar Boy's game.

As the sun set, tears welled up in Petey's eyes. But as suddenly as a summer shower gives way to a rainbow, his face brightened and broke into a happy grin. A'nt Pig was sauntering down the sidewalk, pushing the Greenes' gate open with a stick she'd been using as a walking cane. "Myyyyy grandmother," Petey cheered inwardly, turning cartwheels in his mind.

Francine looked up from her knitting. "Oh, Maggie. You're coming around for a visit?" She tried to hold the disappointment from her voice. She had hoped to have a full weekend alone with Petey, to expose her older grandchild to a different way of living.

"Yeah, just come 'round here to see 'bout this ol boy. He giving you any trouble?"

"No, he's no trouble at all. None at all. Have a seat."

Petey edged over to the cushioned chair A'nt Pig sat in, and leaned on her leg with his chin in his hands. Francine put down her knitting and turned to Maggie Floyd. "Could I get you some lemonade, Maggie?"

"Thank you. I could use a little something to drink." In the next moment, Bernard Greene looked up from his Evening Star newspaper, dateline Friday, October 12, 1934. "I was just reading here in the paper where a colored boy was seriously hurt falling out of a tree. Went up there after his pet kitten, they say. Fell 15 feet. Broke his spine. May not live, it says here."

"Lord, lord!" A'nt Pig sucked at the back of her front teeth and shook her head. "I feel for the boy's people."

"Excuse me, Maggie, but I've had a long day. Doing some extra work lately. I'm going to turn in now," Bernard said wearily, rising from the porch swing.

As soon as his other grandparents were no longer in hearing range, Petey leaned closer to A'nt Pig and whispered desperately.

"They crazy 'round here."

A'nt Pig looked at his earnest little face. "What did you say?"

"They crazy 'round here."

"What you talking 'bout?"

"They takes baths in the middle of the day. What day you supposed to take a bath? Saturday, ain't it? We took one *today*!"

Hearing A'nt Pig's chuckle, afraid she was not convinced, Petey rushed to add: "And they goes to sleep in the middle of the day, too! I want to go home."

Forcing herself to smile graciously, Francine came back out with two glasses of lemonade, handing one to Maggie. "Thank you. You sure he ain't been giving you no trouble?" A'nt Pig asked.

"None at all. Of course it's time for them to get ready for bed now. I thought you and I could sit here and have this lemonade after I take them inside."

Petey nudged A'nt Pig's leg with his knee right before she asked him, "What you gone do, you staying or going wit' me?" She already knew the answer, but went along with the charade for Francine's sake.

"I want to go home."

Francine could not hold back her disappointment. "But you haven't been here but one night . . ."

"I just want to go home," Petey insisted, as A'nt Pig rose heavily from the soft porch chair. "Okay, go get your things." Petey ran happily inside and changed into his old play clothes, leaving Sugar Boy staring after him on the porch.

On the five-block walk home, tears of laughter streamed down A'nt Pig's face as Petey told her about the restrictions at his Grandma Greene's house. "You comes inside for lunch then you can't play no more after lunch. They sleeps when the sun is out. And they takes a bath on Friday!"

A'nt Pig wiped her face with her sleeve. "I know you didn't want to sleep. That means you gotta stop talking. You the talkingest boy I ever seen. Yo' mouth is either gone get you rich or get you killed one day. Yo' mouth just go yappitty yappitty . . . just like a clatter pan in a goose's ass. I *know* you didn't want to go to sleep."

At high noon the next day, Petey was tearing up and down 11th Street with eight or 10 other boys when A'nt Pig hollered to him from her doorway. "Come here, Bo." As he came in the house, she was sitting on the couch, patting the space beside her. "Sit down here for a minute and tell me what you been doing out there."

Petey started talking, and within moments, was sound asleep, with his head near his A'nt Pig's lap on the couch. Maggie Floyd looked over a stack of papers, numbers slips, for the next hour.

When Petey awakened, he had no idea he'd had a nap. He jumped up talking, as though he'd just sat down. "I'm gone go back out there to play. I'll see you when Granddaddy get home."

Smiling as Petey bolted out the door, A'nt Pig said aloud to herself, "And **he** sleep when the sun is out. It just don't never *look* like no nap."

*   *   *

CHAPTER 3

Lessons at Home and in School

"A'NT PIG, WHY everybody call you A'nt Pig?"

Petey was sitting on the linoleum floor of his grandmother's kitchen, playing with one of the 10 alley cats who walked in and out of the house freely, easily coexisting with the dog and an injured wren A'nt Pig had also taken in. When she found the-broken-winged bird in the yard, she brought him inside and lectured the cats as usual, as though they were her children.

"If I see aar one of y'all messin wit' this chap, don't come 'round here no mo'. I'm telling y'all, he gone live here just like the rest of us, 'til he get well and fly on to find his people." But the bird did not leave as soon as he recovered. Once he was well enough to try his wings, he kept coming back through the open window, or in behind the cats or dog when they used the flap cut into the kitchen door for them. And whenever A'nt Pig sat still long enough or took a walk down the street, the bird viewed the world from her shoulder.

"Well, Bo', when me and Allen first come up here from Newberry, South Ca'lina, in 'round 1915, I had my niece with me. She called me A'nt Pig, so everybody repeat after her. Even my own four chi'dren. That's all I ever been up here is A'nt Pig."

Petey put the grey cat down and got up to watch A'nt Pig prepare the chicken for frying on her "cook stove," which had six eyes on top, an oven, and a bin for ashes at the bottom. He knew if he didn't come over, she'd tell him to in a minute. She always wanted him to watch what she was doing so he could learn. "I'm gone learn you how to cook and sew when you a little older, cause you ain't gone keep no woman long. I'm gone teach you how to take care of yo'self," she had insisted when he complained that cooking and sewing were for girls.

"But what about Pig. Why they call you Pig?"

"Oh. That's 'cause I was a fat little girl. People call me Pig ever since I can remember. I went to work for some white folk live up the road from my house when I was 'bout 8 years old. Never went to school. Only came home every other weekend." A'nt Pig lowered the heavily battered, cut up chicken parts into the large, black skillet filled with sizzling lard. Petey moved back a step to avoid the popping grease.

"Them people called me Pig, too. 'Pig, wash these clothes. Pig, take care the baby. Pig, iron Mr. Hamill shirts. Pig, hoe in the garden. Pig, cook dinner.' I couldn't wait to grow up and get away from all that hard work them people had me doing. And they wasn't payin no money, hardly. Mostly they'd give me food and clothes to take home. Guess tha's why I don't wanna wash no white people clothes now. Now, I takes in the washin' and ironin' and hires Miss Sarah 'n them to do the work. Then I pays them outta what I gets."

Petey looked up to see his grandfather stepping into the living room. Allen Floyd, a tall, muscular man with black skin and a bald head, poured water from a bucket into a basin on the kitchen counter to wash his callused hands and dust-streaked face. As a construction worker, his job meant eight straight hours of hoisting a hod—two sacks on either side of a solid bar—filled with bricks, up ladders to white bricklayers who completed the top stories of buildings for a contractor. No black men were hired as bricklayers in Washington in the 1930s.

"Hey, Petey. What you learn in school today?" No matter how worn out he felt when he came home, Allen Floyd always took time to give his grandson a bit of undivided attention. On Saturdays, he took Petey with him on his errands, which sometimes included a stop by the home of his secret sweetheart, Miss Ada Mae. On Sundays, he walked Petey to Sunday School at nearby Mount Zion Methodist Church; then he would take a street car over to Emmanuel Baptist in the Southwest section of the city, where he was a deacon. A'nt Pig joined Petey at the Methodist church for 11 a.m. services.

"I learned how to write y'all's names, and I'm gone teach y'all after dinner," Petey announced proudly, swinging from his grandfather's wide hands then skipping into the living room to set up his imaginary classroom—two chairs for his grandparents facing the "teacher chair," where he would sit. In Petey's "school," A'nt Pig always got the answers faster than her husband.

"I still say you cheat me, Petey. You grade your grandmother's paper better and move her chair up 'cause you like her better," Allen teased, settling in at the small kitchen table.

"Huh unh, naw, that ain't it. No I don't give her the answers, Angallen," Petey pouted self-righteously. Just as everyone had made Petey's grandmother their aunt by name, Allen Floyd had become everyone's uncle. Soon after moving to Washington, the words ran together convolutedly, making him "Angallen," to relatives and friends.

After a dinner of fried chicken, fresh-baked biscuits and collard greens, Allen Floyd was ready to fall asleep. But Petey pulled his grandparents over to their school chairs set near the open window. A'nt Pig wiped her hands on her apron and watched as Petey slowly copied his grandparents' names on wide-lined notebook paper then handed over the sheets for them to repeat. Both adults leaned close to the paper, holding thick pencils, and carefully followed their kindergarten grandson's print.

As usual, A'nt Pig finished her assignment before her husband. Her face and eyes held the awed expression that comes with an unexpected accomplishment. With an uncharacteristically soft voice fit for a library, she held up her page.

"Look Petey. M-A-G-G-I-E. Ain't that right?"

Petey smiled broadly, as he had seen his teacher, Miss Minnie Lee, beam when her students did A-plus work. "That's right!" At first his pleasure turned to confusion, then he decided that the thin tears trickling down his grandmother's face were tears of happiness. At age 55, she had finally learned to write her name.

*   *   *

Petey loved playing school with his grandparents, and he loved real school, too. He had fun in kindergarten, putting the classroom's small, painted turtles in little girls' pockets and scaring them half to death; coloring, singing and learning to write at Thaddeus Stevens Elementary School.

The four-story school building, on 21st Street between L and K Streets, six blocks from Franklin Delano Roosevelt's White House, became Petey's stage, proving grounds, and, in many ways, his haven during years that brought turmoil at home.

When he moved into first grade, at 5 1/2 years old, his teacher, Alice S. Glass, recognized his innate intelligence and made him feel very special. One mid-October day that year, he ran into the house after school, and instead of immediately changing into his play clothes to blast back outside, he excitedly filled A'nt Pig in on the news.

"I'm gone be the *witch* in the Halloween play!"

A'nt Pig stood at the stove in the kitchen, stirring spices into a pot of beans. "Why you the witch, Rabbit?"

"'Cause the witch got *all* the lines. Talk *all* the talk. Can't nobody say the lines better than me," Petey boasted. "And I can read better than the rest of 'em, too. Listen:" He grabbed his primary reader and bounced up to a chair at the kitchen table. "Jane has a kitten. The kitten's name is Tommy. Tommy says meow, meow. Jack has a dog. His dog's name is Billy. He says bow wow."

Barely concealing her pride, A'nt Pig turned to her grandson who looked up grinning. "Yeah. Thas real good, Petey. But you know what? They sent word 'round here that you been eating that paste y'all use at school. You better stop that, you hear? Go on up and take yo' school clothes off, now."

Petey jumped down and marched off with a frown, announcing, "I'm gone sleep in the bed with Granddaddy tonight. I'm not sleepin' in yo' bed." His grandparents' room held two double beds, two identical chests of drawers, and two wardrobe closets. Whenever he was mad with one, he "punished" the other by climbing into the adjacent bed.

He wanted to say, "I can eat that damn paste if I wanna," but the last time he sassed his grandmother, she whipped him hard with a rope she reserved just for punishments. Out in the back yard, he kept a cardboard box discarded when a neighbor's new piano was delivered. After that last spanking, he had raced out to the box to vent his anger. His brand of venting was not allowed in the house.

"You no-good motherfucker. I'll kill yo' ass when I get big. Old grey-head bitch! Beatin' me! Old bitch!," he had yelled non-stop, pretending to face A'nt Pig, while rolling around in his special hide-away, alternately pounding on the ground and rubbing the welts the whipping left on his thin legs.

He knew he could not use those words in A'nt Pig's house. Only his father encouraged cursing; in fact, he *required* it of his sons, as evidence of budding manhood. Whenever Petey had refused to curse the year before, Ralph Greene Sr. severely berated him, calling him a "faggot," and "the only sissy in the family."

The next door neighbor heard Petey's wild profanity through the cardboard walls of his sanctuary, and dashed over to alert Maggie Floyd. In mid-cuss, Petey looked up to the rim of his open box to see his grandmother peering down at him. Wishing he could close himself up in a shell, like one of the turtles at school, he swallowed hard and whispered faintly, "Oh gyaddamn!"

A'nt Pig shook her head from side to side and released the chuckle she had been trying to suppress. "Come on out so I can get in that box," she said. To her, fairness demanded no further punishment; Petey had not broken another rule. After all, he was not sassing her or cursing in the house; he was in what A'nt Pig and Angallen called Petey's "cussin' box."

*   *   *

Shortly after 5 a.m. the next Saturday morning, Petey skipped down the street behind the delivery trucks that started rambling into the neighborhood with deliveries of coal, wood, ice, and food to homes and corner stores just before dawn. The milkman and the doughnut man were Petey's favorites, because they always looked for him to come ask for their wares, and they encouraged his outlandish profanity.

"Hey, boy. What you want today?" The doughnut man always seemed glad to see Petey, his ragged shirt falling loosely off his tiny shoulders; his pants baggy and cuffed; his big, black shoes scuffed and untied; his tightly-curled hair uncombed and overgrown.

"I want two doughnuts from you, Mister Doughnut Man."

The middle-aged white man hoisted his pants over his protruding stomach and gestured with freckled hands toward his friend who drove the milk truck. "Well, tell this man here to kiss your ass."

"Kiss my ass, you white motherfucker," Petey said bodaciously, hitting the side of the truck. He was absolutely sure the aging milkman would laugh as he had done every Saturday morning since Petey moved to Georgetown and started getting up with A'nt Pig when the rooster crowed, and running to find the delivery men.

"Well if that's how you gone be, cussin' me *and* hittin' my truck, I ain't giving you no milk, you little bastard," the milkman answered, through his own and his friend's guffaws. Reaching inside his truck for the milk, he added, "Unless you tell this damn doughnut man to go straight to hell."

Petey complied, then grabbed the glass bottle and the two large plain doughnuts his grown-up buddies readily passed his way. It was time to go find Freddy and Emell, to start the day's real mischief. Until the older kids came out, maybe he and his two buddies would play kick ball in the 23rd Street alley.

*   *   *

By the time he was 7 years old, Petey had established himself as a boy whose weapons were his dirty mouth and a pocketful of rocks, both sufficient to hold at bay most neighborhood boys his age or younger. But because older guys would often ignore him,

Petey began to devise more outlandish methods of securing attention—a talent that ultimately led to his success as a comedian but was also the genesis for his involvement in petty crime.

His deep, never-ending desire to be recognized, to be center stage, led to Petey's first arrest, at age seven, one early fall Saturday in 1938—all because the big boys wouldn't let him play.

Into the windows of creme-colored apartment buildings and two-story houses near the 23rd Street alley rushed the sounds of boys hollering and laughing over their football game. The teens hiked, punted, raced and cavorted along the open alley that served as their usual weekend playing field. Only one younger boy had been allowed in the game, and no one paid attention to the 7-year-old who stood pouting, arms folded across his chest on the sidelines.

"Hey, y'all better let me in this goddamn game. I know I can play as good as that motherfucker," Petey shouted, angrily jabbing the air toward the youngster his age who won entrance to the game under the aegis of an older brother.

"Aw go the fuck on, Petey. Ain't nobody studying you," a 15-year-old yelled, then ran backwards to catch a pass.

Frustrated, Petey kicked a rock toward an empty lot facing the alley. When the rock landed near a large, old, leafless elm tree, Petey saw a way to occupy his rage—an idea formed around a tree-hole right at his eye level. He began stuffing trash from the vacant lot and the alley into the hole. Chewing gum wrappers, tissues, newspaper, rags and a few dry leaves, all fed the plan that held his complete concentration.

With zealous determination, Petey then picked up an empty soda bottle and stomped off the lot to a corner gas station. The station owner glanced without caring as a little boy emptied into his bottle a few drops of gasoline from each of the pumps on the island. Minutes later, Petey crept quietly into A'nt Pig's kitchen and lifted two long, wooden matches from the box that always sat on the back of the stove.

His mind churning with scenes from newsreels and movies and the conversations of adults sitting outside on crates talking late into the evenings, Petey strode purposefully toward his tree. Filled with his second-hand knowledge of fire-starting, without hesitation Petey sprinkled the gas from his soda bottle over the trash in the hole of the worn-out tree. Then he struck a match.

Whoosh!

For about 10 seconds, Petey stood alone, frozen with fear. He had known gas could ignite a fire, but he thought his fire would start off small, and be contained, as a fire in the pot-bellied stove at home ignited slowly on its coals. The teenagers immersed in their game noticed nothing, until raging flames began to leap out from the top of the tree.

The moment the first boy ran toward him, yelling, Petey's alarm intensified and his bladder gave way. He was rooted to the spot as water flowed down his leg and from his eyes, and children ran toward him with fingers firmly placing blame. And they shouted, "Ooooo! Ohoh! Petey! Look what you did!"

"What's going on down there," an elderly white woman hollered from her second-story window in the Landmoore, an apartment building at 1123 24th Street. "I'm calling the cops on you boys!"

He wanted to run but his legs refused to obey. He wanted to move away from the fire, but felt trapped like a moth hypnotized by a flame. Then, what seemed like only seconds later, "Petey did it! Petey did it," was all he could hear as two white policemen came and lifted him from the spot he had thought he might be welded to forever.

On the short walk to the police car, Petey looked around at the faces of his friends, trying to find sympathy. He saw accusing, frightened eyes staring back, then one of the boys ran off toward Petey's house. Inside the police car, on the way to the Third precinct, Petey thought, "Nobody gone help me now, 'cept A'nt Pig. And I know she gone beat the shit outta me."

A half-hour later, Petey looked up over the counter at the precinct to see his grandmother's stern glare. The navy blue scarf around her head seemed to be pulled tighter than usual, and her face loomed down, unsmiling and ominous. Tears welled up in

his eyes again as he looked back and forth from the policeman to
A'nt Pig. It was like looking from the devil to the deep blue sea.

"You better do something to this boy," the officer said, glancing
up from the short report he filled out on the incident.

"You ain't got to tell me. I'm gone do something to him, all
right. You *know* what I'm gone do. But y'all got to let him out of
here," A'nt Pig said, her voice even lower, deeper and slower than
Petey usually heard it. He could sense in that voice an indication
of the kind of beating he would get with the knotted rope she
kept for his punishments. He knew she hated coming to the
precinct for him, and he thought it must remind her of the troubles
of her own son, Clayton, and her son-in-law, Ralph.

True to his expectations, A'nt Pig administered a severe beating.
Although Petey tried to miss the rope a few times by jumping in
the air as it sailed around his calves, he felt sure each lick landed
more heavily than the last. For the next several days as his whelps
faded, children in the neighborhood teased Petey about the tree.
Nothing else had happened to top that, yet.

On the following Tuesday evening as Petey and A'nt Pig sat on
the steps outside their house, one of Petey's classmates teased him
about the tree before skipping on down the street. By then, A'nt
Pig's anger was gone. She smiled at Petey, shook her head and
said, "Boy, ain't no telling what you gone get into when you leave
out this house in the morning. I just don't never know."

*   *   *

CHAPTER 4

A Whipping to Remember

PETEY'S NEED TO be center stage extended inside the classroom, too, all through his years in school. At Stevens Elementary, sometimes he would disrupt the lesson just so the teacher would call him to the front of the class to apologize. Standing before the other children, feigning remorse for his actions, gave him great pleasure.

"I'm sorry class. I promise not to do that again," Petey often intoned with a straight face and clear, strong voice, year after year. Then he would strut down the narrow aisles back to one of the small chairs with an attached desktop that filled the lower grade rooms. In fourth grade, a boy named Earl Spencer sat beside him. After Petey's frequent apologies, he and Earl would crumple forward into their desktops to conceal snickering behind cupped hands.

But something happened during fourth grade, the fall before he turned 9 years old, that almost cured Petey of misbehaving in class. Two weeks before, A'nt Pig attended a meeting at the school, where parents had been invited to get an early reading of their children's progress.

That early October evening, A'nt Pig tied her hair in her favorite brown scarf, laced her bulky shoes loosely around her ankles, and walked the three blocks from her house on 23rd Street to the school building on 21st, between L and K Streets. She climbed to the second floor and entered the fourth grade classroom.

After visiting with several other parents, Petey's teacher, Miss Ollie Kimbrough, placed her hand on A'nt Pig's elbow and steered her to the wall to view Petey's artwork. A'nt Pig stood several inches higher than Miss Kimbrough but she regarded the smaller woman with respect. Miss Kimbrough, caramel-colored and wearing her hair in a neat bun, spoke in a low, soft voice.

"Let me tell you something Miss Floyd, about Petey. He's the smartest one in the whole class but he just talks all the time. He takes the other children's attention. I can't get the children to do a thing once Petey decides he wants their attention."

A'nt Pig smiled knowingly when Miss Kimbrough acknowledged Petey's intelligence. She looked appreciatively around the room, as though she knew what Miss Kimbrough must be going through, trying to teach nearly 40 restless 9- and 10-year-olds the lessons and the discipline they needed. Like the rest of the adults who came to the open house for parents that night, A'nt Pig placed a high value on education. She believed it would pave the way for her Petey to have a life without the burdens she and Allen had to carry.

"I'm gone see to it that you never have to bow your head to the white man, like your granddaddy and I had to do," she often told Petey. "Don't never bow your head 'less you fixin' to pray."

A'nt Pig turned her dark, determined eyes to Miss Kimbrough, seeing the younger woman's exasperation. She gestured toward Petey's name on the bottom of one of the papers adorning the bulletin board, a nature scene of autumn with leaves of red, yellow and brown. "Well, if this joker give any of y'all any more trouble, it's a store on the corner. You know the one. We ain't got no phone, but if you call the store and aks for that Jew in there, he'll call me to the phone."

The day after the parent-teacher meeting, Petey's behavior seemed more cooperative, but each day thereafter, he got bolder in his attention-getting manuevers. He whispered jokes to the children who sat near him, and when Miss Kimbrough's back was turned, he threw paper across the aisle or crouched near his seat as though in preparation for the 100 yard dash to the chalkboard up front.

In the middle of a math lesson Miss Kimbrough quietly slipped out of the room one day two weeks after the PTA meeting. She left one of the cooperative students in charge, but as soon as the door closed behind her, Petey took over.

He ran up to the front by the blackboard and began to dance wildly. He bucked and whirled, popping his fingers and humming a tune he imagined the adults would dance to that night in one of the clubs near 7th and T Streets. One third of the class cheered and laughed loudly. Another third giggled uncomfortably, keeping an eye on the door. And yet another third frowned in disapproval.

In mid-twirl, Petey caught Earl Spencer's eye. Earl gestured frantically toward the door just as the other children slowly turned to look and a hush began to settle over the room. "Ain't nobody but the teacher," Petey thought, continuing his twirl unfazed. "I got something to tell her anyway. What she got to say can't be no better than what I'm doing. Anyway, all she'll do is make me stand up here and apologize."

Then, a split second before he looked over his shoulder toward the door, he thought of another dance step to show the class, and yelled out to his buddies, "Let me show y'all how to do the Wing."

The last word stuck in his throat like a chicken bone. Miss Kimbrough stood in the doorway, all right. But beside her stood Maggie Floyd, with a familiar, knotted rope in her hand. Up and down her arms, Petey saw flour and dough. Immediately, he knew she had been making bread, using the bag of Washington self-rising flour he'd carted home in his wagon the day before.

With horror, he tore his eyes away from his grandmother to look at his 39 classmates. In their faces, he read surprise, anxious anticipation, and "Ooo I'm glad it's you and not me in this trouble."

The chatter going on in Petey's mind captured his attention. "You can flee if you want to, but before you decide to flee, just understand that there is no place on God's earth that you can go and not have to return," one voice warned, and continued. "This woman is going to double cut your butt if you run. I'm your good conscience. I'm telling you, damnit boy, stand your ground."

The bad conscience chimed in. "To hell with that. Run!"

Again, Petey heard the voice of the good conscience: "You can pay him attention if you wanna, but I'm telling you! Stay!"

Confused, embarrassed, scared to death and unable to run even though he wanted to, Petey's face dissolved in a deluge of tears.

A'nt Pig seemed to shake the floor as she stomped toward Petey with a growl. "Stop that crying, boy. That ain't nothing but the devil coming out of you!" Through his veil of tears, Petey saw his classmates' mouths drop open wider as A'nt Pig snatched the teacher's high-backed chair then plopped down and grabbed Petey by the neck in a single motion. Just as smoothly, she pushed his head down between her scarred knees, dropped his pants and opened the flap on his dingy BVDs.

"Oh no, my red ass is shining to the ceiling of this classroom," Petey had time to realize before the first lash of the rope hit his bare behind. The stunned gasp that the children and Miss Kimbrough sucked in seemed almost practiced in its uniformity and unanimity.

As the rope made a loud whacking, cracking noise that sounded like "Ayeow!" to Petey, he heard A'nt Pig's hard angry question. "You want to dance, do ya?" Crack. Another sound. Awwhow! "I don't sendya here to dance. That's why you ain't got no soles in yo' shoes now!" His behind felt as hot as the tree he'd set on fire the year before, but the rope kept slamming across his bottom, harder and harder, as though A'nt Pig's rage would never abate. He wiggled frantically but everytime he tried to move, her knees tightened their vice-like grip, pressing his ears so tightly against his skull he thought they might dent his head.

The fury of the whipping sent a tremble through Miss Kimbrough. She stepped forward cautiously, reaching her hand toward A'nt Pig. "Miss Floyd . . . I . . ."

With shocking suddenness, A'nt Pig lashed her rope out toward the teacher's wavering fingers, warding her off. Then with another forceful slam of the rope across Petey's rear end, she barked at Miss Kimbrough. "Don't send for me if you don't want me to whip him. And don't tell me how to whip him!"

A'nt Pig pulled Petey up by the shoulders. Tiny beads of sweat formed around the edges of her face. As he stared at his grandmother, snot, tears and saliver dripped from Petey's reddened face and open mouth. He sniveled and shook with fear. How could a person look hard and frosty cold and boiling mad at the same time, Petey wondered.

"Pull your pants up," A'nt Pig commanded, then turned to Miss Kimbrough. "Do you want him to sit or do you want him to stand?"

Still shaken from her near brush with the rope, Miss Kimbrough stammered. "Just let him do anything he wants to do, Miss Floyd."

A'nt Pig rubbed the flour off her arms onto her apron, but kept her eyes on Petey. "Where is yo' seat?"

"Ah . . . ah . . . ah . . ." The wracking sobs would not let him speak, but his grandmother showed no warmth or sympathy. Only anger and frustration.

"Shut up! Get back there," A'nt Pig ordered, still furious, pointing toward the empty seat she saw in the row where Earl Spencer sat looking like he had just seen a thrilling horrow show.

Petey had no time to feel the pain of the welts that cut through the tender skin on his thighs and behind. He had to worry about facing his classmates, who began to relax into the wicked smiles and laughter he dreaded. He heard his grandmother rebuke Miss Kimbrough one last time as she headed out the door.

"Don't call me if you don't want me to come. You see I was making dough, trying to get dinner ready for this nigguh, and his granddaddy be coming in soon. You calling me and then talking 'bout don't hit him! I'll hit you if you call me again and try to tell me how to hit him." She shot one final command to Petey. "Make sho' you come straight home and take them clothes off."

He knew she did not mean for him to get undressed for another whipping. She just meant he should put his school clothes away, as usual, and change to his more threadbare outfit referred to as play clothes. At the time, he had two outfits for school, a play outfit, and a Sunday outfit. He never kept his school clothes on after school unless someone intended to take him downtown to buy something new. And he never wore his Sunday clothes during the week unless a recital or other special program was scheduled at school.

He tried to focus his thoughts on his clothes, but Earl Spencer's voice broke in. "Hey man, I know how you feel. Ooooo. I didn't know you wear BVDs." Petey looked helplessly around the room, but not a face mirrored his sadness. A classmate named Gaskins whispered gleefully, "She wore your ass out!"

And a girl sitting beside Gaskins turned up her nose, tossed her pigtails and announced self-righteously, "That's what he needs. Always cussin'. I'm so glad he got beat. I'm so glaaad. In the cafeteria the other day, he shook his privates at me. Bet he don't never say his prayers, anyway, do he?"

Petey thought about how he knelt down to pray by his small bed every night, but he never wanted to admit that at school because he thought it showed a soft side. At school, he pretended that having a father in jail didn't bother him; being poor didn't bother him; having a mother who was known to drink and fight didn't bother him. At school, he wanted to be a big shot with a bad mouth who could handle anything that came his way.

Miss Kimbrough called the room to order, but for the last hour of class, children snickered uncontrollably whenever they looked at Petey. They couldn't wait for school to end so they could tell the rest of the children about his grandmother's visit. Soon, the neighborhood would know. That time, being in front of the class, being the center of attraction, had not held its usual reward for Petey.

After about four days of ribbing over the beating, Petey put a stop to the reminders. When a little classmate skipped by calling out in sing-song, "Petey got a beatin', Petey got a beatin'," Petey grabbed a brick and hurled it at the boy. At the same time, he hurled one of the insulting rhymes he heard older men use when they "played the dozens," or "signified." Petey left the taunter on the playground in tears by making the ridiculous claim, "I fucked your mother on the bottom of the sea, and the crabs 'round her pussy sang do re mi."

Everyone stopped teasing him after word got around. Kids who didn't know him well wanted to avoid his caustic retorts; his friends stopped teasing him simply because they needed his company. With Petey around, they never had to face a dull moment.

* * *

CHAPTER 5

The Last Cowboy

DESPITE THE FREQUENT whippings, Petey viewed A'nt Pig as his best friend. She, for the most part, accepted the fact that devilment was in his blood and gave him free rein to come and go as he pleased.

Petey could join Freddie Coles, Junior Lee, and Emell to roam the neighborhood, explore in Rock Creek Park, ride the trolley on dollar passes, and play dare-devil games on barges anchored along the Potomac River, all day long without reporting his whereabouts to A'nt Pig. Tacitly, he knew she would not worry about him. It was understood that he would always come back to her, and she would be there for him, his number one champion, no matter what.

Frequently, she proved her posture in ways other adults seldom understood. While other children knew if a neighbor saw them misbehave, that could mean an immediate beating from that adult then a later one from the parent, Petey knew only A'nt Pig punished him. "Don't put your hands on him. If he do anything, just come on tell me," he heard her warn others, even his own mother and aunt, on many occasions. And when someone reported on him, he knew that did not mean an automatic beating; she would first hear his side.

One such incident stuck in his memory all his life as an example of his grandmother's fairness, her role as protector, and her tendency to seize every opportunity to teach him a lesson about the value of money.

Money, the desire to find ways to earn it, keep it, cheat for it, take it, all consumed a major part of A'nt Pig's time and thoroughly infected her precocious grandson well before he turned 9 years old. So it was no surprise that Petey placed himself outside the Sanitary grocery store with other pre-teen boys or alone on Saturdays and other heavy shopping days, offering to cart groceries home for neighborhood shoppers.

One day when Petey stood at his post while most of his young friends and the older boys were off playing, a neighborhood elder known as Miss Davis emerged from the Sanitary with three large paper bags bulging with groceries. Petey stepped up politely, set them in his wagon and rolled knowingly toward Miss Davis's house, not far from his own.

By the time they walked the 20 blocks from the store to Miss Davis's home, the burdensome weight in Petey's wagon had convinced him that he would get at least 50 cents for hauling this load. It seemed that his decision to forego the alley football game had paid off, and he could tease his buddies about missing a great haul.

After Petey set the bags on Miss Davis's kitchen table, he wiped his hands on his pants and waited in excited expectation for his big tip. But instead of hearing coins clink into his outstretched palm, he saw Miss Davis pluck an apple from a nearby bowl and hand it to him as payment. Anger welled up against Petey's sinking heart as he looked from the apple to Miss Davis. He placed it on the table, returned his cold stare to Miss Davis's wrinkled face, and instinctively mumbled his reaction:

"You greyhead bitch."

About a half-hour later, Junior Lee huffed up to where Petey stood outside the Sanitary. "Hey, man," he panted, barely concealing his excitement, "A'nt Pig want you. I think you in trouble. Man, what did you do to Miss Davis?"

Petey trudged off without comment, but Junior Lee, not wanting to miss out on the prologue, offered his company. "Man, I'm gone walk on back here with you, hear?" Outwardly, he feigned sympathy for whatever Petey might face; privately, he relished the thought of seeing Petey get punished, so he could take that choice information to their peers.

When they entered A'nt Pig's living room, Junior Lee, wrapped in the proprietary importance of an emissary, took a corner chair as Miss Davis jumped up from her seat to point an accusing finger. "There he is now, you punish him," she insisted.

"Hold it, Miss Davis," A'nt Pig injected. "I want to hear what he got to say." She spoke directly to Petey, without a trace of predetermined conviction in her voice. "Boy, what you say to Miss Davis?"

"A'nt Pig, you know where Miss Davis live at?" Nodding, she answered, "I know where she live at," and waited for him to continue his story. "You know where the Sanitary at?"

"Yeah."

"Well, Miss Davis had three big bags of grocery and I took 'em all the way to her house and she gave me a apple!"

"What did you do?"

"I called her a greyhead bitch."

Miss Davis's light brown, wizened face darkened with a strange, satisfied rage, and she sputtered, "I told you he said it! I told you!" Her case proven, she waited now for the satisfaction of seeing the child punished.

Her anticipation could not have been any greater, however, than that of Junior Lee, who sat in the corner salivating over the prospect of seeing A'nt Pig give Petey the kind of spanking Junior Lee had only heard about from Petey's classmates the year before. But the old woman and the young boy felt pangs of disappointment similar to Petey's at the sight of the apple, when they heard A'nt Pig say to her wide-eyed, worried grandson:

"Go to your room."

All Petey's nervous anticipation faded into an inner smile. He knew the case was closed. Forming his third finger and thumb into the O.K. sign, Petey signaled to Junior Lee that the show was over. Taking the stairs two by two, he thought of how he would explain his early conclusion later: "When she told me to go upstairs,

I knew the worst I was going to get out of this was a reprimand. If I was going to get indicted and found guilty, A'nt Pig woulda gave this lady the decency to see me get a spanking."

Miss Davis and Junior Lee walked out into the afternoon sun with drooped shoulders and lingering confusion. Petey made sure they both had time to get to their own houses before he came down the narrow staircase to hear the lecture he knew would be waiting for him. But instead of criticizing him about his use of profanity, A'nt Pig gave him a lecture of a different sort, one she would repeat time and again until she thought he had it right.

"Didn't I tell you 'bout taking nigguhs' orders? I told you when you up there at that store, take *white* people orders. These nigguhs ain't got no money. They don't want to give you nothin, or they *cain't* give you nothin, you understand?"

"Yes, A'nt Pig."

"Humph. I'm telling you!

*   *   *

As the years passed, like other boys his age, Petey came to love going to the movies on Saturdays. He and his friends would pay their quarters for an all-day session of movies and newsreels. Petey often was the only one in the group paying close attention to the newsreels, seeking information he could use later in conversations with adults, to show off his intelligence.

But while he relished seeing the news, no one enjoyed the cowboy movies more than Petey; and, unlike the other boys, Petey immersed himself in his fascination, *becoming* a cowboy once back at home. Summer evenings would find Petey's young neighbors shooting marbles, or playing hop scotch or Hide Spy; they'd find 12-year-old Petey straddling his stick horse, galloping up and down the 23rd Street alley in his cowboy gear—hat, chaps, boots, spurs, and holster and gun, courtesy of A'nt Pig.

Boys crouched in the dirt around their marbles would hear Petey clopping toward them, loudly commanding "Whoa, boy," to his stick with the horse's head, then adding, "ErrrErrr," for the galloping-to-a-halt sound effects. To a polite, "Hi, Petey," from anyone walking by, Petey would answer, "How you doin', Pardner?" For extra measure, Petey kept a guitar slung across his shoulder as he stood near his friends, pretending to be a sheriff or a gunslinger.

But one day, a recent movie featuring rustlers and cattle drivers fresh in his mind, Petey decided he no longer wanted to be a sheriff or a gunslinger. A plan forming in his mind, he raced down to a corner store and bought 15 cents worth of bologna, about a quarter inch thick.

Then he set about assembling what he could use as a herd of cattle: tearing off pieces of meat, he lured 10 stray, flea-bitten, rough, hungry mutts to a garage at the end of the nearby alley and locked them up. "Now, these steers are in my stockyard," he decided proudly, turning his attention to the rest of his plan.

Hours later, all the neighborhood children who were allowed to stay up after dark continued their day-time games in the warm summer twilight. "Let's play Hi' Spy," Emell called to Petey, before running with two more boys toward a group of girls playing hop scotch under the lamppost at the end of the street.

"Naw, I'm going on to bed. See y'all."

Petey's answer surprised Emell, but he didn't have time to ask about it; he wanted to find a girl to partner with in the game some called Hide and Go Seek. Sitting on her porch enjoying her pipe that evening, A'nt Pig, too, reacted to Petey's unusually early return.

"What's wrong, Rabbit? You sick," she asked when he trudged up the steps with a serious, heavy countenance. "I'm just tired," he lied. "I'm gone go on to bed now."

Upstairs, Petey took off his regular play clothes and donned his cowboy outfit, black mask, black hat, spurs on black boots, two guns in a holster, and a black cape tied at the neck. So A'nt Pig would not see him, he climbed out of his second story window to the roof of the woodshed just below. In one hand, he held his stick horse and a thick, crumpled wad of newspapers; in one pocket, he placed matches.

By this time, the children had abandoned their game of Hide Spy in favor of marbles and other games in the dirt at the mouth of the alley. Petey made sure they did not notice him at the other end, where he crept to the garage, his stockyard. Timing moves he practiced in his head all day, Petey turned his rolled newspapers into a torch, almost simultaneously releasing the dogs into the alley. Galloping behind the barking, howling herd, he waved his flaming torch and yelled, "Eiyaaa Eiyaaa," casting himself in the role of a professional rustler of cattle.

The children looked up and saw fire! And dogs! Barking wildly and running right toward them. The girls and boys could not know that the dogs, equally alarmed and confused, meant them no harm. So the children panicked, and darted into the street, running without thinking, along with the dogs. One girl, named Wilhelmina, ran right into the path of a truck. From mid-way down the alley, his torch held high, Petey watched in horror as the girl fell, struck in the middle of the street.

A whispered "Errrr," escaped his lips as he yanked the reins of his stick horse, whirled around and, through force of habit, rhythmically lipped "boggedy woggedy," as he galloped back to the woodshed in his yard. He threw his horse on the shed's roof, hoisted himself up, and fell into the window breathlessly. Fear of discovery blocking out all rationale, Petey threw his hat across the room and leaped into bed fully dressed, pulling the covers tightly under his chin.

His heartbeat registered the minutes like a grandfather clock on his pillow, while he prayed no one would come. He cautiously let out his breath after what seemed like about 20 minutes, but gasped it back in when he heard a loud noise downstairs. "Oh my God. The posse is here. They coming for me. The vigilantes coming to get my ass," his mind screamed out while his body remained stiff as an embalmed corpse.

"A'nt Pig, Petey got that girl hit by a truck," he heard a child's voice accuse hysterically.

"Naw, Petey in bed. I don't know what you mean."

"No, A'nt Pig, it was him," the child persisted, to Petey's accelerating dread. He thought surely his panic would cause him to lose consciousness or wet the bed when he heard A'nt Pig answer:

"Come on. I'm going to show y'all where he really is. Don't put that on my boy. Come on upstairs."

In the seconds it took the crowd to ascend the stairs, Petey mentally undressed a hundred times, so his full regalia would not give him away. He silently cursed himself for not at least shoving the hat under the bed. But, with no time for action, he remained petrified, clutching the covers with bloodless knuckles.

A'nt Pig entered the room and held the kerosene lamp aloft so the children could see Petey in his bunk bed, eyes closed tightly as though deep in sleep. "Now, y'all see him right there. There he is, where he been all night."

But Junior Lee, the same Junior Lee who relished the thought of seeing Petey pay for cursing, noticed something awry, and yelled out, "He got his boots on. Look!" Then ran over and snatched the covers back off, exposing the black cape, guns and holster, black boots and spurs, and Petey, red with fear and embarrassment.

A'nt Pig turned and left the room, the "posse" filing quietly behind her to go out and soon learn that Wilhelmina was okay and would be home from the hospital that same night. A'nt Pig would have to pay the doctor's $50 fee.

When Petey woke and went downstairs that next morning, he found A'nt Pig sitting in her favorite chair. Without raising her voice, she commanded:

"Bring me the hoss. Bring me them guns, and all that mask and stuff. Your cowboys days is over."

Petey knew he had no room to negotiate. He would never have his beloved cowboy trappings again as long as he lived in A'nt Pig's house. Years later, he remembered the definite finality with which he viewed that phase. Explaining his proficiency at card-sharking, he told his best buddy in the Army, "When I put down my guns, I picked up the dice and the cards. I was about 12. I said, 'Fuck it. Let's gamble.'"

Late that same summer, Petey developed a fascination for alcohol that would take him to the edge of oblivion time after time in his adult life. Drinking looked like fun to Petey when he saw teenagers and older men use their intoxication as a ticket to uncontrolled carousing, cursing and cavorting.

Petey watched with amusement as men staggered, laughing, in and out of houses like his, where people bought bootleg liquor. He eyed them loitering in alleyways, playing the dozens and catcalling to anyone wearing a skirt. And he envied the men he saw when he peered into beer gardens and late night joints where liquor flowed freely, courtesy of high-rolling hustlers who showed off wads of money and sported pretty ladies on their laps.

Saturday mornings gave Petey and his best friend a golden opportunity to "play drunk." They would comb through trash cans, retrieving a bounty in near empty fifths, and pour the corners into a single bottle until they got enough for each to take a stiff swig. Then, though not intoxicated, they would stagger along alley walls and slur their speech like the men they pretended to be.

By the time school started that fall, Petey considered himself a seasoned drinker who could "handle his liquor." So when he and three classmates stumbled upon a cache of seriously strong bootleg liquor hidden in mason jars in the woods off P Street, near Francis Junior High School, at recess, Petey did not hesitate to suggest an afternoon party. They rounded up one of the 8th grade girls who let herself into the house after school because her mother worked late, and three other 13- and 14-year-old girls adventurous enough to play hookey, then headed off with the booze.

Shortly after 3 p.m., the young hostess told her party guests to go home. She wanted ample time to clear and clean the house before her mother got home at 5. Everyone did go home, except Petey, who stumbled instead back to school, where he ended up in a cussing match with a janitor.

*   *   *

CHAPTER 6

Good Ol' Days

IN SPITE OF the nearly unbelievable antics Petey pulled, he managed to live the relatively normal childhood of his contemporaries. They roamed the town on streetcars, played in the woods of Rock Creek Park, and formed neighborhood teams for football and baseball. In the mid-40s, when Petey was in his early-teens, he coached a 12-and-under team to a championship against nearly impossible odds.

Before he adopted the rag-tag crew of feisty youngsters, he'd been playing on a team called the Potomac Rams, made up of guys aged 15 to 17, although Petey was 14. The younger guys didn't have anything to do, so they began hanging around the Potomac Rams during practice, throwing rocks or talking loud, trying to aggravate the players on the 15 to 17, 18-20 or 20 and over teams.

One evening after practice, Petey loped over to the younger boys. "Y'all want to play football?" he asked in a voice just beginning to settle into the gravelly tone he would later boom from stages, radio and television. To a series of nods, he added, "Y'all wanna play football for me?"

"Yeah, we'll play for you, Petey," the youngsters smiled, pushing and shoving each other.

"Okay. I'll have to get y'all some jerseys and stuff, so all y'all bring me back a dollar each tomorrow. We gone have practice then I'm gone go get y'all some uniforms."

The next day, each boy proudly turned his dollar over to Petey, then trustingly listened as Petey determined who would play what position. That evening, Petey took the money to a game of craps, hoping to increase it to buy uniforms and equipment. Instead, he lost it all.

"When we gone get them jerseys," the boys asked each day at practice for two weeks, until finally their patience expired. "If you don't get our jerseys, we want our money back, or we gone get our big brothers on you, Petey," a kid named Big Stu threatened.

"Y'all shut up and look at this play," Petey said, drawing on a blackboard at Francis Junior High and stalling for time. "I'm gone get y'all in the Boys Club league, you'll see."

At practice the next day, Petey took the team for a walk up U Street to 12th to the Boys Club, where neighborhood teams could enter to play against each other and against the Boys Club team. Harry Pope, the adult in charge, asked, "Who's the coach." Petey answered, "Me."

"Who's the manager?"

Again, Petey said, "Me." And the owner? "Me."

Finally, Mr. Pope put down the form. "You don't have an adult."

"No, I'm in charge of everything," Petey said, trying to put as much authority into his 14-year-old voice as possible.

Harry Pope shook his head. "I'm sorry, you've got to have a grown-up." Petey and his band of followers marched out, anger steaming off their scalps. They walked right into Jabbo Kenner, the head counselor at the Boys Club.

"What's the matter with y'all?" Jabbo Kenner asked Petey.

"Mr. Jab, Mr. Pope won't let me put this team in the league up here, 'cause we ain't got no grown-up."

The man Petey would later always refer to as Big Jabbo put his arms out to the group. "Come on. I'll take care of it."

Opening the door, Jabbo spoke to Harry Pope. "Hey, look. You know this is my team. These are my boys from over in Georgetown where I came from. I'll take care of them." Without pausing, he reached for the forms that would allow the team to get pants, cleats and shoulder pads. Each team still had to get its own helmets and jerseys.

Once outside, Jabbo pulled Petey to the side. "You got 'em. I'll come over there from time to time to talk to you, but I want you to bring me a championship, and I want you to bring it to me this year."

Petey smiled broadly at his team, and they all set off happily for the long walk back to Georgetown. Still, Petey could not forget the problem of the jerseys, because the boys asked him daily for their shirts or their money back.

The next day, Petey approached Barney Sessle, a Jewish man who owned a lunchroom but also was a hustler A'nt Pig wrote numbers for in the neighborhood. Often, Petey worked in the lunchroom, guarding the sodas against theft from neighborhood kids.

"Hey, man. I need $100."

"If you don't get the hell out of here, asking me for $100. What is wrong with you?" Barney glared at Petey as if he'd just come from Saint Elizabeth's mental hospital.

Petey knew his explanation would hit the right chord. "You know all them little niggers be coming in here trying to steal the sodas? Well, I got 'em on a football team to keep 'em busy and we need some jerseys."

"Get on out of here, boy," Barney said, turning his face to hide a smile. A short while later, he sent one of his messengers for Petey. Peeling ten crisp 10-dollar bills from his roll, Barney commanded, "Y'all better bring me a trophy."

Petey made a beeline for a discount sporting goods store where he bought yellow and blue jerseys for 25 players, spending about $50. The other $50 went toward a pair of fashionable pants for Petey.

When the team saw their jerseys, they couldn't have been happier. But after a few practices, the boys were getting better and better at football but the jerseys started looking worse and worse.

"Y'all know what? These jerseys ain't good enough. I want y'all to start serving papers and doing whatever you need to do so we can raise enough money to get some new jerseys and some helmets," Petey told his loyal team one afternoon after practice.

"Since they the Rock Creek Indians, I think they should have red jerseys," Joe Lee chimed in. Joe and a few others from the Potomac Rams had taken an interest in Petey's team, regarding it as kind of a farm team to the older squad. The guys agreed, and started working toward buying red and white jerseys with matching helmets for the games they would play at 10 on Saturday mornings against other teams in the Boys Club league. The Rams played at 1 o'clock, which gave Petey a little time between coaching one team and playing on the next.

Among the guys on Petey's young team were Big Stu, whose real name was John Harvey; Jackie Lyle; Sylvester Gadson; Petey Matthews; Big John Brown; Leroy Carver; Pedro Parker; Philander Young; Benny Smith; John Sedgewick; Robert Morgan who everyone called Bobby Doe; Gerald Brown who the kids called Tony Pappalina because he could speak with an Italian accent; Howard Markhum; Leonard Dixon; Bo and Billy Peters; Leon Smith whose nickname was Ping Pong; Benny Smith; Sam Lynch; Leslie Gore who they called Mickey, and more.

The games, held at Banneker school grounds on Georgia Avenue, generated attention throughout the neighborhood. Little girls followed the team across town to cheer, and parents kept their ears open for news of success. Would the Rock Creek Indians win, or the Northeast Avalanches or the LeDroit Park Falcons? Or would it be the well-equipped Boys Club team made up of kids from all the city's neighborhoods.

At 8 a.m. on the morning of the first game, Petey assembled his team for the walk from Georgetown to Banneker, near Howard University. Shortly after arriving on the field, Petey's team gawked as the Boys Club in-house team hopped off the bus that brought them from 12th and U to Banneker's field on Georgia Avenue. They immediately fell into a routine of running around the field and throwing the football in choreographed moves like the pros.

"Maaan, look at them big guys!" Petey said in a low voice. "They'll kill our ass . . ." Without waiting to see how his team felt, Petey stomped off to the Boys Club official who had matched the teams for competition.

"What is y'all doing? These ain't nothing but kids!" he demanded, speaking of his team of boys who were just two years younger than he.

The adult in charge stared back. "Look, we didn't ask you to get in the league."

Petey's boys frantically waved him back over. "We want to play! We ain't scared. We came all the way over here."

Calling for a show of hands and seeing every boy raise both his hands to play, Petey kicked into positive gear. "Okay, let's get this show on the road."

All doubt left Petey's mind when he glanced over at the opposing team and saw Harmon Wolfe, a kid who had defected from the Rock Creek Indians to join the Boys Club team. Petey knew his band of ruffians wanted more than anything to get back at Harmon.

He gathered his team for the Lord's Prayer, then snapped his fingers for them to put on their helmets, harness their motivation, and take the field.

The final score, 19 to 6, in favor of the Rock Creek Indians! Less than two hours later, the Potomac Rams beat the Yellowjackets, giving Georgetown double crowing rights.

That night, Petey's bandits couldn't wait to go by Harmon's house near 18th and T streets to rib him. "Yeah, man. You got off our team, but we kicked your ass." Handsome and affable, Harmon didn't really care. He took it all in stride. These were his friends from Stevens Elementary and Francis Junior High.

In the afternoon after the win, Barney treated the team to hot dogs and sodas. "Glad you won, but that still ain't the trophy. Y'all bring me the trophy," he admonished lightly.

The following weekend, the team faced the LeDroit Park Falcons, coached by an adult, J.O. Williams. Wearing burgundy and gold, the team looked professional. Big Stu looked to Petey for confidence. "They got the Banks brothers and the Bird brothers," he said.

"Yeah, but we still gone win. We gone catch 'em off guard. We been practicing since early this morning, so we not gone work out on the field. Just let me do the talking," Petey told his team.

J.O. Williams, the opposing team's coach, came over to Petey. "Your team gets the field for 15 minutes to practice, warm up."

"Naw, that's all right. We tired. We don't want to practice," Petey faked, laughing inside with the knowledge that his guys just put in more than two hours running drills, getting ready.

"Y'all go kick the ball a couple of times and come on and lay back down," Petey said, stifling a yawn, totally confusing coach Williams.

The final score, 21 to 7, in favor of the Rock Creek Indians.

But the fairy tale record of wins ended when one of Petey's best players, a boy with the nickname of Eel, moved to D.C.'s Northeast section and joined the team there, the Avalanches. His brother, nicknamed Hotsy, continued to play with Georgetown's older kids, the Potomac Rams. But Eel took his considerable talent at wiggling away from any grasp over to Northeast, and put fear in his former Georgetown teammates.

Piled into an old trash truck for the ride from Georgetown in Northwest to a field in Northeast, Petey's team talked itself into serious doubts about winning against the one boy who had helped the team to victory in the first two games. True to their expectations, the Avalanches under Eel's leadership beat the Rock Creek Indians 19 to zip.

Their shoulders slumped and their ears burned from Petey's fussing, but the team pulled itself back together. By the second round of games leading to the championship, the Rock Creek Indians had lost only one game, the one to Eel's team; the Avalanches had lost one to the LeDroit Park Falcons; and the Falcons had been beat once by the Indians. Each of the neighborhood teams had better records than the Boys Club in-house team.

In his typical over-the-line fashion, Petey had stuck two ringers on his team in preparation for meeting the Avalanches when he knew his team would face them for the championship. He'd pulled two 14-year-olds from the Rams, both of whom looked like they were 12.

For the first half of the game, the score remained zero to zero. Finally, Mickey Gore called the quarterback sneak, after letting John Montgomery run the ball for a few plays to get the team in scoring position. Then, at the two-yard line, he went over for a touchdown.

With Petey's team ahead 6 to 0, it seemed to Petey that the referee started showing favoritism to the Avalanches. After one penalty too many, unable to restrain himself, Petey ran onto the field. "You calling all this bad-ass shit on these kids," he flailed at the referee. Petey's heart knew the adults did not want to see a team coached by a kid make history by winning the championship.

"You don't tell me how to . . . Get off this goddamn field," the referee shouted, losing his cool completely in the face of an upstart teenaged coach-manager-owner. "Don't come on this field again!"

Petey's team grabbed him, afraid for what he might do. "That's all right Petey, we got 'em." But Petey's sense of justice erased all reason from his mind. The next time the referee made what looked like an unfair call, Petey charged back out on the field. His action, whether fair or not, earned his team a 15-yard penalty and allowed Eel and his team to score.

The game ended with a 6-6 tie and a decision that the teams would be co-champions. At first, his team fumed. "Man, we had 'em. You messed us up. You made us lose the championship." But when they got to the Boys Club to collect their trophy at a banquet the next day, they forgave him. Petey forgave himself, too. Falling back on one of A'nt Pig's southern sayings, he grinned to himself. "A half a hog is better than none."

As soon as they got back to Georgetown after the award ceremony, the Rock Creek Indians marched into Barney's lunchroom. Petey held the prize aloft. "You asked for a trophy for your $100. There it is."

Barney teased, "You went and bought that thing, didn't you?"

The kids laughed, then settled in for the hot dogs, sodas and candy Barney treated them to for giving the neighborhood a championship. The team kept the winning spirit, and under another youthful coach, Chubby Lewis, they became the Rock Creek Indians basketball team next season. Ironically, Chubby would later become a guard at the D.C. Jail.

*   *   *

Of course playing sports typified childhood, but Petey went one better by taking leadership where it had never gone before. Nearly four decades after the fact, he could hardly stop smiling as he concluded his childhood sports stories.

Petey's voice: Showtime at Halftime

"It was a big thing for me to have a chance to play on one team and then run this other team. Right where Howard University is now, there was a stadium called Griffith Stadium. We were the first little black niggers to play in that. What happened, two big teams were going to play there, the Willowtrees and the Lincoln ACs, one Sunday. I went to one of the owners of one of the teams and asked him what did they have for halftime. Well, it wasn't like they had big halftime bands. So, I said, 'Well, I got a team and I can get a game with a team from LeDroit Park, and we'll play at halftime.' Ain't but 15 minutes. The man said, 'That's a good idea.'

"But we had become so good, wouldn't no other little team play us up there that Sunday. So, what we had to do was break our team down. Them gold and blue jerseys we had at first, half the team put those on and the other half put the red and white jerseys on. People in the stands see these little motherfuckers come out! I took four or five guys off the team I was on and put them out there, too.

"I got it all like Barnum and Bailey. It's all show. Everybody on my team know what they gone do. We got about 10,000 people in the stand. Everybody that Sunday gone know when to miss a tackle, know when to make a slick catch. It's all show business now. Solid. And we gone end it 6-6. We gone let one team get 6, but it's gonna be a 95-yard run and all that. Went off like clockwork. And this goddamn Bobby Doe, bless his soul, he gone now. We had hooked it all up, and everybody was doing what they supposed to do. The crowd was going wild. And the last man to get the ball was Bobby.

"We give it to Bobby 'cause he was a nice looking kid. Could run, too. He shook his little helmet off, the crowd was going wild, 'cause players was diving at him like they were trying to tackle him. And that motherfucker! They laughed at Bobby because he tripped over his own feet. The guys gave him hell. Said, 'You couldn't make a fixed touchdown!' But the crowd loved it.

"And again, I don't want to beat my own drum, but that's how far advanced I was. I know this ain't no time to play no real game. We got 15 minutes. You can show off, and that's really what they done. And then they lived with that for a long time. 'We the only ones that played at Griffith Stadium.' It was a real highlight."

Chapter 7

A'nt Pig on Thad

WHILE THE RELATIONSHIP Petey had with A'nt Pig was dependable, unchanging and filled with unquestionable love, the direct opposite was true of his relationship with his parents. Ralph Greene Senior spent time with his sons on those rare occasions when he was out of prison, but his volatile personality rarely left room for his sons to feel comfort in his presence.

As for Petey's mother, a penchant for late night drinking and partying often left her unable to care for the children who lived with her—Clayton and Thad, and later, Joyce and Perry, children she had with another man. She turned at least once a month to A'nt Pig to help carry the load of feeding and clothing children whose fathers either could not or would not help. On those occasions when Jackie and her family lived in A'nt Pig's house, Petey never let the younger children forget who was king.

Sometimes, however, the spotlight left Petey and centered squarely on Thad, four years Petey's junior and four times more likely to instigate real trouble. Thad drowned about 10 of the kittens who purred under and over the furniture in A'nt Pig's living room. He set fire to a bedroom doorway so he could leap in, fully attired in a fireman's outfit, and rescue a sleeping doll. And he earned whippings so fierce, Petey thought his brother would surely be knocked into retardation.

Even A'nt Pig worried about the severity of the beatings her daughter Jackie administered. "Stop hitting that boy in the head!" A'nt Pig barked at Jackie time and again. "Just hit a child on his

ass. You knock that boy up side the head too much! That's why
the child ain't got no sense now."

But, Petey thought, if Thad had anything to say about it, he'd
choose a crack over the head instead of A'nt Pig's brand of punishment.

*   *   *

"Boy! You wet this bed again? You too old to be peeing in the
bed, and I'm too old to be washing sheets every day. Come here,"
A'nt Pig yelled at Thad one cold winter morning. "Now suck this
heah sheet!"

Thad stood before A'nt Pig, his full lips sagging and his eyes
wide in disbelief. "Boy, I said suck this heah sheet. Suck it dry!"

Large tears welled up in Thad's eyes, but with Petey watching,
Thad shuffled over to the sheet A'nt Pig held in her strong hand,
and obeyed. He never wet the bed again.

Although A'nt Pig openly played favorites, letting everyone
know she loved Petey more than she loved anyone else, she
showed her affection for the others by trying to teach them good
habits, in her own inimitable style.

Petey and the other children constantly teased Thad about his
weight by calling him "Fatass." "Mama, A'nt Pig," Thad would whine,
"Petey an'em callin me Fatass!" Petey would stretch his eyes and spread
his hands wide in innocence, claiming, "Uhunnh. What you talking
about? I called you Thaddeus. That's your name, ain't it?"

After this ribbing had gone on for months, A'nt Pig decided
she would put Thad on a diet. But each time she looked around,
he was getting a dime from an adult and running to the store to
buy an ice cream on a stick, called a "Choc-Cow." One hot mid-
summer day, she ambled to a corner store and returned with a
huge container holding several gallons of ice cream. She lowered
her heavy frame to a chair on her porch, then yelled to Thad, who
was playing marbles with Petey and his friends Emell and Freddy
in the dirt at the end of the block.

Intuitively, Petey knew this was something he didn't want to
miss. He remembered an earlier time A'nt Pig brought home a

large number of hot dogs and made Thad eat them all, to break him of the habit of only asking for hot dogs for dinner. He signaled to his friends to follow him home, where Thad stood gaping at the ice cream A'nt Pig placed on the top step leading to the porch.

"Here, boy. I'm gone cure you of eating ice cream all the time. Eat all this," she demanded, without a hint of a smile.

"Thad look like he died and gone to heaven," Petey said, hunching Emell, while Thad dropped to the top step, grinning widely and scraping a large spoon across the hard surface of his favorite treat. As the older boys watched in fascination, Thad ate like a man who'd just spent weeks in the dessert, deprived of food, stopping only to laugh out loud every two or three minutes.

Petey watched the event like a reporter covering a White House state dinner, offering running commentary every 30 seconds. "I think ol' Thad gone get out on A'nt Pig this time," Petey whispered to Freddy. "Look like he gone eat *all* that shit!"

But after about 15 minutes, Thad slowed down, stealing a sideways glance up at A'nt Pig. "Oh oh, he looking kinda Donald Duckish now," Petey decided.

"Eat it! Eat it!" A'nt Pig scowled, forcing Thad to dig in with renewed vigor but with obviously less joy. Five more minutes passed before Thad moaned, rolled onto the ground, and pleaded, "Ah, ah . . . I can't eat no more."

"Eat one more spoonful. Eat it, I said!" When she saw that Thad's quivering lips would allow him to consume no more ice cream, A'nt Pig stood to go inside. "Get up boy. I know you won't be aksing for no more ice cream for a while now. Get your fat ass on up off that ground." She stooped to pick up the container that was just under half full, then faced Petey and his friends. "Here, dogs, go ahead and tear it up. I know that's what y'all been waiting for." Thad ran away at the mention of ice cream for the rest of the summer.

In church, however, Thad ruled. He could make Petey laugh, then clear his face of any traces of a smile, and leave his brothers to take the fall for laughing in the sanctuary.

Years past Thad's death, Petey reminisced: "Thad was really sick and crazy. We'd be sitting in the house, and he'd do something dumb. One day, my grandmother say, 'Something burning in here.' She happened to look around, it's Thad! He had went and got a dollbaby, put the dollbaby in the room upstairs on our bed, and put some kerosene all around the door sill, then lit the door. He had seen a show on television about a rescue, and he had a cape on. He gone go in and save that motherfucking baby in the fire.

"Boy, when my grandmother got through beating him! Thad had been up there talking to hisself. 'It's a child up there!' We got some water and put the fire out. The door was charred and shit. Boy, I felt sorry for him. I guess he was around 8 or 9 years old. Whenever we didn't see him, my grandmother would say, 'Where's he at? Go find him,' 'cause that boy would be doing something crazy.

"One time he killed a bunch of my grandmother's cats. She had about 28 of 'em, and he choked some of them to death. He got 'em one day behind the couch and just killed 'em. I was glad. Me and my brother Clayton wanted to give Thad a medal for that, 'cause A'nt Pig had too many cats.

"She'd walk down the street, they all be behind her. She'd turn around and talk to 'em. 'I told y'all quit following me, 'cause I ain't got no money to buy all y'all no food. Wait 'til I come back, I'll bring y'all something.' They'd stop. She talked to 'em just like they was people. They'd sit all up on top of things. They were a trademark in our house, and had been there over the years. It was a new breed of 'em Thad killed. He must have killed about 10 or 15 before my grandmother saw him. She beat him with the same rope she used for all of us, and she beat him half to death that time.

"But Thad was the quietest one of all my mother's children. And turned out to be the best safe-cracker ever to crack a safe."

Chapter 8

Sibling Rivalry

AS ADULTS, PETEY and his brother Clayton spent years estranged from one another, only to renew their closeness within ten years before Petey's death. While triggered by grown-up slights, the mistrust and distance were born of childhood hurt and misplaced envy.

Initially, Petey envied Clayton. In fact, when Petey's mother placed the infant Clayton in a bassinet at A'nt Pig's house during a visit when Petey was just over a year old, Petey lobbed a glass baby milk bottle at Clayton's head. His mother wound herself up to whip Petey unmercifully, but A'nt Pig interceded with a stern rebuke.

"You gived him to me to raise. I'm the onlest one gone whip him. Don't you never lay a hand on him." A'nt Pig stood over Jackie, her eyes hard and hot as coal from the wood-burning stove nearby.

By the time the boys were 11 and 12, Jackie had born children with a man other than Ralph Senior. Her fortunes took a turn for the worse, and she could no longer care for the children who lived with her—Sugar Boy and Thad, Petey's full brothers, and Marion, Bobby, Perry and Joyce, his half siblings. Even coming to A'nt Pig's house for extended stays couldn't bring her to financial health.

When the children would pile in to A'nt Pig's with Jackie, friction inevitably erupted. And this time, all the children directed their envy toward Petey. To compensate, A'nt Pig occasionally gave one of the other children Petey's old toys. Each time, Petey raised hell.

"Let that chap keep that ol' gun," A'nt Pig would command.

Looking back on it, and even at the time, Petey understood A'nt Pig's strategy. He spoke of it wistfully, fondly.

"When she'd make me let him keep it, that would give him a little sense of getting out on me. But after they'd leave the room and we'd get by ourselves, she'd slip me a dollar or something. My grandmother just loved me. It was no question in nobody's mind. She showed it in all kinda ways. It was nothing that could take the place of me."

Naturally some of the tension grew from having so many people packed in such a small amount of space. Often, A'nt Pig found herself taking in her grown son, two grown daughters, and a host of grandchildren at the same time.

Her house had two bedrooms upstairs, a kitchen, a dining room and a living room downstairs. When the troops moved in, the dining room became a bedroom with a roll-away cot where A'nt Pig's son Clayton would sleep. In the living room slept Jackie, her sister who was called Big Sister, and two of the children. Upstairs, in the room usually reserved for Petey, the rest of the children crowded onto his double bed. As for Petey, he always had the sole luxury of sleeping in A'nt Pig's bedroom, in her double bed with her.

After months of scratching to make ends meet, and failing, Jackie decided to send Sugar Boy to live with childless relatives in Yonkers, New York. The couple, the LeBoeufs, could give Clayton the food, the clothes, the comfort Jackie thought he deserved and knew she could not provide. Clayton could not see it that way. He viewed the arrangement as an exile. He was being sent to New York, while Petey stayed in D.C. with A'nt Pig. His hurt and resentment brewed on low boil just below the surface for years. It finally exploded in an adult argument with Petey that would drive the brothers apart for decades.

As a teenager, though, Clayton remained conflicted about his circumstances. Sometimes he even appreciated the solid, rigid lifestyle the LeBouefs tried to instill.

Petey tells a humorous story that symbolizes the emotional conflict his brother grappled with ever since their mother sent him away.

Petey's voice: Clayton's Return

"Once one of A'nt Pig's relatives died, and all her people from South Carolina came up and the ones living in New York came down. Clayton, Sugar Boy, came down with the people he was living with.

My grandmother was the Allied Supreme Commander when the family came for this funeral. People were staying with various relatives or they stayed at the Dunbar or Whitebar hotel. These 'bamas had money. They would have suitcases with rope around 'em and all kind of chicken and grease on 'em, but they had money.

"Couldn't talk no English. T'was, T'wasn't. Names like Uncle Bubba, Cousin Joe, Cousin Sweet Hog. By this time, Sugar Boy had been away about three years. He was 14 or so, but I could see he was running that family. Had a baaad suit on, nice hair cut. Me and my brother Thad were looking at him, then looking at each other thinking 'oooo, this boy has gone crazy.'

"We had a dog who was a puppy when Sugar Boy left. We still had the dog, so Clayton say, 'Jesus Christ! You still have that mutt here?' I looked at Thad and said, 'Oh my God, this nigger done turned white on our ass.'

"But we young and everyone is sitting around after the wake. The adults talking about hog-killing time and whatever else they do down south. But I'm thinking about the dance that's going to start at my junior high school, Francis. I tell my mother, not anybody else, and she gives us the 35 cents it costs to go. But the lady that's raising Sugar Boy says, 'No, this is no time to be frolicking. Our cousin is dead.'

"We sat down, disappointed, until my mother came over saying she wanted us to go to the store for her. She's younger than most of these people and she sympathizes with us. When we get outside, she says, 'Look, go 'head to the dance but come back before too long.' Sugar Boy doesn't get it. When we pass the store, he stops. I said, 'I don't know why you're stopping here. We're going to the dance.' But he was afraid to disobey. I said, 'Well you take the bread and milk and go on back.' I go to the dance and jam like crazy.

"When I get back after 11, they all sitting around. Miz LeBouef grabbed me. 'You went to the dance after we forbade you to go.' She's got a rope in her hand, 'cause they believe in whipping. But I know my grandmother has never let me down. She walked between us, saying, 'Hold it. The one you raised came back and is upstairs in bed. I'm raising this one. I'm putting shoes on his feet, clothes on his back. Nobody else, not even his mammy, touches him. When his ass needs whipping, I whips his ass.'

"She nodded to me, 'Go in there. Your food is on the back of the stove. Eat your food and go on to bed.' She know and I know I ain't done nothing wrong. But this aunt, Miz LeBouef was so mad, she went and woke my brother up and they stayed in a motel.

"After that, Sugar Boy thought I had all the freedom in the world. When they got back to New York, he ran away and came back down to DC. He knew my clothes wasn't up to par like his and my house wasn't as nice, but he thought there wasn't no rules for me, I was free as a bird. Of course there was rules for me, but my rules had more flexibility than his did.

"From the week that he was visiting, his life looked stagnated to him. With all that good stuff he had up there, he wanted to be like me . . . 'til he got down here and after about a month, he tried to RUN back up to New York. He didn't know how poor we were. He and I talk about that now, and laugh.

"A long time ago, people thought me and Clayton were twins. Whenever Clayton sees a Washington, D.C. tag on a car in New York, he'll go to 'em and say, 'Y'all might know my brother.' Or sometimes before he can say that, they'll say, 'Man, you Petey Greene's brother!'

"He was on an elevator in DC one time and he asked these broads, 'Y'all know Petey Greene?' And one of the broads say, 'I'm his boss. He work for me,' which I did. But when he got off the elevator, he told his buddy who was with him, 'He might work for her, but ain't nair a nigguh in Washington is his boss. He ain't got no boss. The president live here, but he ain't even the boss.'

"And that's the thing my grandmother used to always tell people, that nobody bosses Petey at no time. She'd say, 'I'm the only boss he got, and the only reason I'm the boss is because he know that I'll wear his tail out, and if he had half a chance, I wouldn't be his boss.'

"My grandmother just knew. She had bigger ideas for me. She wanted me to be a lawyer or a preacher, because she'd get to listening to me talk, and at night, when all my friends would be at my house laying on the floor, my grandmother would be over in a chair looking at her next day's numbers or talking to somebody grown. Then, after my friends leave, my grandmother used to tell me, 'Boy, you something!' She woulda been listening to how I kept all the attention focused on me. The greatest thing God ever gave me was my verbal skills."

*   *   *

Petey wasn't bragging. He had thousands of stories to back up his matter-of-fact assessment of his natural-born talent. Often, he used these stories in speeches to gain support for Efforts for Ex-Convicts, a group he started after his release from prison. Or when he moved around DC as a field worker for the United Planning Organization, an outgrowth of Lyndon Johnson's anti-poverty programs. Later still, he'd recount personal episodes ending with a moral on his Gospel Radio talk show.

But there were others he hadn't shared on such a public stage, and he wanted to write them down. Relaxing on the baby blue carpet of the living room in his spacious home in Fort Washington, MD, Petey talked to the woman he had chosen to write his life story.

With a stream-of-consciousness style that often spread one story out over several two-hour sessions, Petey recounted outrageous vignettes of his days first as a teenaged private then a sergeant in the U.S. Army. Hilarious tales of using B'rer Rabbit smarts to outwit either Army stockade guards or those at Lorton prison. Or sometimes, he'd spend hours talking about his grandmother and things she would say that applied to the day's news or events 20 years past her death. His most poignant story was of his grandmother helping him kick a heroin habit.

CHAPTER 9

Cold Turkey Withdrawal

PETEY'S BROTHER CLAYTON regarded Petey as strong, shrewd, peerless, even when he also thought Petey was selfish. Petey saw himself as strong, too, in almost every phase of his life except addiction. When it came to kicking habits, he found his strength in A'nt Pig. And her God.

With uncharacteristic somberness, Petey told the story of letting his grandmother help him kick his first terrible habit, and how he found that same strength decades later to kick the second one.

Petey's Voice

"The only time I ever seen my grandmother cry is when she found out I was a dope fiend, and she didn't let but two tears run down her eyes then. That's after somebody had convinced her what drugs would do to me. Once I seen her cry, then it dawned on me that I had done something to her that nobody had ever done. She didn't even cry at my grandfather's funeral. I even seen a man pull a gun in my grandmother's face and tell her, 'If you don't get my goddamn money, I'm gone blow your brains out.' She say, 'Well you gone have to blow 'em out nigguh, 'cause the money won't be here 'til tomorrow.'

"And one time my uncle, he was half crazy and drunk, he took a ax and just told her, 'I'm gone bust your goddamn head open.' And she said, 'If you don't put that ax down and get out of here.' He just dropped the ax and it fell. He put his head in her lap and started crying. Still, none of this made her cry.

"But I had been using drugs for about three years, and she used to think that all my drug addict friends were the best guys in the world because they were quiet and they would always bring her fruit and stuff like that. She just couldn't understand why they didn't get enough rest at home. She used to think that when they nodded, that they be sleepy. And they used to stay upstairs in the bathroom too long. She would say, 'Them boys, I don't know what they do up there.'

"They'd be shooting up. So what happened, my mother was a diabetic, and the drug dealers had moved to Southeast Washington. My mother was living in the 1800 block of Frederick Place, off Alabama Avenue. I went over in Southeast to get some dope, and I was getting sick. I remembered watching my mother shoot that insulin, so I know she had some works in her house. I went over there. My mother didn't even know I was a dope fiend. When I got in there, she said, 'I ain't got no money.' I said, 'I ain't looking for no money.'

"My sister and them were there. I went upstairs to her medicine cabinet and got her hypodermic needle. Drugs were coming in gelatin capsules then. So I had ran it up and got it in the end and was about to take off, but I hadn't closed the door all the way. I'm sitting on the side of the bathtub and my sister come down the hall. She saw me and went downstairs. She was green as grass. She told my mother, 'I didn't know Petey was a diabetic, too.' Mama said, 'Petey ain't no diabetic. Shut the hell up.' My sister say, 'He up there with your diabetic stuff.' My mother said, 'Oh my God!'

"I heard her when she was coming up the stairs. 'Get out of my house, you no-good . . .' Shit, I didn't pay my mother no mind, and when she got there, I was just sitting. She was cussing, 'You no- good motherfucker. Goddamn you. This is my house and your sisters and brothers are here!' She called my grandmother and told her, 'You know he's a goddamn dope fiend.'

"But all that cussing and hollering and screaming never fazed my grandmother, because whatever happens, I'm gonna have the last word. By the time I got home, my mother had already called. When I got in there, my grandmother say, 'You know your mammy called over here today cussing about you used some dope or whatever.' I said, 'Don't pay her no mind. She's crazy.' And I went on upstairs. Dope was good then. I was still high. You could be high for damn near a day with that dope during that particular time.

"When I came back downstairs, she said, 'Sit down, Rabbit. I want to talk to you.' By then, she had asked a nigguh on the corner named Thomas about dope, and he explained it to her. Specifically, he told her a dope fiend was a drug addict who wasn't about a thing, and you don't want none of them around you, because they steal and shit. At that time, a drug addict was the worst thing in the world.

"I sat down and she said, 'They tell me you on that dope. What do it do to you?' I say, 'Grandma, I don't know.' She say, "How long you been using it?' I told her I started while I was in the army. She say, 'Well, is it good for you?' I say, "I really don't know, but it makes you feel good. You see them nigguhs come in here be sitting around, that's what we be doing.' She say, 'They use it too?' I nodded. She say, 'It'll make you steal from me?' I shook my head, but she kept on. 'Well, that's what Thomas say, that it will make people steal. You know I don't want you doing nothing like that.'

"And we just got on into talking, into a good, deep grandmother-grandson relationship. And by her being shrewd as she was and listening to me talking and putting together what Thomas said, she began to understand that this wasn't nothing for her Petey to be doing. As we were talking, tears came out of her eyes, and she said, 'Well, if it's good for you, I'll buy you all you want.' I said, 'It ain't good for me.'

"And when I saw the tears, I knew then that I wasn't gone use no more drugs no more in life, because here's a woman like I said, I'd seen my grandfather die, she didn't cry; I'd seen nigguhs threaten her and she didn't cry; and I'd seen us hungry and cold with no heat, and she had never been anything other than a strong, black, grey-headed woman.

"Going through my mind was 'Here's a woman that love me, and I done done something that nigguhs couldn't make her do, got her crying.' So I had about six pills of narcotics, heroin, and I say, 'Grandma, I ain't gone use it no more.' And we just hugged. She say, 'Well, if it's good for you, I'll get it for you. But if it's gone take you away from me, don't use it.'

"I took the pills to a friend, a dope fiend. When I walked in, the broad asked me, 'You got any drugs?' I say, 'Yeah, here six pills.' She say, 'Well, my ol' man gone to cop,' meaning he was gone to get some dope. 'And I'll give 'em back to you when he come back.' I said, 'No, I don't want any.' She say, 'Are you crazy? You high now, but 'round 7:30 or 8 o'clock, you gone be sick. When the last time you took off?'

"I told her I took off 'bout 11:30. She say, 'Shit, man, you gone get sooo sick. You can always come and get it back.' I told her, 'Fuck this stuff. I don't want it.' She know I'm gone want to stop that nose from running, them eyes from watering, and keep them little cramps out. That ain't nothing but a sickness, and goddamn shore if a hit won't fix it.

"I gave her those pills and went back home and upstairs to my room. At 6:30, 7 o'clock, I was thinking she was wrong. But 'round 10, I shore nuff was getting sick. 'Round 11:30, boy I was going through some changes up there. So my grandmother got out of bed and came in there. She could hear me moving around in that room. We lived in rooms next to each other and she could hear me going back and forth to that bathroom. Trying to throw up, but I didn't have nothing down then.

"She came and I told her that's what it was. If it had been an ordinary stomach ache, an ordinary sickness, she would have had a remedy for it. But I explained to her that it was from them drugs and the reason I was going through it was because I didn't want no more. The next morning, it was really something. I'd be having chills one minute and be sweating the next minute. She kept coming back and forth. And then it got worse.

"My buddies came around the next day, and they was telling her, 'Just let us go up there and talk to him, we can get him well.' She came up and say, 'Your little buddies down here.' I told her to tell them to go away. I don't want none. She went and told them.

"And so, for the 18 or 19 days I was laying in that room, back and forth to the toilet, once she got the gist of what was happening, she know how to take care of me. She started bringing me warm milk. Just warm milk. The lady was the smartest lady in the whole world. And she had the Bible. She would just sit right in the chair beside my bed. I had a old fucked up ass dog, that bastard. He laid right there, had been my puppy all my life. He would lay right there. Just him, me, her. And the Bible.

"She wouldn't let nobody up them stairs. My mother came over one day. 'I'm going up there and I'm gone tell him . . .' She say, 'You ain't going up nowhere. You done done what you had to do. You done told everybody all up and down the block. So everybody know he's a dope fiend now. Now you satisfied.'

"One nigguh did come up there. He's dead now. Sclerosis of the liver. He was my friend. She let him come up because she liked that nigguh. He wasn't no dope fiend. He was a drunk. He used to come up there and sit. Name was Freddy Coles. He'd look at me and say, 'Hey Jack, anything I can do?' I'd say, 'Naw, ain't nothing.'

"Wasn't nothing he could do. Just come to talk to me. He'd say, 'How you feel, Jack?' I felt like it wasn't gone be no more tomorrows. I thought I was gone die each night, because of the severe cramps I was having in my stomach and the gauge of my body temperature.

"The thing that was most frightening was that I would just go from being hot to being cold, from cold to being hot, and them cramps in my stomach. Eyes running. Nose running.

"I remember the day I woke up and didn't have no pain. That's when I should have turned Christian right there. Because I was born again. I could not believe it. My grandmother had done a lot of praying for me, and I woke up that morning and I put my feet on the floor and right then, I should have said, like I would have said now, 'Thank you, Jesus!'

"I just felt good. I went in and took a bath and shaved. My grandmother heard me moving around upstairs. She came up and saw me in there shaving and she said for me, 'Thank you, Jesus!' I came out the house about 11 o'clock in the day. I'm telling you, it was just like coming back from outer space. I walked all down around the river. I just walked. Ain't never been so happy in my life. I was thinking I ain't never gone fuck with this dope no goddamn more. I felt so at ease with myself.

"But it wasn't until about 30 days later, I was walking home and I fell right down in the street. That pain starting hitting me again. I had pains for 'bout almost a year. They used to reoccur. Just reoccur. I'd just ball in a knot 'til they go away. But I didn't want to go back to it. I knew what I had went through in that room for 18 or 19 days. This wasn't nothing but some bullshit.

"And that's when I made sure I didn't become a dope fiend no more. I became a drunk. And my grandmother told me one time when I was drinking and acting crazy, 'I wish you would use that damn stuff again. At least you didn't act like a damn fool when you was using that stuff. Now you drinking this wine, you just acts like a raving maniac.'

"When it come time to give up drinking, I didn't have one thing like my grandmother's tears to help me. But everytime I would go on a drunk, I would wake up and wouldn't nothing be in my favor. My bills would be behind. My skin would be all bust open. My lips would be white and burst all open. My bowels would be all sloppy and my whole physical system would be down.

"Then I would have to catch up on my bills and things. It started taking me longer and longer to get back into the mainstream. My hangovers would become longer. My sicknesses had become longer. I knew this was going to hurt me.

"I had to reason with myself that you ain't just a every run of the day nigguh no more. You have a television show, a well-liked television show. It's seen in 53 cities across the nation. You have a radio show. You are a heavily respected man throughout the city, not only in the black community but the white community. You live as good as any motherfucking college person. You have so many things going for you. Eventually, you ain't gone make it back from one of these drunks, or you gonna do something crazy while you out here, because you are lucky and fortunate enough that you haven't been called up for some of the things you've done.

"I used to be drunk, go all up on 9th Street, take my dick out, piss all on the tables and all that kind of simple shit. Then I used to go all uptown. In people's after-hours joints, pissing on the floor and shit. They'd throw me on out, knowing I was drunk, and I'd go on to another joint and cuss people out. Drink up liquor in bars and wouldn't pay the check. And all of this would go on for about 10 days or however long I would be on a drunk. Sometimes I would stay on a drunk as long as 28 days.

"When I was living with my wife Judy, and Petrie and Pine, they couldn't take it. So, she left, you know. Then I started living by myself. After I would get sober and look around, I would sit and talk to myself and say, 'Jack, you don't want all this nice shit you got. You must don't.' And then I used to have to wear shades sometimes when I go on television.

"So I decided that I would much rather enjoy all of this, and I could enjoy it being sober. I had a lot of friends tell me, 'You are a Dr. Jeckyl and Mr. Hyde. When you ain't drinking that liquor, you can sit on that radio and that television and you are the sharpest, most mentally alert nigger I ever seen. But man, soon as you got a hangover, you repeat yourself.'

"When I'm sober, like I've been for the past 37 months, I can handle all situations. I'm an excellent cook. I'm a damn good reader. And I love to write. Excellent housekeeper, too. When I'm sober.

"My grandmother knew that this was going to happen to me, years ago. She prepared me for all of this. She told me years ago, as a little youngster, that if you ever in life become somebody of note, a big person, the bigger you get, any kind of power you get, the more humble you become. She say, 'Because if you have any type of recognition, son, and you start sticking your chest out and chewing people up and showing off, destroying people or think you destroying people, then it's just a matter of time before some Judas gets to you. And there you go. So, if you ever become big, always take your time out to just listen.'

"I hope somebody's life changes because of mine."

*　　*　　*

Chapter 10

Tales of Petey's Past

THE PEOPLE PETEY most wanted to inspire—whose lives he wanted his to guide—were the vulnerable ones, the poor ones, the ones whose existences reflected his childhood. He rarely talked about himself without radiating a measure of pride in how far he'd risen—to heights that seemed impossible when he was a poor boy in Georgetown in the 1930s.

Petey's Voice

"I lived on the edges of trouble all my life. When I was about 4 or 5, A'nt Pig had me picking up numbers. I used to walk right past the police, going in a lady's house named Miss Daisy, to get the numbers. She would tie them in a hanky, put 'em in a little box and send 'em round to A'nt Pig.

"The police was sitting in the car, waiting to see people come in my house. My grandmother would say, 'Now listen, you going 'round to Miss Daisy, Miss Ethel, Miss Perry. They gone give you money. You just bring it right on in.'

"I'd be coming up the street, my grandmother be standing out there talking to the police. Leaning on the car talking to them. Making sure they couldn't get to me. I'd say, 'A'nt Pig . . .'

"She'd glance at me, nonchalant, 'Go on in the house. I'll be in there to fix your food.' Then she'd turn back to the police. 'And officer, y'all try to get me a Thanksgiving basket, hear? 'Cause I know y'all police got them baskets.'

"A'nt Pig would come on in the house. I'd just go in my little shirt, pull all them numbers out. My mother would act like she was upset. 'He's just a child!' My grandmother would say, 'And you putting your feet under the table, eating everything that I put there. Don't start that. 'Cause you too big and trifling to go get these numbers yourself.'

"So by the time I got to school, I knew all about numbers. When I got to junior high, I had my own little scheme. I wasn't doing numbers on my own in elementary. I was getting into different kinds of trouble. The first thing I done that caused me some problems was mess with them turtles.

"We had two live turtles in the back of the room, a couple of goldfish, hamsters and that kind of thing. The teacher would let us play with them. One day, me and another little boy got one of them turtles, and we put it in a girl's coat pocket. They had coat rooms then, where you put your coat in.

"Boy, I'm telling you! That girl put her hand in her pocket, got to screaming! Little teeny child. Scared that little girl to death. The little boy, my little partner, told. I think that was the first reprimand I got. The teacher, Miss Lee, she gave me a fit!

"Then I moved into the first grade and I was in a lady's room named Miss Alice Glass. A.S. Glass was her name. She looked like a white woman. Had a daughter named Hermione. And that was the first woman I believe that knew I was a talented person. They had a Halloween play and she made me the witch, 'cause the witch had all the lines. Talk all the talk. And I was very successful with that.

"When it came to reading, I was ready. When it came to penmanship, I didn't want to be writing. I got tired of that. I just wanted to read all the time. 'Jane has a kitten. The kitten's name is Tommy. Tommy says meow, meow. Jack has a dog. His dog's name is Billy. He says bow wow.' All that stuff. I loved to read and I loved to talk. Miss Glass saw that in me. My papers used to be all nasty, and when we would use paste, I'd eat that stuff.

"I had fun in school. I really did enjoy being in pageants and plays. And I had fun on the playground. I used to like to watch boys fight, get them in a fight. Signify, then stand and watch.

"Another reason I liked school, it was nice and warm all the time. You know, we didn't always have too much heat. The main reason, though, I was the center of attraction. The whole time. Any school I was in, I was the center of attraction, even though I wasn't playing no whole lotta sports. Sometimes I would cut up in school just so the teacher would make me stand up in the front of the class and apologize. I just loved being up in front of that class! But there were times in school when it really hit me how poor we were.

"Our teachers knew who the leaders were, they knew who was smart, who was studious, and they could make book on your ass. A junior high school teacher told me, 'You are going to jail. You are destined to go to jail.' She didn't like me.

"I had read an article about her in the paper and it said she was frigid. She and her husband were getting divorced and her husband made a statement that he was leaving his wife because she was frigid. I read it in the Afro newspaper. He was a prominent doctor and she was a prominent school teacher. I asked a girl named Wilhelmina, 'What do frigid mean?' She said, 'It means she doesn't want to have sex.' I say, 'What you say? She don't like to fuck?'

"So I took that section of the newspaper with her picture and the doctor's picture and put it in my locker. It was a helluva messy divorce. I think I was about in the 8th grade. Not long after, we had to turn in this English report, and I knew I shoulda got an A on it. It's no question. Let me get this point straight to you—I might as well: I was not a dumb guy in school. At no time, in no subjects.

"But when everybody got their books back, I had a B. I went off. I went up to her and said, 'You gave me a B.' She said, 'Well, it's not neat.' I lost it and told her, 'You ain't nothing,' and I ran to the locker, got that paper and came back. 'You don't want to fuck,' I hollered, with all the children sitting in the classroom. I was about 13 years old. I said, 'You always take it out on us, that's all you do.' That lady fell back down in her chair. I got scared and ran on out all the way home.

"The counselor came to my house the next day and said, "Ralph, you can come on back to school.' I told her what happened and she said 'You are not supposed to do people like that.'

"I saw that teacher's picture in the paper the other day. You can't put her name in the book because she's still living. She just didn't like me because I was always cutting up in her class. I was doing the work, but playing around. One day, she called me and a kid named Benjamin Burton up to the front of the class. He was a pianist. He could really play.

"She started in, 'Now you take this young man here, Benjamin Burton. Look how neat he is. He has a necktie on, his hair is combed, shoes shined, and he plays piano well. One day he will probably be in Carnegie Hall. But you take this hoodlum,' pointing to me. 'Look at him. Shoes open, collar open. There is nothing gentlemanly about him. He is destined to wind up in the penitentiary.'

"I just looked at her. At that particular time, in front of class, you put up a front. Then you go somewhere and cry, you know. But these are some of the things I look back on in my life and can appreciate. I couldn't appreciate it then, but I can now. It makes me understand much better that people have feelings.

"I know she would have liked to have been to that reunion we just had, like the other teachers I invited. She could never be like Miss Phillips or Miss Wells or Mr. Walker. They can call me on the television or the radio and tell me, 'Keep going.' Because that lady knows what she done to me. She just didn't like you if your background was not up to her standards.

"We had another teacher like that who used to talk about your mother all the time. Like if we'd do something wrong, she'd say, 'Oh, I can understand that. You probably see your mother and father do it all the time. I know you hear that cussing at home.' That teacher was in elementary school.

"But teachers like that were in the minority. Most of them were compassionate and concerned and would come to your house or get you to come and cut they grass. Not me. I ain't cut no grass.

Teachers would give you they lunch and stuff. Like Miss McNair. Miss McNair would be sitting there eating. They would eat in their rooms because they would keep bad motherfuckers in like me. I'd be done messed up, so I can't go to lunch. Lunch is an hour, so I can't go until there's only 15 minutes left.

"I'd be sitting there, then she'd make me go get her tray. When she'd finish, she'd have half a biscuit or something left. 'Miss McNair, can I have that biscuit?' I'd eat it and the jelly. 'Thank you, Miss McNair.' So the next day, she'd keep me in and get two trays, one for me, one for her. She thought I wasn't getting nothing to eat at home.

"That was elementary and junior high. I went to Cardozo for high school. People used to say you had to be light skinned to get into Dunbar High School, but that wasn't true. I imagine the rumor started when some black motherfucker got a bad grade and he just had heart enough to tell the teacher out loud, 'If I'da been light skinned, you wouldn'ta failed me.' And it just caught on. But it wasn't true 'cause I know some really black people come out of that school. 'A' students.

"It was a class school. People used to send their children from all over the country to go to Dunbar. Odessa. Ed Brooke. Benjamin Davis. All them come out of Dunbar. Dunbar was something to come out of. It was a prep school within itself. Featherstone come out of Dunbar, too.

"The school for the gangsters to go to was Armstrong. Right across the street, but it was two different elements. Gorillas went to Armstrong. Dunbar's colors were red and black; Armstrong's colors were orange and blue. Then, I went to Cardozo. You could go to Cardozo if you was a player. It was where the broads went, 'cause it was a clerical school. 'a s d f semi-colon lkj' on the typewriters. And typewriters with no letters on the keys. This is where I went."

CHAPTER 11

A Brick-Hard Lesson

ALTHOUGH PETEY WAS fond of saying he only had an eighth grade education, in fact, he graduated from Francis Junior High then attended Cardozo High School until he was nearly 17. Less than a year before graduation, he convinced two winos to pose as his parents. Their signatures allowed him to enter the Army as a minor. Petey left behind the days of leading cheers at football games, marching in the Cadet Corps, and disappointing teachers who knew a good student when they saw one but couldn't corral his brilliance.

Lounging on the baby blue carpet of his spacious home nearly 40 years later, Petey laughed about the reputation he created at Cardozo.

"They used to call me a last advisory genius, the smartest one in school. To hell with the first two advisories, they don't mean nothing. But the third? All I got to do is get me some Bs, I'll be all right. When it come time to do my school work and it was down to the wire, I'm the first one speaking when the teacher hit the desk. 'Good morning Miss So and So . . . Yes M'am.' It's time to go to work!

"My buddies would say, 'Greene, you gonna do this work?' I'd tell 'em, 'Shit-ass yeah, I'm gone do my work and gone ask the teacher can I move from back here with you crazy motherfuckers, 'cause you don't want to do nothing. And I will get killed if I stay back.'"

Most teachers saw Petey's potential, tried in vain not to laugh at his jokes, and often pulled him aside to encourage a different path. However, the printing teacher, Jerry Green, disliked Petey intensely. He saw no redeeming qualities; rather, he thought the teachers who liked Petey had their heads in the sand. And he hated the fact that they shared the same last name, his without the e.

One afternoon after most classes had been dismissed, Petey sauntered down a school hallway bouncing a basketball. As he passed the print classroom, Petey was oblivious to the hatred bearing down on him from Mr. Green's eyes. At the last minute, Petey's peripheral vision caught Mr. Green reaching out menacingly. Before Petey had time to react, Mr. Green had grabbed him by the collar and launched him headfirst into a thick exit door.

"Students are not allowed to bounce balls down the hall. You know better, Greene. Get on out of here." Jerry Green spat out the reprimand before returning to his last period class. Shocked and embarrassed in front of a group of girls standing near the building, Petey brooded for less than a minute before blindly storming toward two bricks loosened from a flower bed's border.

Petey sidled around to the side of the building where Mr. Green and his students pored over printing theory. In summer, teachers kept their windows opened. Petey positioned himself on a stoop with a direct line of fire through the window, cocked his right arm back and lobbed a missile toward Mr. Green's head. Just as the brick left Petey's hand, a yell whipped his attention to his left. It came from a girl who'd followed him around to that side of the building. "Mr. Green," she screamed. "He's gonna throw . . ."

If her alarm had sounded a split second later, the brick may have hit the print teacher in the back of the head instead of on the shoulder, as he turned toward the commotion outside his window. The second brick hit him square in the chest.

Petey ran like a rabbit chased by wolverines, silently vowing never to return to the school. For the next week, he roused himself at the proper time, left the house dressed for school, then proceeded to play hookey until the last bell and time to go back home. This lasted until the following week. On route home with his friends, Petey's stomach coiled into a knot at the sight of Wilmer Stewart, a detective assigned to juveniles.

Instructing his friends to tell his grandmother what happened, Petey followed Wilmer Stewart into the waiting car for the ride to the Receiving Home where the city processed juvenile offenders like Petey with warrants on their heads. He spent one night before Jackie Greene, under orders from A'nt Pig, bailed him out.

On Easter Monday, Petey prepared for court. His family cautioned him to change from his fashionable new shirt into something more suitable to a child, and expected his academic record to be of some help to him. The surprise came when they learned that his saving grace would be a teacher, not his grades.

"The thing that helped me in that case was a teacher stood up for me. A teacher told the court that the other teacher was wrong. The judge, Judge Bentley, say she never saw no shit like that, a teacher standing up for a pupil against a teacher," Petey recalled in later years. "Miss Wells stood up for me. She had seen the whole thing. She said, 'Petey came down the hall bouncing that ball, no question about that. But Jerry was too harsh. He didn't have to do what he did.'"

The system considered assault on a teacher a grave offense, but Miss Wells and her honest appraisal probably saved Petey from going to jail. Instead, he got a year's probation, assigned to a probation officer he came to despise. When his friends asked why he stopped visiting the probation officer two months later, he explained: "He kept trying to rub my leg all the time. I told him I would tell my mother on him, a white bastard."

A year later, on the next Easter Sunday, Petey and his friends joined a melee on the zoo grounds. When he realized several picnickers had been seriously hurt, Petey made the decision to run away to join the Army. If he had to face charges in the zoo disturbance, all he saw for himself was jail until age 21. There would be no Miss Wells to stand up for him this time.

Chapter 12

In the Army Now

THE GRIM-FACED corporal barked the order. "No talking. Lights out." Little did he know this was a useless admonition. Petey Greene, at 16 passing as 18, well-formed though thin, could no more keep his mouth shut than the other young men could resist asking for his risque jokes.

Earlier in the day, in the processing area waiting for more new recruits to arrive so a full complement could be assigned to a training area, 40 young men nervously assessed themselves and each other. In their first lonely days away from home, they quickly learned that Petey Greene could brighten anybody's mood.

"Psst. Hey D.C.," came a whisper across the spartan dormitory room in Petey's direction. "Tell us that thing 'bout that signifying monkey." Always ready to perform, Petey softly chanted the raunchy poem about the monkey who instigates trouble for every living creature in the jungle. Soon, quiet snickers turned to peals of laughter, interrupted immediately by the return of the exasperated corporal.

"All right! If I have to come here one more time, all you motherfuckers will have to pay!" Ignoring the corporal's bellow as soon as his back turned, several young men whispered at the same time. "Finish it, D.C.!"

At 3 a.m., 40 young men found themselves out of bed, running laps around the barracks. The corporal considered this punishment. The young men teased each other about their underwear. "That motherfucking Greene can roll," the guys confirmed to each other. As Petey began to make his mark, even some sergeants and corporals privately agreed.

Always, there will be a few people who hate the one on stage; so constantly running his mouth, attracting a crowd, and convincing a newfound friend to clean his rifle all earned Petey his share of simmering enemies; and he knew it.

Never one to consider brawn where brains would do, Petey called two of his Washington, DC homeboys to his side one humid afternoon, once they had all been assigned to a company for basic training.

"Hey John, hey Bobby, come here. I know you can't fight a pound and you know I can't fight. Y'all know we are a long way from home. We in Fort Dix, New Jersey."

"Yeah, what about it," Bobby stared.

"Well you can't fight, you can't fight, and I can't fight, but only the three of us know that," Petey continued, nodding at Bobby then John.

"So what?" John threw in, impatient for the point his former high school buddy dragged toward.

Petey blew smoke from a long drag off his Lucky Strike. "Well, none of these motherfuckers up here know we can't fight. So, here's what we gonna do. If one of us get in a fight, a'er one of us, even if we fightin' a ant, all three of us gone jump on that motherfucker. Do you understand?"

Bobby and John looked at Petey then each other, then back at Petey, answering in unison, "Noooo no." To Petey's raised eyebrows, John explained. "'Cause we know you going to be fucking with somebody. So, you just be by yourself!"

Without missing a beat, Petey swiped a handkerchief across his face, and retorted. "Okay, now you heard what you saying, right? You know it's just a matter of time before I get one of these big motherfuckers to be on my side, like I been doin' all my life. One of y'all gone get the shit slapped out of you one day, but don't ask me for no help."

The two former classmates conferred quietly then turned back to Petey. "Okay. Just don't you fuck with nobody. Don't start no shit. But if we just have to rumble, we gone do it like you said."

Bobby and John turned to leave, hearing Petey's last bit on the subject. "Solid. But don't y'all do no reneging. I say we just establish the fact that we are from DC and we are together." Petey strutted off to stir mischief elsewhere on the base.

One day later in the week, Petey joined a poker game in the drab barracks. John sat on his bed cleaning his rifle while Bobby spit-shined his boots. As he'd predicted, Petey had found a loyal friend, Private Patterson, who cleaned his rifle and polished his boots for him, freeing Petey to gamble and drink when he pleased.

Out of the corner of his eye, Petey caught a soldier named Tom, from Nashville, TN, steal two cards out of the deck. "Goddamn! This nigguh done stole them two cards and here I am sitting here with four queens," he thought to himself, heart racing, keeping a poker face.

Betting whittled down leaving only Tom and Petey in the game. "I got something for your ass. I call your $25, what you got left?"

"$15," Petey answered gamely.

"Well, put that in, too." After eyeing the pot, Tom bragged, "I got four aces!"

"Hold it," Petey shouted. You can't win that money, boss."

"What you mean, motherfucker???"

"Well, houseman, count them cards." Under the table, Petey's knees began to shake, because he could see a vein straining on the side of Tom's head. "This nigguh is getting ready to get dangerous, nose beginning to look like Brock Peters," Petey said to himself. He eased toward a thick soda bottle he intended to use if necessary.

Tom still argued that the win was his, until Petey jumped up, screaming, "Fuck you, man," and threw the bottle, hitting Tom on the enlarged vein. As Tom lunged for Petey's throat, Bobby practically flew across the room and popped Tom on the forehead with a boot. John emerged immediately with his rifle butt aimed at Tom's gut, then all three DC boys jumped on Tom, kicking and hollering.

The game's house man and other card players pulled Petey, Bobby and John off the dazed Tom within minutes of the fracas. Everyone walked away muttering, "Hey man, don't fuck with them crazy motherfuckers. If any of you bother one, all three of 'em come after you."

At the end of basic training, the three headed off to different camps; Bobby and John to Camp Campbell, KY, Petey to Fort Meade by way of a stint at Cook and Baker School first. But their reputations followed them.

*   *   *

Not Quite Cooking

At Cook and Baker School, Petey became friends with a Puerto Rican classmate named Jesusti Vincent, out of Brooklyn, NY. This was his first non-black friend ever, but a love of drinking liquor united them. While Petey considered himself to be slick, Jesusti actually was slick. He convinced Petey to help him steal the final exam, led him to break into the office, and showed him how to copy the answers. But Jesusti advised that he and Petey should not make anywhere near perfect scores.

"We're going to put these answers inside our jackets, but you're going to make an 80 and I'll make a 76 on the test. Miss enough. Okay." Jesusti—Petey called him Jesus—knew these scores wouldn't raise any eyebrows from the professor, who probably expected even less of the restless teens in the class with older cooks required to take it.

When time came for the final scores to be read out in class, the professor stared in disbelief. "Well, I'm going to say this. There is some shit going on here, but we are going to graduation Monday. I'm not going to say anything to the colonel. I just want all you fellows to know that something went wrong here."

The highest score went to a long-time soldier who really could cook. The second highest, a 94, went to Petey Greene. Several other guys who actually excelled in cooking couldn't pass the test at all because they couldn't read and write. The newly required test interrupted years of Army cooking that had been second to none.

True to his word, Jesusti settled for a 76. "Hey Greene, what if that man ask you right in front of everybody to boil a motherfucking egg, man, what the fuck were you thinking?" The two friends sat on the steps outside the dormitory smoking, congratulating each other on graduation, knowing their future paths would not likely meet.

"Man, when they call my name as second highest in the class, I know all y'all are going to be thinking 'What kind of shit is this here," but I am going up there, get my little certificate, and be outta here to Fort Meade, MD. As a cook," Petey crowed.

*   *   *

"I'm Ralph W. Greene, R8-13275832." Petey stood his full 6 feet 2 inches, handed the paperwork to the man in charge, and looked around the Orderly room.

"Oh yeah, you the new cook," a private said, calling in to let the sergeant know Greene had arrived. Giving Petey a skeptical appraisal, the sergeant sent him on down to the Mess.

"Hello. I'm the new cook."

The head cook took one look at Petey and saw right through him. "Oh boy, I can see already you ain't about a goddamn thing. Look at this shit they done sent me. Come on in here and get your hat and apron. Go on and be back here in the morning. Lord have mercy."

The next morning, the head cook handed out duties down the line.

"You got the meat. You got the potatoes. You got the peas. Greene, you got the rice."

His hat cocked at a jaunty angle, like a tam, Petey looked anything but skilled at culinary tasks. Especially not rice, which he knew needed to have each grain standing alone.

"This is a big ol' bag of rice, and I gotta start cooking it for dinner while people still eating they French toast for breakfast. I know they fucking with me, giving me this rice," he told his bunk-mate that evening.

After letting Petey struggle with the rice a while, the head cook feigned exasperation. "Come here. Just don't fuck with no cooking. Here's what you can do: be in charge of the milk. Just bring the bottles over here and set them out. I think you might also be able to handle the fruit cocktail. Tear off the lettuce slices and spoon the fruit cocktail on them. You got that, Greene? And we'll let you supervise the guys on KP."

This landed right up Petey's alley: because he was a cook, he felt he could boss the guys on KP around, since they merely had to work in the kitchen. And they were the same fellows he teased with in the barracks.

"You goddamn KPs, don't be up there all day sleeping," he'd command in a gruff voice. "Aw fuck you, Greene."

The head cook let this go on a few days, then called Petey over early one morning. "Look here, Greene. See all this meat we got here? We need to make it stretch to feed more people, so I need you to go over there to C company and tell that man to send us the meat stretcher. Tell him we getting ready to run out of meat. Got to stretch it so everybody can eat."

Although the clock struck nine, already the sun blazed in the Maryland sky. Once he reached C company, Petey sought out the sergeant. "Excuse me. Sergeant Johnson said he got to get that meat stretcher 'cause, uh . . . ."

Raising his cleaver over a mass of red meat, the head cook at C company turned to look at the teenager in front of him. "Goddamn, man, you know you a little too late. We had it yesterday, but G company got that motherfucker now. Go on up there and ask the sergeant. Tell him I sent you."

Mopping sweat from his neck, Petey trudged to G Company. "Sergeant at C company said you got the meat stretcher."

"Goddamn, boy! We didn't even keep it. They sent that motherfucker to us but we loaned it on to I company."

Tired and irritable, Petey made it to I company. There, a sergeant informed him of the same bad news. "Look here, man. We just sent it over to L company." At L company, the sergeant looked at Petey's sagging shoulders, falling white hat, and explained, "What happened, it was supposed to come to us, but they sent it over there to the WACs."

Once he arrived at the WACs company, the first woman he encountered asked, "Which company you say you in?" Catching his breath, Petey answered, "H."

"And where'd you go first? C company, then G, then I? Can I tell you something? They done fucked with you long enough. Ain't no such thing as a meat stretcher."

A palpable disbelief enveloped Petey, as he struggled to come to terms with the joke the sergeant initiated more than two hours before. "What did you say??"

"Ain't no such thing as a meat stretcher. That's why nobody had it. They send a rookie just because they know all the oldtimers will get the joke." The WAC smiled sympathetically as Petey shrugged, saying "Well, I'll be going back now."

Instead, he headed straight for his barracks, took a shower, and ducked around the wall, ready to take the 27-mile trip to Washington, D.C. It was 11:30 a.m. Time enough to find a party.

The next morning, he sauntered into the kitchen, right up to the irate sergeant. "Motherfucker, you went AWOL. You going to the stockade. You had no business leaving!"

"Yeah, okay," Petey answered nonchalantly, showing no concern as he was led to the corporal. "What's wrong with you, boy, leaving here at 11:30 in the day and going away? Where did you go?

Looking the picture of innocence with wide eyes, Petey answered. "Well, Sarge right there sent me to get the meat stretcher. When I got up there to get it from the WACs, they told me they had just sent it to the Pentagon. I went to the Pentagon. And the man at the Pentagon told me there wasn't no such thing as a meat stretcher."

Petey could hardly keep a straight face, knowing he'd used A'nt Pig's wiles to get over on the pranksters. And the corporal himself fought back a hearty guffaw, managing to say to the sergeant, "I told y'all 'bout playing." And to Petey, "Get the fuck on out of here, Greene."

*   *   *

Sometimes, the joke stayed on Petey. Like the time he was awakened by a rough shake of the shoulder. "Hey, hey. What's your name? You see this boiler right here? And this one? I want hot water in these motherfuckers all night long. Better be hot water. If I come back in here and see your ass in bed . . ."

Gaping at the stripes, Petey saluted, "Yessir, sergeant." He stayed up all night, keeping hot water in the boilers. Next morning, hardly able to keep his eyes open, he confided to another soldier. "Yeah man, that's a mean sergeant over there. Made me fix all them hot water boilers."

"What sergeant? Man, that's Priestly. He ain't no sergeant. That black motherfucker was probably on detail to do that shit and got you to do it while he went to town. 'Cause you the new guy."

At first, Petey hated Priestly. Every time they'd see each other, they'd snarl. "I'm going to break your red ass," Priestly would growl. "No, you are going to kiss my red ass, you black motherfucker," Petey would rejoin.

But not long after Priestly pulled the hot water tank stunt, he came to Petey's defense, challenging guys who were cheating in a poker game. He saw them cheating, then won the money back and gave it to Petey. Thereafter, they were inseparable.

After about nine months of spooning fruit cocktail and pretending to order the KPs around, Petey was reassigned, first as a jeep driver, then as a colonel's orderly.

*   *   *

Looking back on those days years later, Petey belittled his own approach to the service and praised the ambition of others.

Petey's voice: Soldiers on Parade

"We were in a segregated army, in the calvary. It went from a horse calvary to when I got to it, it was called a mechanized calvary. This was armored cars and half-trucks and so on. They gave the white boys these tanks and personnel carriers, PC 139s. Came with all the track wheels. We're supposed to have some too, but they had us cutting grass, doing shit like that.

"Well, me and my crew, we didn't give a fuck. We didn't want tanks and shit. Fuck them tanks. We cutting grass and jammin' and fucking broads. We hung out in Annapolis in Boon Town all day long.

"But you got some other motherfuckers that didn't come in there to cut no grass. They came in there to *soldier*. They *wanted* tanks and shit. So they kept pressing. They got a petition and went to the general, and when we know anything, goddamn! They gave 'em these tanks. I was madder than a motherfucker. They gave us these ol' raggedy-ass tanks. Within a month's time, them nigguhs had them tanks shining and rolling, with goggles on and all. They told me and my partners, 'Y'all better learn how to get in with this, 'cause either you are going to be with us or you going to be doing guard duty.'

"They put me in an M-39, PC, personnel carrier. Then they had me as assistant tank driver. They say I'm the only motherfucker in life turned a tank over. Said they should have put me out the army for *that*.

"Once we got the tanks, we started going on maneuvers every six months. Our girlfriends would start going with other guys, 'cause we stayed in the woods all the motherfucking time. Maneuvers lasted 90 days. We'd come back for 60 days and go right back for winter training.

"But now we had another edge. Any time they had a parade, they'd call for our asses. I remember the greatest parade I ever participated in. A general died and they buried him in Arlington cemetery. We had to go down Pennsylvania Avenue. It was 1948. His name was General Blackjack Pershing, and he was a calvary man.

"I was driving a jeep, had a dark green helmet on, braid, yellow scarf, yellow gloves, yellow leggings, boots, and the people on the street say, 'There Petey, there Petey! I was riding like a motherfucker. Just riding."

*   *   *

Serving in Jest

To entertain his army buddies or strangers, Petey put his own spin on age-old jokes, recited "Signifying Monkey" rhymes, and kept audiences spellbound by "calling the trains" like an announcer in Grand Central Station. But he also relied on the conversations, nuances, and cadences of everyday life to form the basis of his humor and keep his cohorts off balance.

In basic training, he listened to the habitual admonitions of irascible sergeants and turned them on their heads. One unforgettable stunt came to him after hearing a sergeant named Hudson bark an order for weeks on end: "Let me tell you one goddamn thing. I'm tired of you men being late getting to these formations . . . Especially you goddamn bolos like Greene. 'Cause Greene, you're a bolo, you know that, don't you? Now I'm gone let y'all fall out. But when that whistle blows, I don't care what you doing, drop everything and come when you hear the whistle."

Finally one day, back in the barracks while other soldiers shined their shoes or read magazines, Petey schemed. To his friend Priestly, he avowed, "I'm gone stop Sergeant Hudson from saying that." Quietly, he disrobed, then sat with his towel draped across his lap. Brrrr. The whistle sounded, soldiers scurried out to formation, and Petey followed, huffing and puffing, breathlessly catching up. Absolutely naked.

"What the hell is wrong with you, bolo??" Sergeant Hudson gasped. Not a soldier outside could stop laughing. Petey faked surprise, answering, "Sergeant, I was trying to take a shower when I heard the whistle, but you said come when the whistle blows!"

"Boy, go put on some clothes."

Perhaps that would have been the end of it for anyone else, but Petey Greene hadn't finished with Sergeant Hudson yet. Another favorite expression the sergeant used to represent speed was "bring me the door." He'd say, "When you hear the whistle, bring me the door."

Of course Petey couldn't let that rest. One day not long after the buck-naked episode, he returned to barracks with "bring me the door" ringing in his ears. Giving Priestly the warning, he unhinged one of the doors in the barracks. As other soldiers filed out when the whistle blew, Petey struggled over carrying a door.

"What the fuck is wrong with you, boy?" Sergeant Hudson blew his top. "Come with me." By the time he paraded Petey over to the captain's office, the anger had dissipated. The First Sergeant waved the incident away, telling Sergeant Hudson, "Well, he didn't break any rules. You did say 'bring the door.'"

"Yeah, well, you say it, too," Sergeant Hudson retorted. And while the two sergeants bantered, Petey went back to his barracks to dream up more schemes.

His antics and sassy mouth weren't always so easily dismissed. During a rifle training drill where each soldier had to show his skill at cleaning his carbine, Petey's clowning finally got on the wrong side of a serious airborne lieutenant named Davis.

Bored by the drill that required inserting a dime in a crevice of the rifle, opening it, and breaking it down step by step, Petey began to slouch.

"You, Greene, how would you disassemble a carbine?"

"Well, you take ten cents . . ."

"What do you mean ten cents?"

"A dime, two nickels, it don't make no difference . . ."

As usual, other soldiers burst out laughing. Without thinking, Lt. Davis lashed out and slapped Petey hard across the face. Shocked into a state of fear, Petey ran back to the dormitory, leaving the rest of the troop speechless. About 30 minutes later, a sergeant came for Petey, leading him to the Orderly Room.

Afraid he was about to be arrested, placed in the stockade, Petey sat on a stiff bench outside while the company commander, the captain and the lieutenant conferred within.

"You know you shouldn't have hit that kid," the captain spoke solemnly.

Lt. Davis, frustration unconcealed, answered, "That little bastard is always fucking up. You should be out there with him. If he's not doing one thing, it's another."

"Yeah, but if the I.G. finds out, you're in trouble."

Petey's ears perked up. He had no idea that I.G. meant Inspector General. But he knew he had a tool.

When they finally called him in and asked to hear his version, Petey looked around, then announced, "I just want to talk to the I.G." Seeing fear form in the lieutenant's eyes, he continued. "I want to see the I.G. about him hitting me."

"Well, you go ahead back to your barracks and we'll take this matter up a little later. We just want you to cool off a while," the captain encouraged.

For the next several weeks, whenever anyone criticized or spoke sharply to Petey, his used as his stock comeback, "I ain't saw the I.G. yet." All the while, he hoped he would never see the Inspector General. He had no interest in reporting the slapping incident. He much preferred to have something to hold over Lt. Davis's head.

Every once in a blue moon, Petey pulled a stunt that won him praise, although it could just as well have landed him in the stockade. As often as not, he had no idea of the outcome when he started down the jesting path.

On guard duty at the PX one night, Petey received instructions not to let anyone in without a tie after "retreat," which meant after 5:30 p.m., dress uniforms were required.

Standing at the door, thinking of ways to choke back the boredom, Petey watched young recruits his age coming in with their ties on one by one. At about 6:45, a Cadillac pulled up. Petey's mind went into warp speed when he saw an officer approaching the door wearing an open collar.

"Pardon me, sir. You can't go in," he said, in his most polite voice and manner.

Almost before the officer managed to say, "Well I'm Captain . . ," Petey added, "It's against the rules for anyone to go in without a necktie."

"But I'm the PX Officer, Captain Wilcox," a tall, lean man, continued. Seeing Petey's unchanged position, Captain Wilcox turned to his wife who stood near the car. "Dear, is my tie hanging on the rear view mirror?"

No tie could be found anywhere in the car, but Captain Wilcox, reasonably, thought an exception would be made in his case. "I'm the PX officer," he repeated.

"Well, the sergeant told me not to let anybody without a necktie in." Petey kept a straight face, but just behind his stiff jaw a snicker danced. He knew exactly what he was doing: toying with an officer over a minor rule. Officer Wilcox had two choices. He could lose face by disregarding a rule in front of a young recruit or he could turn around and go home for a tie. He chose the latter, but before leaving, asked for Petey's name.

"Private Greene, 13275832, B Company, Sir."

Later that night, Petey held a group of friends in awe with his story of jerking the officer around. "I got that man," he crowed, just before an orderly entered the barracks calling his name.

"They want you, Greene. What did you do to the PX officer?"

As he entered the PX, First Sergeant Hudson, already familiar with Petey's reputation, assumed the worse. "Goddamn you, bolo, what did you do this time?"

Ushered into a room where he saw Captain Wilcox and several other officers, Petey assumed his perfect-soldier pose. "Private Greene reporting, sir."

"Stand at ease, Greene. Do you know any of these officers?" Captain Davis swept his arm to encompass the other men.

"Yes, I know that one right there. He told me he was the PX officer," Petey responded, nodding toward Captain Wilcox.

"Why did he have to tell you?" Captain Davis knew the answer, but wanted to hear how Petey would defend his action.

"I was on guard duty, and Sergeant Coley had told me don't nobody go in after 5:30 without neckties. He didn't have on a necktie."

Captain Davis scowled, then spoke slowly and deliberately, as if lecturing to a dense child. "Didn't he show you he was the PX officer? And weren't you guarding the PX? All you had to do was let him in."

Petey knew that he had been within his rights but was "talking silly" in defending his actions. Still, he enjoyed the game.

"But Sergeant Coley is the Sergeant of the Guards, and I was on guard duty," he said, eyes wide with practiced innocence.

Captain Davis's exasperation spilled over, and his voice quickened. "That's not the point!"

Out of the corner of his eyes, Petey saw Captain Wilcox's smooth face break into a grin.

"Well, if you get a few more recruits like him, we don't have too much to worry about. You're dismissed, Private Greene."

Thanking everyone and quietly exiting, Petey heard First Sergeant Hudson whisper toward him. "Bolo, this is the first time you ever got a good commendation. Get on out of here."

CHAPTER 13

Party in the Army

PETEY COULD DANCE. In junior high and high school, the boys admired him because he could play the dozens better than anyone in town, curse like a sailor, run the numbers, and drink most any grownup under the table. None of that impressed the girls, but they loved Petey because he could dance. Nobody could cut the rug better than Petey Greene, and even the guys paid him grudging respect for that.

His pals in the Army, high school-aged or just past, felt the same way. They enjoyed having Petey in their group because he could talk shit and attract the ladies on the dance floor.

Petey's crew—Murray Turner, Fred Ewell, Clyde Syka, Herbert C. Rodrigues, Nathaniel Richardson, Robert C. McNair, Gusso Andrews, Wallace N. Murphy, Curtis Davis, Eugene Gunn, Eugene Seafer, and Caldwell Priestly—lived to party. Annapolis, MD, 19 miles away from Fort Meade, attracted the young soldiers. There, they found themselves in competition with young sailors, based right in Annapolis, both groups eager for the hands of the high school girls who frequented the dance clubs.

The girls could take their pick because one club, Cozy Corner, catered to soldiers and the other, Alsop's, reserved itself for sailors. Civilians kept the other two popular clubs in business.

"Man, these girls playing both ends against the middle," Petey said to Priestly one night after they'd ducked away from a fight outside Cozy Corner between a soldier and a sailor over a girl. "The soldiers and the sailors get to fighting, and the civilians don't do nothing but sit back and laugh. They got the edge anyway, 'cause they with these broads in high school. While we fightin', they get the girls and go on 'bout they motherfuckin' business."

The next day, Petey and his crew sat on the side of their tanks at midday, taking a break, talking. Petey had decided to do something about the conflict over the girls.

"Man, we can't keep going down there fighting these fools."

"Well, we can't be no punks." Ewell, brow furrowed, looked around for support.

Petey had the stage. "We got to talk to them motherfuckers."

Richardson nodded in agreement, asking, "Who gone talk to 'em?"

Not surprisingly, Petey volunteered. "I'll do the talking. I know the sailor who control the rest of 'em. Name is Settles."

Getting up dusting off his pants, Priestly made a quiet pronouncement. "Okay, but just for safekeeping, I'm taking one of my 45s."

That evening, a car full of soldiers pulled up to Alsop's. Sailors standing outside the door glared. Petey spotted a sailor he knew— a sailor who dated the sister of the girl Ewell dated.

"Hey, Brown, man, I'm looking for Settles."

"Go on in, man. He inside."

But beyond the door stood Mr. Alsop, who wanted nothing more than peace in his club. "Hey, Greene, you know you can't come in here."

"I just want to see Settles. We got to talk." Everyone stopped talking, transfixed by the soldier at the door. Settles walked over to see what could be so important to bring Petey Greene to Alsop's. To get away from the crowd of sailors and soldiers surrounding the door, and diffuse what looked like the beginnings of a rumble, Petey and Settles walked down the graveled Calvert Street.

Petey started. "Hey man, we've got to come to some type of understanding. It's no use of us keep fighting each other as servicemen, because, man, you know some of these guys might marry these broads. I ain't gone marry none. You might not . . ."

"Well, man, I really do like Phyllis," Settles interrupted.

Petey saw his opening. "My man Priestly go with her sister. And y'all always bumping heads when you taking Phyllis home and he taking Sylvia home."

Settles, still unsure of where Petey wanted to take the conversation, saw the merits in some compromise. He relaxed his clenched fists. "Well, I don't care, as long as he don't bring none of you chumps down there to mess with Phyllis."

The diplomat in Petey opened up full swing. "Well, he feels the same way, man, long as you don't bring none of them sailors down there to mess with Sylvia. What I'm saying is that we have to come to some type of understanding. Let's do it like this: Whoever get to town first just get the broads, and whoever can pull, pull. Then, when somebody get real heavy into one of these girls, then we just let 'em know that this chump ain't playing. You see his woman ain't hanging out no more, so just raise."

A slow grin crept across Settles's face, he and Petey shook hands, and from then on, the soldiers and sailors started hanging together.

$$* \quad * \quad *$$

The merger between the soldiers and sailors meant good business for the club owners and a different story for the girls who had been waltzing between the two. The former enemy camps inaugurated their new friendship with a big party at the Dixie Hotel. They called it The Servicemen's Party.

Witnessing the great success of the hotel party, Petey blew smoke from his nose and bragged to Priestly about the follow-up fun they'd have at the clubs. "You know I went and told Alsop that soldiers would be coming in there, and I told that man at Cozy's the sailors are no longer off limits here. Man, I done made the MPs and the SPs happy, too, 'cause we won't be fighting no more. But the civilians are drugged! They real mad now. Their days of getting the girls while we fightin' is over!"

The partnership solidified to the point that when the soldiers at Fort Meade had a big football game against Howard University, their sailor friends drove up in a convertible, chauffeuring the soldiers' girlfriends.

"Y'all brought liquor and some girls you know ain't going back with you. Don't matter we losing this game, we jammin' and having fun," Petey laughed, talking to his sailor friend Settles and wrapping his arm around Sylvia Brown, the Annapolis girl who had captured his heart. Priestly sat with Sylvia Dorsey, his special lady.

Sometimes, though, their dates weren't quite so open.

* * *

Petey's voice: Girls on the Floor

"I can remember, we had three girls at Fort Meade one night. Me, Priestly and Spencer were together with three girls out of Annapolis. We brought 'em back to the NCO club. Everybody jammin'. So, 'bout three o'clock when the thing was over, we took the girls to the army barracks, over to our company, and put 'em upstairs in the squad room.

"All the fellows slept out in a big open room, so we put them in the squad room where NCOs stay. It was a weekend, so you know nobody but hoodlums in the barracks. Everything was cool. The next morning, we get up early and we tell the dudes we got three broads upstairs. No bullshit. They coming down, they gone use the shower and everything.

"Guys say, 'They fine?' We say, 'You know they fine!' Everything was going good until here come First Sergeant Wilbur Young. Sergeant Young been in the Army 30 years. He was sho' 'nuff a soldier, you understand. His wife wouldn't let him get out the army. He could have retired, but she say 'If you retire, what you gone do? Stay in the army.' So he been there 30 years.

"Now, he go to church up the street, because he lives on Post, not in our company, though. When he heading to church, being an old soldier, he just gone walk down through the company and see what people are doing. 'Where is ol' Greene?' Always giving me hell and always giving my mob hell.

"We got these girls there, and we don't know this fool is in the company. The girls have got relaxed, they down there fixing their hair and everything. He coming in the front door, saying 'Hey, how y'all?' The dudes can't get to us in time to tell us that Sergeant Young is in the barracks. If you ever been in the army, you know you walk down the long barracks and at the back, you can go downstairs to the latrine, as they call it, or you can go on out the back door.

"While he is standing there talking, ain't talking about nothing, one of the girls happened to come out the squad room and she looked down. A dude tried to tell her to get back, 'cause the sergeant is down there. She is ducking back, but ol' Sergeant Young kinda looked up and saw her dress. He said, 'I don't believe what I just saw up them stairs.' We up there with the girls and here he come, up them steps. We scared to death.

"He hollered for us to come out, so we opened the door. But by this time the girls had their clothes on and everything. 'What is these women doing in here?' He was so mad. Of course I had to do the talking. 'Sergeant, let me tell you what happened. We just came in here five minutes ago, 'cause these girls came to get us to go to church, and we didn't have our clothes and stuff together.'

"He still fussing. 'I don't care! These women ain't got no business in here. This is the military. I know you had to have something to do with this, Greene. Get these ladies out of here!'

"He was just a spit and polish man. We know we are going to have to hear about it all week.

"The girls were so young, it's a big joke with them. They were 17, 18, and in high school, living in Annapolis or what at the time was East Port. It's all Annapolis now. But at the time, the East Port girls and the Annapolis girls didn't get along, although they all went to the same high school."

*   *   *

The East Port and the Annapolis girls disliked each other the way the soldiers and the sailors once did. What fed the resentment was competition over the servicemen, many trying to date a girl in Annapolis and another in East Port at the same time. Petey was a classic example. Before he left Fort Meade for a stint in Korea, in fact, he had begun to date more than one girl in each town. But all the while, his favorite was Sylvia Brown.

The first time he met the East Port girls, he behaved rudely. It happened one night at one of the Annapolis beaches that in segregated times was reserved for black people. The two beaches, called Cobb's and Sparrow's, side by side, attracted patrons from Washington, DC, Baltimore, and other parts of Maryland. Bands and entertainers such as Dinah Washington and Jerry Butler performed there, and servicemen often went down for the midnight parties.

"Man, it gets cold down here at night. A nigguh could freeze 'less he drinking that steam. Much as I love to dance, I'm ready to go now 'cause it's too cold," Petey complained to his friend Charlie one night at the beach. But Charlie had other ideas.

"Hey, listen Jack, I got these girls I promised to take back to East Port. They in the car already. I'ma take them to East Port and come back for y'all."

"Man, get these bitches out the car! Is you crazy?" Petey spewed, talking through the liquor he'd consumed all night.

"Look, the girls is all right. I'm just gone take 'em right up there and come back and get y'all."

"You ain't gone come back and get ME! I don't care nothin' 'bout these crazy motherfuckers . . ."

Charlie, face flushed with embarrassment, turned to the girls whose anger he could feel warming the car. "Don't mind him . . ."

One of the girls felt so insulted, she reached for the door. "Well, he ain't gotta talk that way. We'll get out."

Unmoved by her offer, Petey yelled, "You goddamn right, you can get out. I'm ready to go now!"

Charlie shook his head, then started the engine of his Chevrolet and backed away, rolling the window up against Petey's vitriolic tirade, leaving him and four other servicemen waiting in the sand. Both he and Petey knew the real deal: Charlie was trying to win the favors of Margaret, the prettiest girl in the East Port crowd. Petey, with Sylvia Brown, already had the most desirable of the Annapolis girls.

All the while, Charlie planned to take the girls to one of their houses in East Port, then return to bring his friends for a private party. But when he returned, he found a still-hopping mad Petey Greene. He'd left the girls in East Port still bristling from Petey's insults.

"Man, them girls is mad with you!" Charlie tried to think of a way to smooth things over before they got back to East Port. He really hoped Petey would begin to date one of Margaret's friends, so he and Petey could hang in East Port instead of over in Annapolis to visit Sylvia and her friend who liked Charlie.

"Fuck them broads," was Petey's reply. Back at East Port, the other fellows all talked with the girls, but Petey stayed in the car. Several girls came out, glaring at him in the back seat, taunting that they would get their brothers to attack him by surprise one night.

"Your brothers ain't gone do nothing," Petey snorted. On the way back to camp, he told Charlie and the others, "I ain't never going back over there, so I ain't got to worry about them or their brothers neither."

Things stalemated. Charlie wanted only to date Margaret, in East Port, and Petey only wanted to see Sylvia, in Annapolis. Double-dating was out of the question, because Margaret and Sylvia did not get along. They were caught in the silent feud of Annapolis vs East Port girls.

The breaking point came when Charlie and Petey got tickets to see George Kirby and The Drifters at the Roth's Theater in Baltimore, on Pennsylvania Avenue. Each guy was hell-bent on taking his favorite girl.

"Well, man, what you gone do?" Petey threw the challenge out to Charlie, whose only comeback was, "Well, what *you* gone do?" Petey settled with, "I'm taking Sylvia. I know you want me to take one of Margaret's friends, but I'm taking Sylvia."

*   *   *

Petey's voice: Friends and Foes

"We got in the car. He say, 'Where we going?' I say, '199 Clay.' That's where Sylvia was living at, 199 Clay. He blow the horn. Sylvia was 16 years old. Fiiine. Oh my God, she was fine. She was brown, big legs, always kept a smile on her face. I just loved her. I had took her from another soldier, who is now down there in Annapolis. Named McKensie. He still living there. He married a baaad broad. I told him the last time I was down there, 'You wouldn't have this pretty woman here, boy, if it don't be for me taking Sylvia from you, nigguh.'

"So we got ready to go to the theater. I got Sylvia, then we went to East Port, picked up Margaret. She got in, they looked at each other, and we drove on. We on 301, which was the Governor Ritchie Highway, going to Baltimore. I've always been direct. I say, 'Hold it. Before we get over there with this bullshit . . .' Charlie loved it, but he tried to act like he could hold me back. 'Hey, hey, come on Greene, don't start nothing.' But he wanted me to keep talking.

"I say, 'Let me tell y'all this. You live in East Port and you live in Annapolis. We know y'all have not been all right with each other, and don't like each other, but you Charlie's girl and you my girl. Me and Charlie's in Fort Meade together and we are definitely gonna be good friends. Charlie ain't gone have nobody in Annapolis since he got you, Margaret. And I ain't gone have nobody in East Port, since I got you, Sylvia. So, case closed. Y'all gone have to learn to deal with each other, because this is the first but it's not the last time y'all are gonna be together. That shit 'bout not talking to each other, when y'all get in school and back with y'all little girlfriends, then y'all can talk 'bout each other. But when you're here, you're friends.'

"Right after that, they both made enemies with their girlfriends, because they became all right with each other. Charlie was so happy.

"Not too long after that, I rode over to East Port with Charlie one night and fell asleep in the car. Charlie and them played a trick on me. I woke up and them girls I had insulted surrounded the car, holding sticks and shit, saying their brothers were on the way to get me. I just sit in the car and looked at them, 'cause they had me. Finally, the guys and the girls went in a little soda fountain, in there jammin', playing records like 'Lawdy Miss Claudie,' and I'm sitting in the car.

"The next day, they laughing at my ass, but Charlie tell me, 'Hey, Greene, one of them girls really like you. Peggy, she told Margaret, but Margaret told her not to mess with you 'cause you got a nasty mouth. Eventually I started going with Peggy. It had become a challenge to me to get over there, and there was something special about Peggy. She's the one I had a baby by."

*   *   *

Peggy Turner and Sylvia Brown were as different as sugar and spice. Peggy's soft beauty and shy manner left her feeling like a comfortable robe to Petey, while he wore Sylvia like a formal tux. At the clubs, Sylvia was as likely as not to be finger-popping with another beau, while Peggy waited quietly for Petey even when she knew he was chasing after Sylvia. She took Petey's rash behavior and Casanova reputation in stride, because she wanted nobody but him. With the devotion of first love, she clung to the hope that he'd choose her in the end.

Meanwhile, Petey busily added to his stable. Besides the dazzling Sylvia and the sweet Peggy, he also started dating Elsie, who was nearly 6 feet tall and whose aunt played saxophone for the Sweethearts of Rhythm. Then, too, there was Margie, the sister of his civilian friend and drinking buddy Jackie's wife.

Occasionally, all four girls would come to Fort Meade to the dances at the same time. Soldiers' resentment of Petey grew by leaps and bounds when they'd ask a girl out only to hear her give the same answer another one just gave: "I go with Petey Greene."

"Greene? Don't you see him over there with Sylvia? Don't you know he go with Sylvia?"

Yet, Sylvia was the only one who played Petey like a fiddle.

One evening, Petey sat on the divan in Sylvia's living room, with Sylvia on his lap. Priestly sat nearby with one of Sylvia's friends, Fran. The door opened and in walked Sylvia's civilian boyfriend, John Saw.

"Okay, Sylvia, let's go."

She uncurled herself from Petey's lap, stepped into her size 6 shoes, and said softly, "I'll see y'all later."

Priestly's mouth dropped open and his mind raced toward the next hour when he'd be back in the barracks telling their crew, "That motherfucking Greene ain't got no heart!"

Hurt, but with undiminished ardor, Petey was right back at Sylvia's the next day, asking her to be his girl, to marry him when he returned from Korea. Once in Korea, he sent her money each month to save for their wedding and first house.

About $6,000 later, Petey learned that she'd married John without telling him. His money was lost, and so were his ties to Sylvia. What tied his mind to Annapolis in years thereafter was his child with Peggy, his first daughter, Renee.

CHAPTER 14

A Classic Time

IF ANYONE HAD asked Petey Greene to name the entertainment capital of the world in the 1940s and 50s, he would have answered "Washington, D.C." without hesitation. He would have been thinking of the spots in the Northwest section of town, not far from Howard University and Griffith's Stadium. Southwest and Northeast sported their share, but Northwest claimed the entertainment mecca.

Along Florida Avenue, 14th, U, Seventh and T, the beautiful people spilled out in expensive furs, going from the Cozy Corner to the Hollywood for hully gully, pork chop music, and on to Abart's for jazz. High heels clicking, laughter ringing, cologne and perfume scents mixing with tobacco and alcohol, big cars driven slowly down the street by high rollers, the scene replicated entertainment strips in Harlem of the same era.

Patrons sauntered to Freddy Woods's Off Beat, the Squeeze In, or Joe Heard's place, behind the Howard Theater. Then over to Powell's, where folk played mellow and raucous tunes on a juke box. On to the Crystal Caverns, known as the Cave, a jazz joint owned by Cab Calloway's sister, Blanche. In the 1200 block of U Street, Tasson's packed a crowd into narrow quarters. The Republic Gardens, in the 1300 block of U, featured a combo each night. The Radio Music Hall, on V Street, Johnson's Flamingo, the Ben Gazza, the Casbah, and Club Balley, where Billie Holiday, Pearl Bailey and other greats performed regularly, added to the Northwest club scene.

Around the corner on 14th Street, anyone with a sweet tooth could stop in the Doughnut Shop. And for real hunger, the nearby Chinese restaurant called the Zanzibar gave the clubs' dining a run for their money.

A short car ride away, in Southwest, the nightlife sparkled at the Stardust and at Bruce Wahl's. Wahl, a debonair, suave entrepreneur, knew the benefit of the personal touch. A customer never came in a stranger the second time. Instead, Wahl captured names and faces with a photographic memory and treated each customer like a treasured friend.

"I began to understand how that club stayed crowded. People used to like to take out-of-towners with them, so they could just show off how they know the owner of that sucker. He would give it up to you, too. 'Hey Bruce.' 'Heey, my man, how you feel?' And call you by name," Petey recalled decades later, when Wahl was being honored for his contributions to black business.

He also remembered clubs in Northeast. Jimmy McFail's Gold Room, where Jimmy himself sang. The Boot and Saddles. Rocky's with shake dancer Delores Proctor. The Cotton Club on Benning Road. And Dikes Stockade, which Petey considered to be ahead of its time. Owned by Jim Dike, the establishment featured horseback riding, dinner and barbecues, and parties at night in the dance hall.

The quadrant claimed another popular spot, known as the Northeast Casino, a large dance hall where Rhythm and Blues entertainers performed. In fact, the place was across the Maryland line, which Petey discovered once after he was arrested for fighting there in his post-Army days. He'd been running his mouth, not fighting, but got swept up in the arrests and had to pay $25 to authorities in Upper Marlboro, MD to be released.

However, in the late 40s, fueled by his father's fascination, Petey succumbed to the lure of nightlife along the Northwest strip like a moth flies to flame. He watched the glamorous as well as ordinary people float in and out of club after club, dollars flowing like wine into the coffers of the black-owned nightclubs and theaters like the Howard that no one imagined would ever fail.

As a young teen, Petey and his junior high school classmates used every opportunity to sneak into the Howard Theater, where Petey hung onto every syllable uttered by comedians. He knew he wanted to take their place more than anything in the world, and one day, he would get there. Finally where he wanted to be, he would fall off the stage in a drunken stupor as an adult in his late 30s.

Before alcohol's demons grew to their full force, when drinking was just the fun thing to do, Petey came to the Howard as a soldier, to sit in the audience reciting jokes word for word along with comedians he'd studied for years.

Although now old enough to enter the nearby popular clubs in his army uniform, Petey most often looked in from the outside. He felt no kinship with the people he saw as elite, light and bright, hoity toities. People he would later jokingly call "Macka Cuckie Lackies," in small, classy clubs. People like Adam Clayton Powell or Charles Diggs, Howard University students at the time.

Instead, he chose to spend his leave time at the Lincoln Colonnade, a fabulous ballroom and dance hall where he could show off his dancing skills and attract red-lipsticked women in their full skirts.

When he looked back on those days, however, the show-off spot he recalled most fondly was Griffith Stadium, on Georgia Avenue, for its annual Capital Classic football game. In the fall of 1949, Private Ralph "Petey" Greene stepped into the stadium with a beautiful woman on his arm. A woman he'd paid to be his date.

*　　*　　*

Petey's voice: *Styling and Profiling*

"We was wearing the Billy Eckstine shirts then. Mr. B., we called him. The shirt had a collar that would roll. You would tie a knot in your necktie, big knot called a Beau Windsor, roll your shirt up over your tie and have the collar showing up over your jacket, you know.

"I'll never forget as long as I live the outfit I wore to the Capital Classic that year. I had a yellow Mr. B shirt with a dark green necktie. A pair of Oxford grey slacks, dark, almost black. And I had a pair of black Nettletons, a long shoe with stitches. They didn't cost but 14 dollars, from down at Rich's Shoe Store. I had a grey Dobb 20 hat, big brim, and a light gray sport coat. Finally, I had a Ragland, a top coat with four buttons down the front, a patch pocket, tight collar that I worn open. I thought I was the sharpest thing.

"I got off the Greyhound bus with a prostitute named Evelyn I knew from Baltimore, who I'd paid to be with me for just that occasion. She and I had become friendly because I saw her lift a soldier's wallet, but I didn't tell on her. She was beautiful, and I paid her just to come with me to that Capital Classic.

"When we got to Griffith Stadium, boy you talk about guys going off! 'Goddamn Petey Greene, where you get the FINE woman from?' Naturally I was talking shit, and by her being a ho', naturally she knowed how to act. Boy, she made me feel so good. She just did something none of the high school girls would have known how to do. She just held me and leaned on me. I was the awkward one.

"And I must have had about $200 on me. The old guys was looking at her and talking shit to me. One guy come up to me and said, 'Man, that ain't your woman. You ain't got sense enough to have no woman like that. This woman is too fast for you.' She understood that this was a walking thing, where you are supposed to be seen. So we walked, and guys were drooling at the lips, too.

"For halftime, they brought in a high school band, Booker T., out of Norfolk, Va. They put all the lights out in the stadium and the band had lights on their hats and shoes. Goddamn if them guys didn't roll. They'd been in the Capital Classic parade earlier in the day, along with the major colleges and dignitaries and all. I guess somebody like Tuskegee or Morgan was playing against each other. I wasn't paying no attention to the game. I just wanted to parade around the stadium in front of 17,000 people with this woman on my arm.

"After the game, we went on down U Street to a couple of bars, then to the Capital Classic Ball at the Uline Arena to hear Louis Jordan. She didn't bump into anybody she knew. Everything was my whole show. We had a real good time."

*   *   *

Some of Petey's friends held jobs as busboys and dishwashers at the white clubs down past 14th Street and Thomas Circle. Clubs with names like Casino Royal and Lotus. Clubs with black performers but no black customers, maitre'd's or waiters. They'd notice the white customers heading on up to the black entertainment mecca, but segregation prevented reverse traffic.

In summer, waitresses and bar maids in DC would head up to Atlantic City, to work in Club Harlem and Graces, owned by a black man, Catfish Greenwall. Out of service and generally doing nothing, Petey caught rides with friends whenever he could to frequent the Atlantic City clubs. Once fortified with liquor, he'd launch into his routine of jokes and rhymes, either from his chair or on the stage between paid acts.

"At Club Harlem, they had a mean-ass special police who didn't like me. Snatched me off that stage one time. So they didn't have no more trouble out of me. The people gave him hell that night. Wanted to jump on his ass, because they liked to hear me. They'd always say, 'Give Petey Greene that mike.'"

That was the story at Club Harlem. Just a few years earlier while he was in service, Petey's unauthorized use of stages ended with much better results.

*   *   *

The Grand Send-off

Prior to the declaration of war against Korea, Petey had never heard of the place. He knew about Japan, but Korea may as well have been on another planet. A scary, dangerous planet. To take his mind off the fear of impending battles, Petey joined fellow soldiers in finding as many parties as they could in the days leading up to their departure.

Once in California, at Camp Stollman, a matter of days before setting sail for the Far East, Petey and three friends heard about a club in Oakland, on Seventh Street. At 10 p.m., Cary Grover, Oliver Cooper, Robert L. Brookes and Petey Greene stepped into one of the classiest spots they'd ever seen: Slim Jenkins.

Each soldier had $500 burning a hole in his pocket, and each agreed they deserved champagne on ice in a bucket, pheasant for dinner, and the best seats in the house for the stage show. The more Petey drank, the sillier he got; the sillier he got, the louder his friends roared with laughter.

The hilarity became so infectious, people at nearby tables began to lean closer to listen to Petey, instead of watching the act on stage. Finally, the owner, Slim Jenkins himself, sent a waitress over to Petey's table.

"Hey soldier, my boss, Mr. Jenkins, says he doesn't know what you telling these people, but it seems like everybody should be in on it since it's so good. There's a microphone and a stage. Go on up," the curvaceous waitress invited.

Although his buddies immediately started nudging him, Petey needed no more encouragement. He bounded onto the stage and launched into his rapid-fire act of calling the trains just like a real conductor.

"We leaving New York City on train number 5, leaving out of New York City at 5:15 for all points south. You got the smoker car, the box car, freight car, day line, club car, refrigerator car, pullman car, and the coach. Leaving out of New York at 5:15 for all points south. Going to Newark, Trenton, Philadelphia, 30th Street stop. Chester, Pennsylvania, Wilmington, Delaware, Baltimore, Maryland, change in Washington, D.C. for all points south going to Quantico, Brookville, Richmond, Petersburg, Suffolk, Norfolk, Newport News, Raleigh, Birmingham, Columbus, Atlanta, Savannah, Jacksonville, Tallahassee, Miami, Key West, and catch a Banana Boat to Cuba. Wahnnnwahhh. Wahhhwahhh."

The audience yelled, cheered, and clapped, so Petey kept going, becoming a chef, a short-order cook in a restaurant.

"I worked as a short order cook and a man came in saying 'I'd like to get two ham and eggs on toast and a couple of black coffees to go.' I said, 'Hey Chef.' He said, 'Hey Greene.' I said, 'Two Adam and Eves in a garden on a raft with their eyes wide open, draw one from the dark, rack him.' 'Next, a lady come in, saying,' I'd like to get two hamburgers with nothing on 'em.' I say, 'Yes, m'am.' I say, 'Hey Chef.' He say, 'Hey Greene.' I say, 'Send two destroyers all alone in the Pacific Ocean.' She say, 'Make that with mustard on it.' I say, 'Hey Chef.' He say, 'Hey Greene.' I say, 'Send them destroyers with a convoy looking.' . . . ."

People kept calling for encores, but Petey finally ended his act, and as he descended the stage, Mr. Jenkins came over. "You don't belong in the army, soldier. As long as you're in town, come on in here every night if you want to. You don't have to pay."

Flattered, Petey expressed his gratitude and filed Slim Jenkins in his memory bank. He split the rest of his time in the Bay area looking for women and gambling.

On at least one occasion, Petey gambled on the wrong thing—and got taken for a ride of the wrong sort.

*   *   *

Petey's voice: Scammin' and Jammin'

"We came out of a joint one night in Oakland, walking down the street. It was Cary Grover, Robert Brookes, Petey Greene and Oliver Cooper, all four of us walking together. Oliver Cooper is out of Jamaica, Long Island; Robert Brookes is out of Pensacola, Florida; Cary Grover is out of Sumter, South Carolina; and I was out of Washington, D.C. We walking down the street and we meet up with four other soldiers.

"Cooper say, 'My man! Goddamn! Out of Jamaica, New York! Hey Baby!' Then Brooks turns to one of the soldiers and say, 'My man!' That guy was out of Brooks's home town. Then Grover say,

'What?' Saw his buddy, from his home. All three of them met three guys from out of their home towns. And here's a nigguh with them named Alphonso English from Washington, D.C. That's the most weird thing I have ever seen in my life. Four soldiers together on the street meet four soldiers and each one happened to be a home boy.

"Me and the dude named Alphonso was laughing about that, and we have laughed about that since we been back home. We talked and joked and they went on their way and we went on ours. Now, we going to buy some pussy, but we ran into the best operation I ever seen.

"We saw these whores. We got plenty money, so we told the broads we wanted to buy some pussy. 'Short time?' 'Yeah, we don't want a whole lot of time.' They say '$40.' We got plenty money, we say okay. That was expensive—that would be expensive if you buying it from your wife—but to nigguhs that's going overseas, it ain't expensive. You want everything. You don't have to pass up nothing.

"We wanted four girls, but it wasn't but two. They told us to stand right there while they walked off. A cab pulled up. 'All right, soldiers, get in.' We say, 'Get in? Fuck you.' 'Did you just say you want to buy some pussy?' We got right in the car and the man took us somewhere. We didn't have to pay him nothing. We get out and we standing on the corner. All of a sudden, there's them two broads.

"They take us around to a house and they had two more broads. We fucked 'em, paid 'em, and they took us back to the corner. The same cab pulled up, took us back, dropped us off, we ain't gave the cab driver nothing yet.

"The next night, though, I got tricked, waiting for the bus to go back to the army camp. Me and Grover and Brooks standing there and a guy came up to us. 'Y'all want a nice girl?' My buddies said 'Shit, no,' but I asked, 'Where the girl at?' He pointed to a fine white broad, sitting up 'neath the wheel of a car. He said, 'Ain't but $20.'

"She was looking over, smiling. The bus was coming, so Grover and Brookes said, 'Come on, Greene.' I said, 'Noooo. I'm going to fuck this white bitch. Y'all go 'head.' They got on the bus. I told the guy, 'Look, man. One more bus coming and I got to be on it by 10:30.' He said, 'All right. Since you got to go, she'll take you 'round and fuck you in the back of the car. You want her to do that?' I said, "It don't make no difference to me, fine as she is.' He said, 'You want her to suck your dick? Give me $25 and you'll get a blow job, too.'

"I said, 'Okay,' because she was sitting in the car looking, just smiling like a motherfucker. I give the man that $25, and he said, 'Go ahead over there, jim. Tell her Al sent you.'

"When I got to the window, I said, 'You saw me talking to Al. He said for me to come over here and get in.' She said, 'Get in where? You'd better get away from here, soldier. You're not getting in this car. Are you crazy? What's wrong with you?'

"I looked back, and that man had disappeared. Then the police came out of nowhere. They asked her 'What's wrong?' and she told them, 'I don't know about this crazy soldier here. He's talking about getting in my car.' They said, 'All right, Mack, what's wrong with you?' 'Nothing, this guy . . . ' 'What guy?'

"By this time, I'm scared. I say, 'Look, man, just forget it. I'm stationed at Fort Stollman and I'm getting ready to go overseas. I'm waiting for the bus.' The policeman said, 'Well, get your ass over at that bus stop. Stand there, you understand. And don't you move your black ass until that bus comes.' I say, 'Yes sir.' The woman was saying, 'The very idea!!! Let me move my car . . .'

"When I got back to camp and told the sergeant about it, he explained that it was a scam. He said the policemen probably weren't even policemen. Said they probably had fake uniforms on. He said, 'You don't know whether he had a badge on or not, do you? You couldn't even describe them. They do that to everybody.'

"It really drugged me for a little while. Then I figured, 'What the fuck.' And I went on down to a tattoo place in a town called Richmond, California, outside Camp Stollman. I was going to get a shaking lady on my arm. But when I looked at that motherfucker waving the machine, I say, "Man, if you don't get the fuck away from me.' None of my friends got any tattoos. I was with them black-ass nigguhs; a tattoo wouldn't even shine up on them. I just wanted to be grown and different, but when I saw that machine, I said, 'Fuck this heah. I knew right then that I didn't want to be white. Tattoos were for white people. A nigguh don't need no motherfuckin' tattoo.

"In the next couple of days, they put us on trucks and took us to what they called The Pier. They let us off these trucks and you got your duffle bag with you and your rifle over your shoulder. Your helmet and your helmet liner is the only thing that's not in that bag.

"Now a duffle bag, if it's packed right, will hold a host of garments and other accessories. But for a trifling guy like me, who can't pack shit, it will be bulging and all that. So, being a slick motherfucker, I had it packed for me, by a nigguh that didn't have no money. Shirts was pressed and all.

"You stand beside your bag, reach and get your helmet, put your helmet liner right there with its number across it; mine was 1089. I'm leaving the United States of America to go fight in a country I had never heard of. But being a versatile, humorous person—God has gifted me those talents, humor, verbal skills and versatility to adjust to any situation—even though fear was in the pit of my little young-ass stomach, weighing no more than a ball 140, which is 140 motherfuckin' pounds, and just started shaving not too long ago, coming out of my mouth was all kinds of jokes and shit about 'kill those Koreans.' And little bits of pee was trickling down my leg, cause I was SCARED.

"I'm standing there with big old black buck nigguhs, all scared to death. There were sergeants barking who had been overseas before. 'All right, goddamnit, we going straight up this gang plank. The days of bullshit is over!' They gave us mess passes and started calling numbers. They finally called mine, 1089. I got that duffle bag, put it over my shoulder, rifle on my other shoulder, and after a while, it's not even bothering me. It's a big joke again.

"They showed us where we would sleep in these hammocks, in a big ol' room, and they tell you about the mess hall. It was 1950, and I guess I was about 18 or 19. I knew about Japan, but I ain't never heard of Korea. I was supposed to get out of the Army, but Truman gave us an additional 9 months. They called it The Truman Year. That gave enough time to get me overseas.

"As I recall, I never worried about much while I was on that ship. All I did was gamble and stay seasick, and gave my chow card to a nigguh with a cast-iron stomach. For 19 days, they were chasing my ass to get on KP. 'Private Greene, 13275832, report to the galley!' Fuck that KP, I gambled all the time, and I walked all over the ship to learn about it. All my life, whenever I'm anywhere, there's a time—no matter how much recreation there is for me—Petey Greene always takes some educational part out of it for hisself.

"The thing we had going for us was that we are going to Yokohama, Japan. We had enough knowledge to know that they weren't fighting in Japan. They were fighting in Korea. But after we was out at sea about 11 days, an announcement came over the speaker. 'Now hear this. Now hear this. At approximately 0800 hours this morning, our course and destination was changed from Yokohama, Japan, to Pusan, Korea.' Everybody on the ship got quiet. Them nigguhs stopped shooting dice. They went to chapel. I just sat right there while they was going, just sitting playing with the dice by myself.

"The chaplain came over. 'Why didn't you go to church?' I said, 'Cap, ain't no use in going to church now. Whatever gone happen, gone happen.' We don't even know whether they fighting in Pusan. They said Korea, and that's enough to scare everybody.

"But, as it turned out, we just going to Pusan to let them unload them tanks and that heavy equipment. We ain't getting off. We back up, spin around and go on to Yokohama. We get off in Yokohama, and when we know anything again, we was in Fujinobe, about 20 miles away, in Quonset huts. We stayed in Japan at least a month and a half. We had to wait for our last pickups, which were amphibious ducks. Those were machines that run on land and in the water. Then we ready to go to Korea.

"Don't nobody know what's happening but them goddamn people in the Pentagon. We don't know 'bout no Inchon Invasion. That's gone make history, and goddamnit, I made that motherfucker, too. Ain't shot nothing, just made that motherfucker."

CHAPTER 15

Korea

INCONGRUOUSLY, PETEY WAS part of one of the Korean War's classic battles: the Inchon Invasion. On route to Asia on the General SS Ballou for 19 days, Petey and his friends gambled, stifled their fears, and bragged about girls they'd left behind. Once he landed on the beachhead in Korea, in an LST landing barge, he faced the serious side of war for the first time.

But, because he was who his grandmother raised him to be, Petey got back in his game as soon as he found his footing. Assigned first to the 76th Engineer Duck Truck Company, then a few months later as a cook in the 74th Engineer Combat Battalion, Petey found ways to transform the experience to fit his style.

"Whenever I go anywhere, I find out who the damn fools is, who I can use, who ain't gone let me use them, who is concerned about me, and then I just make it work," he would explain in later years. And if he couldn't find the humor in a situation, he'd create it.

*   *   *

The tales he brought back from Korea were the stuff movies are made of. From falling into latrines to "adopting" two children who hung around the camp, to eating foods he'd never have eaten at home, Petey wove his army experiences into comedic routines:

Petey's Voice: Dogging It

"I ate a dog in Korea. We were right outside Seoul, the capital. We'd been there about three or four weeks, and we was getting a lot of drugs in Chinatown. Brown heroin. Hit you right in the pit of your stomach. You got to throw up, boy, and after you through throwing up, you be higher than a motherfucker.

"I had two friends, a nigguh named Monroe out of New York, 125th and 7th Avenue—that's all he ever talk about, Harlem, the Apollo Theater. I used to tell him, 'Man, fuck Harlem.' The other guy was out of Chicago; named Hooper. The three of us used to be together all the time. We met these three Korean broads who were middle class, with clean dresses and all. We used to take 'em little gifts.

"One night they invited us over to they Mamasan house. We knowed they was middle class, not welfare, as I say. They had little lanterns in a hut with sliding doors, built up off the ground. And they heated the floor.

"The floor was made of concrete and the heat was in there. You put the blankets down on the nice warm floor to sit on. Well, they'd squat, not sit. They were the squattingest people in the world.

"Then they would make bowls of warm milk sake that would make you drunker than a motherfucker. By us messing with the drugs, Hooper and Monroe didn't want much sake. I wanted it all. Bowls of it! It look like clam chowder and was gooder than a motherfucker. Wish I had a gallon of it.

"Anyway, we sitting there talking and the Mamasan cooking rice, make every grain stand for itself. Uncle Ben ain't shit compared to them goddamn people. So it come time for us to eat. They had this animal, you could tell it was a torso, just laying up on a platter. We had our little bowls of rice in front of us. Papasan was serving, poured something like gravy over the meat. I didn't know what it was, but it was gooood. I told Moore, 'This is good. I thought I'd never eat no lamb.'

Moore said, 'This ain't no lamb, this is turkey.' Hoop say, 'I don't care what it is, I just want another piece.' We having a good time, singing. I'll never forget. We all singing 'She ain't got no yodel' and all that. A Korean song. Another one, 'Ay de young, kokeronomaganda.' Now what that mean, I don't know, but they singed it everywhere you go, with a big 'Nomaganda' at the end.

"I always get things fucked up. I said, 'Papasan, what meat is this?' The girl spoke English, so she asked him, and translated his answer. She say, 'Korean say Majoogo. Japanese say Kangee.' I asked, 'What do American's say?' 'Americans say Arff.'

"Moore yelled, 'He means a dog???' The three of us jumped right outside that house and threw up. It goes to show you how your mind works. If he don't never tell us it was a dog, it wouldn'ta never made us sick. All three of us got sick. And on the way back to the Army camp, Hoop and Moore say, 'Greene, don't tell nobody.'

"I say, 'I ain't gone tell nobody.' Shiiit. I say to myself, 'As juicy as this is, I got to tell every motherfuckin' body in camp.'"

*   *   *

Petey's job as cook allowed him time to sit around and scheme. Once, he held back second servings so he could amass food to trade for free sex from women whose soldier-pimps charged outrageous sums. The longer the demolition crews had been away from the towns, the higher the fees got for sex with Korean women in tents set up a little distance from camp as the soldiers moved along the demolition route.

At first, the Republic of Korea, ROK, soldiers assigned to KP didn't want to refuse seconds to the brawny, ravenous soldiers who'd been blowing up mountains all day, clearing the way, building bridges. "If me say 'no seconds', GI punchee," the man who Petey called Number 804 complained when Petey explained his plan to amass extra food. Petey hadn't told them what it was for, knowing they resented the situation that created the prostitutes.

"If anybody tries to hit you or says anything, you tell them to see me," Petey responded, trying to establish control. But the Korean soldier saw right through him.

"No, you all the time yabby yabby yabby. You no come."
Which Petey translated to mean, "We know you can't help, you
can't fight, all you can do is talk shit." The Korean soldiers already
called him Sergeant Yabbity Yabbity. "Look. You want to stay on
your job? No seconds. Tell 'em to see me."

His plan worked for a while, until Number 804 found out
what was happening, ratted Petey out, and put an end to the game.

Koreans played a part in Petey's next escapade involving food,
too. This time, it was a crew of civilians who followed the
demolition squad to clear away the bricks and debris. About 150
old people would form a brigade to clear 100 miles a day, by
hand. The Army paid them in rations, large grass sacks of rice and
three or four hundred cases of sardines in oil.

When the Army trucks moved, they hooked the trailers that
carried the food supply for the Koreans and pulled it along.

*　　*　　*

A man whose childhood included numerous hungry nights
often finds ways to avoid the same fate in adulthood. Petey was
such a man:

Petey's voice: In the Can

"So what happened, sweetheart, we get cut off up in a place
somewhere called Kuneree Pass or something. This might not be
the right name, but I know we got cut off from the rest of the
troops. And we couldn't move because the enemy was over here.
We was jammed, and we ain't got much food anyway. We jammed
for damn near a month.

"But now the food is done dwindled all the way down. When
we get round 'bout the second week and that food was running
low, I happened to be walking to the latrine. That's a cut in the
ground. And I passed by one of them trailers. Our food is running
out, but these people got a trailer load. I steals a case of sardines.
They ain't got to give us none of these, and *didn't* give us none.

"I take it and digs me a hole down by the river, back in some little forest. Our food is steady running out. I would feed the troops whatever we had, which would be a half cup of coffee and maybe three grains of powdered eggs. It's getting all the way down. I mean, it's not bullshitting. This is not in the movies. This is in Korea. And I'm a cook.

"Men walking around talking crazy. I used to come out, look to my left, look to my right, look up and down, then ease down to my stash. I had a little can opener. Must have been 48 cans in there. Opens me two. Eat, and wash my mouth out with dirty water from that river, 'cause I don't want a scent from that food.

"I'd come back and when it's time to eat, say, 'All right, let's move it. Here you go, take your rations, soldier.' After everybody sitting there, eating whatever they had, I'd be talking shit. 'Goddamnit, boy, you got to be a man to be in this motherfucker. All my life, I been a man! I'm a gangster!'

"Around 9 that night, when everybody's guts be growling and grumbling, I'd ease to my stash, knock me off two cans. Come on back. We be sitting around, I be talking shit about Washington. 'Let me tell y'all. When I get back, I'm gone get seven 'ho's. Want me to tell y'all a toast . . . Signifying monkey, deep in the jungle . . .' I'd be buck dancing, all on top of the jeep.

"Guys would say, 'Man, how can this motherfucker do it? He is baad!' So the thing was out that Greene was strong. The lieutenant called me one day, saying, 'Greene, we really want to see if we can get you an honor, because you are lifting the morale of these soldiers. I just want to tell you to hold on, because we got word that they're going to break through pretty soon.'

"Let me tell you how I fucked up. I always fuck myself. I must have had 32 cans left, and it was the first time I'd ever done anything by myself and wouldn't tell nobody. 'Cause I know it was dangerous to let anybody know. That's how hungry everybody was and how low the rations was.

"The cooks ain't got nothing to do, 'cause they ain't got nothing to serve. I had served the coffee and the soldiers had one hardtack, a kind of a cookie. So a guy came through saying, 'Man, I wish I had something . . .' I say, 'Nigguh, stop crying! Look at you, 6'10, 200 something pounds. Give that nigguh my rations!' A soldier named Key say, 'Are you crazy?' I rolled my eyes, saying, 'I'm tired of these nigguhs crying all the time.' He say, "D.C., I wish I had asked you for it.' I say, 'Fuck that shit. Just give me a cup of coffee.'

"But that's how I fucked up. That evening, I'm down by my stash eating like a motherfucker and somebody said, 'You bastard, you.' I looked back and it's the First Sergeant. A rolly polly man named Sergeant Redd. He had followed me and caught me. He told me later he knew when I give that hardtack away. He had his reservations about me all the time, because I was always so happy and shit.

"I said, 'Well, Sarge, you know I can get in serious trouble for stealing this stuff from those people. You ain't gone tell nobody, are you?' He said, 'If you don't get the fuck out the way!' Me and him sat down there. He got six stars, he's a First Sergeant. He ate about six or eight cans of my sardines. First thing he wanted to do was take some back to his tent, but I told him he couldn't do that. We must have dined together for about two days, and then the breakthrough came.

"Then he couldn't hold it. He told everybody, but I didn't get in no trouble. They made a big joke of it."

*   *   *

They already knew Petey's style. They'd seen it as soon as they landed in Korea. Petey had been uncomfortable sleeping on the ground in his sleeping bag, so he'd gone to a little town and taken an Army cot from an old Korean man. The next time his squad put up their tents and rolled out their sleeping bags, Petey erected his cot. "I told y'all I ain't never slept on the ground in my life," he crowed.

Word travels fast, and before another night passed, a sergeant pulled rank. "Where'd you get that cot, Greene?"

"I brought it with me from the States," Petey lied. All his buddies encouraged, "Take it from him, Sarge," because they had already tired of Petey's bragging. As Ain't Pig always told him, "Yo' mouth gets you in all kindsa trouble!"

Stung by the loss, Petey marched right to the lieutenant. "Lieutenant, Sergeant King got a bed. Got a cot. I thought officers was supposed to have it."

"Where did he get it?"

"I don't know, but he said he's the only one here with one."

The lieutenant sent for it, but before he could pick it up, the captain got word, and commandeered it for himself. Petey, thinking, "Wow, that cot shouldn'ta meant so much. I made it more than what it was," congratulated himself once again for stirring the hornets' nest.

Chapter 16

The Down Side

SOMETIMES, THOUGH, EVEN Petey's ability to laugh at himself and others couldn't take away the hurt of war. And the horror did not always come from the enemy without. Often, simple human error inside the camp caused death and injury.

Petey's battalion crossed mine fields on route to mountains they would demolish and bridges they would build. The procedure for clearing the minefields had to be strictly adhered to, or soldiers could be maimed and killed. A group of soldiers carrying mine detectors would advance to clear the mine fields before the rest of the troops proceeded.

More than once, something went wrong. The first time Petey witnessed this kind of tragedy, a truck in the line ahead of his hit a mine along a route that had been declared clear. The truck blew up, not killing the soldiers instantly but leaving them with injuries so serious, they died before help could reach them.

The next time involved the demolition squad, called in to blast a hole through a mountain so the US Army could march to its destination in an hour instead of taking a 10-day detour around the mass. The demolition team would bore holes in the mountain's base, put detonator caps inside, then instruct everyone to stand back a distance.

"If they say get back 50 feet, I get back 150 feet," Petey wrote to A'nt Pig after seeing his first mountain blown to bits.

Now and then, a detonator cap would be defective. "Fire in the hole," an expert would yell out. One bleak day, a young soldier out of Roanoke, Virginia, went back too soon. Just as he got close, the cap detonated. Nearly half the mountain rained down on him as crew members raced to pull him away.

Gently, they laid him in the back of a jeep, trying to get him to the nearest Mobile Surgical Unit, a hospital set up in a tent. "Don't go fast, don't go fast," the soldier whispered desperately, washed in blood, gripped in a vise of pain and fear. Within minutes, he died.

In his next letter, Petey told A'nt Pig: "I was sad that boy got killed. I'm even more alert now. When they say get back 50 feet, where I was getting back 150 feet, I'ma get back 200 now. And when they say wait 20 minutes before you go near a fire in the hole, I'ma wait 'til tomorrow."

On occasion, injuries would be self-inflicted. Petey's friend Private Watson, out of Philadelphia, made himself a notable example. A small man with a reputation of fighting men 10 times his size and winning, Watson befriended Petey when they both waited in Camp Campbell, Kentucky, to be moved through California, through Japan, to Korea. After a few months in Korea, he urged Petey to transfer out of the mess hall to become an assistant driver on Watson's truck.

"Watson so short, he got to sit on pillows to drive," Petey wrote to Priestly, who had stayed in Annapolis. "All he ever want to do is drive. Ass hanging out, double clutching, got his hat cocked on the side. He just as crazy as he can be."

One cold night, Petey and Watson shivered in zip-up sleeping bags in their tents, fighting back tears. They couldn't make fires for warmth because the enemy was too close. In fact, Petey and Watson could see the enemy's fires in the near distance. By the time he went for guard duty, Watson's resentment boiled over.

Ten minutes later, he came back to the tent, summoning Petey to follow him outside to witness an act of defiance. There stood a glowing fire, flames licking skyward, fueled by five gallons of gas and some ammunition boxes.

"Put that fire out," the lieutenant on command yelled.

Watson turned steely eyes his way. "Don't touch it." To his fellow soldiers, he encouraged, "Come, get warm. Get warm, everybody!" Minutes later, Watson's superiors led him off to the tent to "rest," the only sensible punishment in the middle of war, a stone's throw from the enemy.

"Hey Greene, you know I'm going home," Watson announced, after gambling with Petey and several other soldiers, and pocketing $700 the next day.

"All I know is, you crazy," Petey replied.

A minute later, a blast startled Petey. He ran outside, only to see that Watson had shot himself in the foot. As he headed to the ambulance on a stretcher, Watson called out to Petey:

"Hey Greene, don't forget me. I live on East North Street in North Philadelphia."

Years later, when Watson came to D.C., he found Petey living as a "winehead bum," as Petey would later describe himself. Watson told Petey he'd unintentionally blasted his entire big toe off through his combat boot, and had never walked again without thinking of that rash, desperate ploy. He also never asked Petey about the $700 Petey had taken out of Watson's bag as soon as he saw the ambulance pull away that day.

*   *   *

The next time Watson saw Petey, he could hardly find anything to laugh about:

Petey's voice: Johnny Get Your Gun

"Watson come to DC with a church group or something, and he asked somebody if they know Petey Greene. That person said, 'All you got to do is go to Georgetown and anybody'll tell you where Petey Greene at.'

"See, I think I told you this before, and if I didn't, I'm gone tell you now: Television and radio just made me popular with the white people. But my name has been a legend in this town all the time, with the black folks. Watson just went to 7th and T and asked a man did he know Petey Greene. Two or three people said, 'He live over in Georgetown.'

"I was doing bad, extremely bad, extraordinarily bad. When I came out of the alley where I had been drinking with some more wineheads, I could tell by Watson's eyes how surprised he was. Jesus Christ! Had his old lady with him and another guy and his old lady. He said, 'Man, where can we get a drink around here?'

"He introduced me to them people, and I could see them people thinking, 'What? Where you know *this* nigguh from?' I took 'em up to a bootlegging joint, upstairs. Old dude named Johnny Jenkins had a joint. Ran it with his lady, Miss Florence. Now I ain't got no money, but I say, 'What you want, man?' Watson said, 'We got money,' but I had to be in charge. 'You can't pay for nothing in my town.' I ain't got a dime.

"Miss Florence asked, 'What you want, Petey?' I looked around, said, 'Where's Johnny?' She nodded toward the back, 'He in there sleep.' I breathed a bit easier, saying, 'Give me two half pints and six beers.'

"Now I got another winehead with me named Spin. He know I ain't got no money, but he just want to drink. When we go to pick up the drinks, I get the two half pints and some cups. Watson say, 'What do I owe?' I'm acting insulted now. 'You don't owe *nothing*. This is my town, motherfucker!' Spin whispered in my ear, 'Now Greene, you know Johnny bought a pistol. You better let them people pay for the liquor.' Johnny is the man in charge of the joint but he sleep. I just looked at Spin, so he said, 'Well, I'ma get me a drink and I'm gone.'

"He get him a drink, tell Watson, 'Nice meeting you, man, I was in the army too.' And gone. So I get another half pint, which is now three half pints, and two more beers. Watson asked, 'You need any money?' I'm still playing the part. 'Man, I don't need no money in here, you understand?' They finished their drinks, and Watson said, 'Well, Jack, if you ever in Philadelphia, give me a call.'

"He felt kinda bad, so he left on out. I had on the clothes that I'd had on for about two weeks. Some old brogan shoes and a old greasy field jacket. I needed a haircut and a bath. I looked just like you supposed to look when you's a derelict.

"When they left out, Miss Florence's head snapped up. 'Petey, you know that'll be seven dollars.' A half a pint of liquor was a dollar and a half, and beers about 25 cent a can on Sunday. I say, 'I ain't got no money. I'll pay you Saturday.'

"Her eyes narrowed and her jaw started twitching. 'I am tired of this shit. Johnny! Johnny! This motherfucking Petey Greene owe me $7 and won't pay.'

"I heard him fumbling with the dresser drawer and I remembered what Spin said, that this man just bought a pistol. Now I'm on the second floor when I started thinking 'bout that pistol, but felt like I was on the fifth floor when I heard him say, 'I'll kill this motherfucker!'

"I'm running to the door and I could hear him coming. When I get down to the bottom of the steps, that ain't enough. It's another door there, because you have to go into something called a vestibule. He's at the top of the steps, firing the gun. A bullet went through my jacket. I say, 'Goddamn!' I'm not out yet. I'm in the vestibule. Whoom! He shoots the glass out the window. When I get the door open and see daylight, I hear him right behind me.

"I run out the door and POW! He shot again. I felt that bullet when it hit me in the leg, but I didn't break stride because it's no time to be breaking stride. As I turned the corner, here's a broad named Louise, walking down the street. She say, 'Hey, baby, you driving reckless, baby. Give me some skin.' But I ran right past, straight home to my little room, a little dungeon I was living in, at A'nt Pig's.

"When I get in there, I pulled my pants leg up to check the damage. What had happened, the dirt and the husk on my leg probably saved my ass. If I had been clean like I am now, it would have been different. But with four layers of eight-week-old dirt, the bullet just bounced off and just grazed me, I guess. It was bleeding, so I hollered, 'Oh my God!'

"My grandmother came running. 'What's wrong?' Staring at the blood, I said, 'I just got shot.' She looked at it and said, 'Shit, get on and wash it. It'll be all right. If you'd take a bath some damn time . . .' So I washed one leg. That's the leg that was wounded.

"But I'm scared to go out until a guy in the neighborhood come around to say Johnny wanted to talk to me. Because I was running fast and not looking back, what I don't know is the police had been riding by. They saw Johnny with that pistol, looking wild in the middle of a residential section, with smoke protruding out the barrel, and he's ugly and he in his T-shirt and bedroom slippers. Somebody told them, 'He was chasing Petey.' Police say, 'Oh my God, hope he killed him.' I had quite a reputation as a drunk.

"They took Johnny and locked him up, then let him out on bond. He sent the guy around to tell me he'd give me a piece of money if I'd make a statement that'll keep him out of jail. First I didn't want to do it, but then I was thinking 'bout Johnny. He was a good dude. He had had a lot of money one time, and had got broke. He was making a little comeback, and nigguhs were fucking over him and shit. Finally I went around there and we talked. He said, 'All you got to do is don't appear in court and I'll give you $100.' I said, 'What can you give me now?' Johnny reached in his pocket, 'Here's $35.' I never got the other $65, but I never paid him the $7 neither."

Petey presenting his Community Hall of Fame award
to Mr. James Brewer

Petey at news conference in Washington, DC

Petey with Sugar Ray Leonard

Petey on a movie set

Petey as graduation day speaker for
Walt Whitman high school
Photo credit: Charles D. Ramsey

Petey shaking hands with graduates of
Walt Whitman high school
Photo credit: Charles D. Ramsey

Dewey Hughes (right) interviewing actor
Calvin Lockhart

Petey with author Lurma Rackley and her son Rumal at Petey's
home a few months before Petey died in January 1984.

THE ARLINGTON JOURNAL

THIS NEWSPAPER WAS GIVEN TO ME YEARS AGO BY THE LATE MRS. VIRGINIA KEITH, A D.C. SENIOR CITIZEN WHO WAS PRES. OF THE SENIOR CITIZEN TASK FORCE AND THE VERY FIRST VICE PRES. OF THE CAPITAL AREA COMMUNITY FOOD BANK. SHE LOVED PETEY!

C. RAMSEY

38 Tuesday, February 9, 1982

Wed

Mr. and Mrs. Strickland

Weyant — Strickland

Debbra Marie Weyant, daughter of Mr. and Mrs. Robert N. Weyant of Falls Church, and Lee Stephen Strickland, son of Mrs. Mary Strickland of Orlando, Fla., and Mr. Warren C. Strickland of Bristol, Tenn., were married in a candlelight ceremony at St. George's Episcopal Church with the Rev. Robert C. Hall officiating. The reception was held at The Country Squire.

The bride was escorted by her father and given in marriage by her parents. Gloria Thorn, sister of the bride, served as the matron of honor. Bridesmaids were Faye Weyant, Kimberly Weyant, and Carol Gula, cousins of the bride, and Shelby Warmell.

Serving as the best man was Jack Weyant, brother of the bride. Ushers werew Robert Weyant, brother of the bride, Harry Thorn, Les Warnell and Dick Mansfield.

The bride is a 1974 graduate of George C. Marshall High School and is employed by Shaw, Pittman, Potts and Trowbridge of Washington, D.C.

The groom is a magna cum laude graduate of the University of Florida, where he received his law degree and received his mas-

Ok

Diane I ter of Mr the late Pittsburg Phillip W Charles I were uni mandale Church. Worden c ring cerei

The br riage by Borgo, n as the ma zel was th

Mr. Ch son's best Al Koken Russell W

The bri Vernon C graduate sity. He WTOP R.

Followi ception w inn.

The co Church.

"Once, if a cracker ever called me a nigger I'd bust a chair over his head. Now I realize that cracker couldn't hurt me as long as he doesn't touch me. So I'm very comfortable with both words."

"I have only two goals. Number one. I want to hear Mr. Phelps on 'Mission: Impossible' tell that box, when it says, 'You don't have to do it,' say, 'Okay, I ain't gonna do it.' Then, I just want to see the Coyote catch the Road Runner."

Prints of newspaper coverage of Petey in 1982,
courtesy of Charles D. Ramsey's files.
Ramsey and Petey worked together at the
United Planning Organization.

"I never hit a home run when I found out you could bunt."

"I distrust wealthy people who say money doesn't mean anything. I test them by saying, 'Hey man, give me a thousand dollars.' They say, 'Man, you're crazy.' "

Petey speaking at a Gospel (choir) Awards event he initiated
Photo credit: Charles D. Ramsey

Petey's dad, photo from Petey's sister, Constance Bailey

Chapter 17

Home From War

IN ONE SENSE, Petey's best memory of the end of the war was the single day he arrived back on U.S. soil. Thereafter, trouble followed him like a deranged shadow.

Petey's Voice: I'm Coming Back

"The first time I ever drank any beer was the day I stepped off the boat in Seattle, Washington, coming home from Korea. We were going through the streets of Seattle and people were lined up, cheering us on, and they threw beer into our trucks. Cold beer. It was a hot day, so I drank some beer, but I hated it.

"People were screaming. Black and white people. The Airborne guys got on the same ship we did, and they had their clothes tucked away like we did. But when they stepped off that boat that day, I'll never forget it. That had to be one of the most envious times of my life. Them airborne guys was clean, polished, everything. Our shit was all wrinkled. Them suckers were in the same boat, but when they stepped off, they had them creases, their boots was shining. I guess they had made arrangements with the merchant seaman to get an iron and shine their shoes. And all I done the whole time was have my thumb cocked, shooting dice.

"When we got off, my mind reflected back to the old Second World War I used to see in the movies, with the Andrews Sisters singing, 'When Johnny come marching home again, hooray, hooray.' I guess if anyone had known I was thinking about that, they would have thought I was crazy.

"I was so glad to be back in the United States but I still wasn't happy, because I was not in Washington, D.C. I was in another Washington, Seattle, for about six days, getting processed and they seeing if you got any diseases, looking at your dick about 40 times. Boy, they looked at your dick more than any time I ever seen in my life. They don't care what you take overseas, but you wasn't gone bring nothing back in. Nooooo. They give you about 10 inspections before you get to the boat in Korea. Then they go through it again when you land. They give you the Tetanus shot and everything else. My dick was so clean, you could stir coffee with it, because I hadn't been doing nothing but gambling."

*   *   *

Losing in Love

Petey went back to Fort Meade for 30 days before being assigned to Camp Pickett, near Richmond, VA. As soon as he could, he connected with Priestly for a ride to Sylvia's house. Just as Priestly had warned him, Sylvia came to the door pregnant, already married to John Saw. To keep the hurt in his eyes from showing, Petey jumped in the car, snapped his fingers, and directed Priestly, "Take me to Peggy's."

When Peggy saw Petey standing at the door of the small bungalow where she lived with her parents and brothers, tears came to her eyes. He hadn't written in months, and she wasn't sure she'd ever see him again. She thought when he found out about Sylvia's pregnancy, he'd stay away from Annapolis forever, and she'd have no way to find him, to convince him that she was the one he should love best, anyway.

Folding her slim arms around Petey, Peggy looked into his wide grin and laughed. She could see he wanted her as much as she wanted him. Her parents and brothers were out, so as Petey waved Priestly off, Peggy took Petey's other hand to lead him into her tiny, neat bedroom at the back of the house. There, gripped in his strong, lean arms, all Peggy's dreams burst into reality. She believed she loved Petey and always would. Petey cared for her, too. Her sweetness and loyalty made him feel special, safe. But more than anything else, he was in it for the sex.

*   *   *

Throughout his life, Petey carried a quiet sorrow he rarely revealed. It rested on a wish that he could go back in time to erase the hurt he believed he caused his first daughter by not being part of her childhood.

Petey's Voice: My First Baby

"I was in Camp Pickett when I found out Peggy was pregnant. She kept writing me letters saying I got something to tell you. I'm young and simple, so I don't answer to tell her I'm in the stockade and can't go nowhere. Finally, she saw I wasn't coming home, so she put it in a letter. 'Since you won't come home so I can tell you, I want you to know I'm pregnant.' I wrote right back and told her the reason why I can't come. I'm in jail. So, then we correspond about the baby. She told me how much time before she's due and when she's getting ready to have the baby.

"Now, I'm getting money in the stockade because they ain't taking all my pay. I know I won't be out until after she have the baby. When I get out, I stay around camp for about 3 or 4 days and win some money gambling. Must have had about $1,500 on me. She's already done had the baby when I go up there. I didn't know at the time that she had the baby in Freedman's Hospital, in D.C.

"When I get to the house, I knock on the door. They know I'm coming. Everybody was in the house. She hadn't been home from the hospital no more than about a week. The father, the mother, the aunts, say, 'Here come ol' Greene.' I walk in with pockets full of money. I have always been a show-off, loved to have money jammed in my pockets. I wanted to give Peggy a lot of money and I wanted to see my baby.

"One of the aunts came up to me and said, 'Here's your baby.' And handed me a big, huge, black, greasy, fat-jawed baby. I folded my arms up, saying 'I don't want to hold it.' This woman pushing the baby toward me. 'Take your baby.' I was saying in my mind, 'If this is my baby, they are not getting no money out of my ass, 'cause I'm gone.' I'm saying in my mind, 'Fuck this big old goddamn Buckwheat-looking baby. I know this ain't my baby. Shiiit.'

"So, Peggy's father, Fish Turner was his name, good man, he said, 'Why don't y'all stop playing. Boy, that ain't your baby. That's this woman's child. Go on in there. Peggy in there.' I went in Peggy's room and there was Peggy, in the bed with Renee, my daughter, laying beside her. Pretty little red baby laying there. I'm thinking, 'This is more like it.' I know this baby is the right size and look like me.

"I pulled out that money, about five or six one hundred dollar bills. 'Here's a little something for you.' I kissed her. I'm young and immature, and simple as a motherfucker, but I know this is the right thing to do. I had a box of cigars, too, to give to her father. Not one, but a whole box. 'Here, take these cigars.' He say, 'You dumb bastard.' But he liked me. His wife did not. That lady hated me. She felt as though Peggy could have done better, with all the soldiers there. She would have preferred Peggy to be with Charlie or Priestly or Millett. Wanted her daughter to have a better soldier than me. That lady knew I wasn't about a damn thing.

"A few months later, I came to visit and Peggy's mother told me she really didn't want to see me in her house again. Said just don't worry about supporting the baby. Go away and don't come back. I was shocked and hurt, but being a young, simple motherfucker, I felt I had to play it tough. I said, 'Well, you ain't said nothin'. Bye.' And I didn't go back."

*   *   *

Petey walked out of Peggy's life with a hole in his heart. He thought about his daughter often, especially after he had two more children. He wondered how she was doing, but didn't see a way to put himself back in her life. Fate took care of it for him.

In 1969, Ebony magazine ran a feature article about Petey's amazing transformation from prisoner to highly regarded spokesman for poor people. Through his work with the United Planning Organization, Petey had emerged as a star in President Johnson's anti-poverty program—a man who came from poverty with answers for getting out of it.

Sixteen years after Petey left Peggy's kitchen, an article in the nation's premier black magazine united him with Renee. It happened because children in Renee's neighborhood read the story, heard their parents say Petey was Renee's father, then teased her at school.

"Your daddy been to jail," they snickered, confusing Renee and sending her straight to her mother for the story. Within a matter of days, Peggy contacted Petey in Washington and sent Renee down to spend time with him.

A beautiful girl with Petey's wide smile, Renee told her daddy how glad she was to finally meet him. Throughout her childhood, she'd heard from her grandmother, "You look just like your no-count father. He ain't nothing." Now, here he was in the flesh, not only holding down a respectable job, but on the speaking circuit talking about his life story and using his comic talent on local stages.

A decade later when Renee got married, Petey's heart almost burst with the pride the two of them could share in who he had become.

In talking about his first-born for his memoirs, Petey concluded:

"The greatest thing for her was to finally see me as a radio and television star, and to be able to say 'This is my real daddy.' When I went to her wedding, I stepped out of that limousine with two pockets full of money, manicured nails and a suit that fit me like I was poured into it. I had a photographer with me, too. That's the way I get vengeance on people, as opposed to cussing them out.

"I knew seeing me like I was made the grandmother think of the time she told me if you don't bother us, we won't bother you. That had to refresh her memory. 'Look at this nigger now, pulling up in a big limousine, got his own t.v. show and shit. And here is my daughter over there, the mother of his child.' And I guess she said to herself, 'I'm the one that broke up all of this.'

"When I got out of that car and started walking to the church, people standing outside moved to the side. I parted the crowd and heard them whispering, 'There he is. That's her real father. That's the one on the television. That's Petey Greene.'

"Things like that make me want to keep on keeping on. Those type of settings made me know eventually I had to lay that liquor bottle down. These are motivators, these are enhancers. Just the parting of a crowd for me is something that I would like to inject into my resume.

"I was so glad God had put me in a position to make my daughter proud of me. I gave her and her husband a clock, cost $350, with a pendulum to it. A friend of mine who is a professional booster brought it to me. Beautiful clock. I started to keep it for myself."

*   *   *

CHAPTER 18

Camp Pickett

PETEY CAME BACK from Korea as a Sergeant. He told A'nt Pig he must have been promoted because "everybody else got killed. They didn't have nobody else to give no stripes to, 'cause I didn't earn them worth a damn. I didn't kill no enemy or nothing."

In reality, Petey had shown himself to be as capable as any other man, as a cook, an orderly, a driver for officers. His superiors did not know of his crooked schemes, petty crimes, or drug use. Instead, they knew he had contributed greatly to morale with his wit and irreverent views. Back in the U.S., though, expectations were different.

After his return from Korea, Petey spent small amounts of time in a number of places including Fort Sills, Oklahoma, Fort Bliss, Texas, Aberdeen Proving Grounds in Maryland, and, finally, Camp Kilmer, New Jersey. He spent his longest, most memorable stretch at Camp Pickett, in Blackstone, near Richmond, Virginia.

While most soldiers viewed Camp Pickett as an Army base, Petey treated it like a college campus, from which he could come and go as he pleased. He landed in the stockade more than once when MPs had to come looking for him. They found him usually not in Washington, D.C., but elsewhere. Second Street in Richmond. Newport News. Petersburg. Farmville. Lawrenceville. Victoria. Chase City. Anywhere young soldiers turned him on to the after-hours joints, the dance halls, the house parties, the women.

As usual, Petey had a friend who wanted to protect him. At Camp Pickett, assigned to the 210 Quartermaster Company, Petey ran into a young man from his old neighborhood in Georgetown.

Robert Steves, nicknamed Steamboat, let everyone know he'd fight Petey's battles. But Steamboat couldn't help when Petey landed in the stockade.

*   *   *

Camp Pickett may as well have been called Camp Prison or Camp Party, because Petey spent little time in any notable endeavor. Instead, his memories of Camp Pickett center on getting high and going to nightclubs, impressing the small-town girls with his D.C.-big city civilian clothes, wide hats, and fast talk. Otherwise, he checked off the days confined to the stockade or the base hospital. In the latter, he spent a year recovering from a near fatal battle against hepatitis.

The illness was discovered almost as a fluke, because Petey did not feel deathly ill. Rather, he went to the base hospital complaining of a sore throat. "They think I got bronchitis or some shit," Petey said to a soldier in the next bed. "I'll be outta here in three days."

On that third day, when Dr. Leo Spaulding came for one last look before releasing Petey, the twinkle normally in his eyes faded. "Lay back down. Let me see your eyes," Dr. Spaulding said in a low, grave tone.

"Come on, Doc. Don't start no shit. My throat feel all right," Petey answered, fearing the panic he sensed from Dr. Spaulding.

Dr. Spaulding, a West Virginia native, made his home in Chicago with his wife Marva, whose first husband had been Joe Louis, the famous boxer. With his light skin, straight hair, and accomplished profession, Dr. Spaulding knew he had to walk carefully in the Army where segregation still reigned. Too many times in life, he'd overheard the whispers, "That boy thinks he's white; too big for his britches." He couldn't afford any mistakes, couldn't give any white officer a chance to act on the jealousy and racism simmering under the surface.

He left Petey's side to call in a white doctor for a second opinion. Together, they stood over Petey.

"I'm going out of here?"

Dr. Spaulding got the nod from his co-worker, then told Petey, "Yeah, you are going out of here but you're not going home. You are going into isolation. Greene, you are almost dead. You've got a highly contagious form of hepatitis, infectious hepatitis."

Petey did not believe it until the doctor showed him how black his urine had become and pointed out the yellow overtaking his eyes and the palms of his hands. He concluded that dirty needles from shooting drugs or contaminated water in Korea must have left him with the germ that festered for months before taking over.

The word "isolation" saddened Petey ten times more than "hepatitis," and he could hardly wait to pass the infectious stage and once again join the rest of the soldiers in sick beds.

"You'll be on strict bed rest and hard candy. Your diet will be high protein, and you will not leave this hospital," Dr. Spaulding instructed, when Petey returned to the general population.

His Georgetown friends Junior Lee, Laurence Norwood, Roland Freeman, and Mohawk came down to visit, depleted the bowl of hard candy, and returned to Washington with a message for A'nt Pig. Petey had given the orders. "Just tell her I'm all right. Don't tell her I'm in the hospital." Even when he called her on the phone, he kept his whereabouts a complete secret.

Out of isolation and in the general ward, Petey assessed his situation. He shared a large room with about 25 other soldiers, only two of them black. Quickly, he made friends with the men he came to know as Jackson from Atlanta and Keith from West Virginia. He also struck a friendship with a white soldier in the bed beside his, Private Cazero.

But the person he admired most there was Dr. Spaulding. Petey smiled with pride every time Dr. Spaulding walked onto the ward in his crisp white coat, picked up the chart from the end of Petey's bed, and instructed the white nurse on dosages of Belladonna and other medications.

"How are you doing there, boy? Running your mouth?" Dr. Spaulding already knew the answer, but delighted Petey every time by recognizing Petey's gift of gab.

His other gift, card sharking, kept him at the center of attention. He'd start calling a simple game of Three-Card Molly on the side of his bed. Other patients would gather around, betting dollars that they could pick where the red card landed. Before long, Petey had a drawer full of money. And always a crowd around listening to his constant chatter.

Not everyone felt so enthralled, and in fact, a few of the white soldiers complained to Dr. Spaulding that Petey teased and annoyed them too often.

"This is what I'm going to do, put you in a private room. Give you a television, everything by yourself." Dr. Spaulding told Petey after one complaint too many.

"No, no, Captain. I don't want no television in another room. I like the big television here where all of us can look at it," Petey implored. A private room might as well have been an isolation chamber, for all Petey cared. In order to thrive, he needed an audience at all times.

"Well, if you don't want a private room, you'd better stop giving these people hell," Dr. Spaulding chuckled. "Otherwise, I know what you want. You want a private room."

"Hey Doc, I bet Joe Louis could kick your ass for marrying his wife," Petey jabbed.

Catching the harmless punch, Dr. Spaulding teased back, "I'm not thinking about Joe Louis. I've got more friends than he does. Last Christmas, I had Nat King Cole over to my house, singing Christmas carols to my little children. Sugar Ray Robinson's my buddy, too. But I'm not impressed with all that. When I was at Howard University Med School, I saw all the famous people down on U Street."

If he hadn't bonded with Dr. Spaulding before, mention of U Street would have done it for Petey. In a conversation about U Street, Petey could shine better than most.

But Petey could not let life boil along on its own. He had to stir the pot. As A'nt Pig had taught him to do, he watched the white guys. Often, they'd tell the day nurse to give them their civilian clothes so they could put them in the hospital's cleaners. Instead, they'd only pretend to go out to the cleaners, return and stash the clothing under their mattresses. At night, after the lights went out, one white soldier would wake the others.

"All right, y'all. Gimme yer money. I'm going to town." He'd put his uniform on, go to town, and return about 3 a.m. with whiskey for the others.

After watching a time or two, and feeling well enough to party, Petey employed the same ruse. When he walked into The Rendezvous club, that night, all his friends cheered. "Greene! Where you been?" What with several people treating him to wine and liquor, and him spending his card winnings, Petey drank himself under the table.

At 3 a.m., armed with two pints of liquor for his friends, Petey tipped back into the hospital ward.

"Hey Greene, you ain't got to tip," Cazero said. "You been caught. Captain Spaulding caught your ass."

Petey froze. "Who told?"

"Nobody. You ain't gone believe what happened. You in some serious trouble."

Everyone woke, turned on the lights, and started talking over each other to recount Petey's downfall.

"Man, them two guys down at the end of the room started fighting and somebody else jumped in, then everybody got to fighting. The nurse couldn't do nothing with nobody, so they called Dr. Spaulding over at the officer's quarters," Keith's voice rang out.

Jackson continued, "When we looked around, Dr. Spaulding coming through the door. He said, 'What the hell is this? I'll have all of you taken to the stockade. Straighten this place up. I don't want to have to come back over here any more tonight.'

"He was walking out, but all of a sudden when he got to the door, he stopped dead in his tracks and started running back toward your bed. He was hollering, 'Greene, Greene!' He thought you was dead, 'cause he know you'da been talking shit the whole time if you was breathing.

"He pulled up those pillows from under the cover and said, 'A son of a bitch! Where is he? Okay, you don't have to tell me. When he gets back, just tell him he is in hot water.'"

The next morning, Dr. Spaulding walked coldly to Petey's bed. "I think this is your last day here. I always thought you had more sense than the rest of these guys in here. But I found out differently. You are practically dead and here you are taking your ass out of that bed going to town. Did you drink anything?"

"Yes sir."

"You don't know how sick you are. Well, I'm not going to have it on my hands. I'm going to transfer you to another ward."

Tears coursed down Petey's stubbled cheeks. "Captain Spaulding, please. I won't give you no more trouble. I ain't never lied to you. I just wanted to go . . ."

Dr. Spaulding interrupted Petey's pleas. "Listen, I stopped those dope fiend friends of yours from coming up here because I knew they would talk you into shooting dope. I am concerned about you. If I give you another chance, it will be the last. I'll think about it."

Petey's shoulders released their tension. He knew he would not be transferred.

Camping in the Stockade

A near-death experience and wondrous recovery from hepatitis may have scared some men straight. Not Petey. The week after his release, Petey and his friend Priestly took the three-hour ride with friends to Maryland, where he viewed as equal priorities spending time with Peggy in Annapolis and going to Baltimore with friends to drink and clown in clubs along the entertainment strip.

Within weeks, Petey landed in the stockade for being AWOL from the 210 Quartermaster Company; Priestly joined him on a forgery charge. Inside the stockade, Petey got another view of what segregation meant in the U.S. Army: the black guards tried to look out for the black prisoners, and the black prisoners behaved like siblings. They argued over crap games, card games, and anything else they could disagree on; but, in the face of authority, they bonded.

They also pooled their creativity and con-artistry to alter their reality. Inside the stockade, sometimes the black soldiers ruled the day.

*　　*　　*

Petey's 's Voice: Near Fighting

"In the stockade, we controlled all the yeast for making liquor, all the narcotics, all the pills, everything that come in there. We controlling the penitentiary. The most important thing about it is that we wasn't hurting no blacks and we wasn't really getting no black marks against us. But in all situations, whitey don't like for nigguhs to dominate nothing.

"What we started doing, we started having football games where the whites play the blacks. With no equipment or nothing. We were just hurting them whites. Had a old football and nothing else. Also, we used to go to church, just so we could fight the white boys.

"We'd go to chapel on Sunday, and an outside chaplain would come in to give the morning services. It's nigguhs and whities in the chapel together on different sides. As soon as he would finish his service and say Amen, he'd walk out and I'd give a signal. One of my boys would lock the door, and we'd get to fighting.

"I mean THEY would fight. Everybody know I can't fight a lick. Those nigguhs used to beat the shit out of five or six of them crackers, to make up for all the shit the white guards would do to nigguhs. I seen a cracker, a little young dude, they called him Blue Eyes, a pretty boy, I saw him just tear the whole sash of a window getting out of that place.

"One day, it came to a head. We met on the yard at the break of day. When I come out the latrine, which is the bathroom, they was out there talking. My boys say, 'D.C., man, these motherfuckers talking about rumbling.' It was eight crackers, saying they tired of nigguhs taking advantage of them. They'd been looking for they yeast and it ain't coming in like it's supposed to, because they had a special pipeline to the bakery. Since I'd taken over, we had gated all that shit. Ain't no pipeline going nowhere 'til it come through us.

"Where the white boys had been getting four pounds of yeast, we'd break it down and they'd get two and a half. We might not give 'em but one, 'cause we got a nigguh we done put in that bakery and he taking care of business in there.

"A big ol' whitey, a 'Bama, 6 feet tall, name Parker, looked me straight in the eyes and said, 'I want to fight you.' I thought, 'Lord have mercy!' He kept talking, 'Since you seem to have all the say-so, I want your motherfucking ass. I think you and me need to fight, cause if you beat my ass, it's all right. But I think I can beat your ass.'

"All my mob know I can't fight, but I say, 'Well, come on motherfucker, it don't make no difference.' One of the guys say, 'Man, you don't really want this cracker, do you? You want this cracker?' I'm scared to death, heart just beating. I say, 'Fuck this cracker!'

"So we squares off. That motherfucker throws up his guards like John L. Sullivan, 1889. I thought, 'Aw, this motherfucker can't fight.' But I also know I can't hit him. So, me and him bullshit, he throwing weak punches and I'm ducking.

"All of a sudden, this boy named Roundtree off 11th and N pushed me out of the way, saying, 'To hell with this cracker!' Bing. Boom. Knocked that man cold. 'Get up, you white motherfucker, you.' Parker say, 'That's not fair. I wanted to fight Greene.' Roundtree into it, now. 'You ain't fighting no motherfucking body.' And turned to another whitey named Mahaffy, from West Virginia, who walked with Parker. 'Do you want any part of it?' Mahaffy say, 'No, no. Greene's all right with me.' Roundtree put his fists down, 'Well, pick that cracker up and get him out of here.'

"I'm so happy, because that boy was gone beat the shit out of me when he got his hands on me. Now, it's an established fact that I ain't got to do no fighting."

* * *

Dangerous Goods

Closing in on Thanksgiving, the inmates chipped in to celebrate. With contraband yeast, they made 20 gallons of "shoots" and placed it in the rafters. With three weeks to ferment, the vat of alcohol would be good and ready, they assumed.

A couple of days before Turkey Day, a team of inspectors, lead by Major Russell, came through. Petey and his friends stood by their beds, completely neat and orderly, when a low rumble sounded over their heads.

"What is that?" Everyone looked at each other, wondering if a freak storm, an earthquake, or an errant fighter jet could be causing such a sound. In a matter of seconds, the rumble became a roar, then an explosion. Piyow! Next, liquid flooded down the side of the wall from the rafters.

Major Russell looked directly at Petey. "How long has that been sitting? Go up there and get it! Take it over to my office."

Once at the office, Major Russell gave Petey a chance to come clean. "Greene, you know anything about this?"

"Not nary solitary bit do I know about it. You should throw it away." Petey kept a straight face, but his insides roared like the fermented beverage minutes earlier.

"Throw it away? Hell no. I'm going to serve it to my guests tonight at home. I was just wondering if you know where anymore is around here." Major Russell grinned, then dismissed Petey.

When Petey got back to his dormitory, he laughed to see everyone razzing the one man who caused the loss. "You dumb ass nigguh! You forgot to put the hose in! You cost us our Thanksgiving liquor, man! You owe us. Better start now making some for Christmas!"

*　　*　　*

Serving prison time in the Army had its perks for Petey because he was detailed to the officer's club sometimes and the hospital at other times. In both places, he schemed to get contraband. He also used those assignments to earn high marks, because he wanted to be selected as Yard Sergeant, in charge of lining the inmates up each day and ordering them around.

Even if he hadn't been in line for good assignments, he had an ace in the hole: a friend from Georgetown was the guard. Leo Drawn and Petey sat in the same class at Francis Junior High School. When it came time for a guard to walk Petey to detail, Leo would slow down to a crawl. "Let's talk about the girls at Francis," he'd encourage. Decades later, when they would run into each other in DC, Leo Drawn never passed up an opportunity to kid about those days at Camp Pickett. "Fall in, Greene," he'd shout, knowing he'd see Petey's wide grin.

While Drawn typified the guards' responses to Petey, a few authorities hated him with a passion. One guard, Stiltner, a white man from West Virginia, even aspired to kill Petey.

Stiltner's nightly routine included cruising through the barracks to make sure prisoners weren't gambling with cigarettes or contraband. One evening, he knocked a pillow off a bed near Petey's.

"Whose cigarettes are these?"

Petey looked up from shuffling a deck of cards. "I don't know."

"I wasn't asking you," Stiltner shot back.

"Well, I was the only one that spoke up." Petey didn't back down.

His face turning red, Stiltner began to walk away. "You know, you are too goddamn smart. You think you got all the guards put to sleep and that you run this place."

Not willing to let the man leave without a parting blow, Petey taunted, "Just go the fuck on. I don't run nothing!"

Two days later, at 9 p.m., Stiltner approached Petey's bed. "Greene, they want to see you down at the captain's office."

With a sense of unease, Petey stuck his feet in his shoes and picked up his shirt. "For what?"

Stiltner headed toward the door. "Just come with me."

As Petey began to follow, Priestly sidled up to him. "Don't go with him, D.C. He gone fuck you up. That motherfucker is drunk and he ain't forgot what you said."

Petey saw the glazed look in Stiltner's eyes, but didn't know how to refuse the command: "Keep moving!" All he could think to say was, "What do they want with me ?"

As soon as they were outside the building, Stiltner grumbled, "You motherfucker, you!"

Petey cowered, his voice raspy, small, nervous. "What did I do?"

Approaching the gate leading away from the barracks, Stiltner's anger intensified. "You just too motherfucking smart, you no-good nigger." Petey's silence and the pints of alcohol Stiltner had consumed combined to ignite his rage beyond reason.

While Petey tried to think of something to say, Stiltner pulled his gun from his holster and cracked it into the back of Petey's skull.

Falling, Petey yelped, "Help! Lord, don't let him kill me! He gone kill me!"

Eyes red, mouth spewing spittle, Stiltner screamed, "Get up motherfucker!!!"

Banking on drawing saviors from inside, Petey yelled louder. "I ain't gone run. Don't shoot me. Please, please don't shoot me."

One by one in rapid succession, lights blazed on inside and inmates spilled out to the fence. "Leave that man alone, you no-good . . ."

Petey still blubbered, hollering, "Don't kill me, please don't kill me." Even through his drunken rage, Stiltner could feel control slipping away. "Ain't nobody tryin' to kill you." But Petey wouldn't be pacified, and continued to yell. "Don't let him take me away! He gone kill me."

Hearing the commotion, officers rushed over from their barracks. Cornered, Stiltner stammered. "I was taking him to the captain, but he tried to escape."

Incredulous, because he knew Petey, a lieutenant challenged. "Greene tried to escape??"

Seeing his opportunity, Petey interrupted Stiltner's effort to confirm. "No, Lieutenant, I ain't trying to excape. Just look at my head. It's bleeding."

The lieutenant's eyes hardened as he caught a whiff of liquor on Stiltner's breath. "What did you hit him with? Have you been drinking?"

"I had a couple of beers . . . ."

"Give me that gun and go to the guard's house!" The lieutenant whirled around. "Take Greene to the hospital."

A couple of days and five stitches later, Petey was back among his cohorts. "Man, you a faggot. Just crying like a baby . . ."

"Kiss my ass. That man had a motherfucking pistol," Petey defended.

Priestly wrapped his arm around Petey's shoulder. "I told you he was drunk. You better try to get him transferred."

Surprised, Petey asked, "Can I do that?"

"Hell, yeah! Go tell them you want to see the IG and press charges."

As opposed to the time in basic training when Petey merely pretended to want to see the Inspector General, this time he really did lodge a complaint. Stiltner transferred immediately, and Petey never saw him again.

Convinced that the man really had intended to kill him, Petey later attributed his escape from that fate to divine intervention. Thirty years later, he reflected, "That's how I know now that God has always had his arms around me."

CHAPTER 19

Making Fun of Time

OUT OF THE ARMY, making nothing of himself, doing occasional comedy routines at parties and picnics in exchange for liquor, Petey woke up in DC jail more often than he cared to remember. The D.C. Jail served as a second home for him during the days Petey described himself as "a winehead bum." He went there charged with public drunkenness so often that when he finally fell to a robbery charge, guards were initially unprepared to treat him as anything other than a jovial sot.

In fact, most of the guards and prisoners liked Petey and his never-a-dull moment style of serving his time. After two years, however, he got transferred to Lorton following a clash with a guard who couldn't take it as well as he could dish it out.

Before that guard, Roy Shuman, came to D.C. Jail, Petey had his dormitory mates and the guards at Cellblock 3 dancing to his raucous tunes. But as usual, adhering to A'nt Pig's advice, Petey categorized the prisoners to select those from whom he could learn something new. He found such a person in Irvin Scarbach.

Scarbach, a former undersecretary of the U.S. Army, represented status and intelligence to Petey. As soon as Petey heard that he and Scarbach shared the same cellblock, the word research took over his mind. Next, his thoughts went to befriending Scarbach, so he could pick his brain.

"Hey Chinch, I done found out about this white man, Scarbach. Let me tell you how he got in here with us. He was overseas, in Poland or somewhere, and those people needed some American secrets, so they put a young Polish girl on him and they started fucking. One night, while he was laying up with her, the door flew open and they took pictures and had guns drawn. And they told him, 'If you don't get us these secrets, we gone send these pictures back to your wife and family.' So he started giving them secrets, and then, naturally, he got busted."

Chinch rubbed his arm absently, wondering how Petey managed to get so much information so fast. "Man, how you know all this?"

"Because I talk to this man. I have watched him beat them nigguhs playing ping pong, but you notice, he don't never bet. These ghetto nigguhs be betting 50 and 60 cartons a game. They so good, they give a motherfucker 19 points at the start. 'You got 19. All you got to do is get 2 points and you win.' Most guys ain't got a chance with them two points, but Scarbach can play some ping pong," Petey chuckled.

Chinch thought back to a week or so before when he and Petey were among the inmates riding to court on the prison bus. Scarbach had been there, too. One of the inmates turned sideways on the drab brown seat, then rose up to holler at Scarbach.

"Man, you sold our country out! You tried to give up the plans to the enemy. Somebody needs to kick your ass!"

With his plans for befriending Scarbach already in place, Petey spoke up immediately.

"Aw nigguh, leave that goddamn man alone. Sit down, you black bastard. You ain't got no country."

Scarbach suppressed a guffaw while the inmate slumped in his seat. In the seat behind Scarbach, Petey touched the man's shoulder. "Hey, buddy, don't pay no 'tention to that motherfucker."

Once the two started talking regularly in the recreation room, Scarbach found a willing pupil when the conversation turned to etiquette at State dinners, foreign affairs, country clubs, and anything in the world Petey had only seen on television.

"Hey Chinch, listen at this. Scarbach say if you're ever at a table and the waiter start to coming around to serve, he will serve over your left shoulder. And he will drape the napkin over your right knee or your right leg. And they got a different fork for the salad and for the dinner . . ." Petey stopped short. "I don't know why I am telling you this, man. You ain't never going to no White House dinner."

"Oh? So you going?" Chinch joked, but in the back of his mind, he thought Petey might very well one day end up at a White House dinner. Anyone as smart as Petey, Chinch always said, should be on top of the world.

At the end of the next decade, Petey Greene did step into the White House, as guest of Grace Olivarez, President Carter's appointee as Director of the Community Services Administration, the federal agency created to serve the poor. Petey escorted her, then kiddingly told a Washington Post reporter that he put a White House silver spoon in his pocket and walked out with it. In reality, Petey respected the place too much to take even a napkin. He had been prepared for this occasion ever since his jailhouse chats with Irvin Scarbach.

"How did you get in this trouble, Petey? You don't need to be in here." Scarbach's blue eyes searched Petey's wide brown ones. Petey turned the tables.

"And you think you need to be in here?"

"No. I didn't give up any real secrets. What I gave, they couldn't do anything with. You know, Petey, it's a funny thing what your friends do to you when you get in any kind of trouble. One day, I'm walking in the embassy, commanding respect. Playing tennis and having lunch. The next day, everybody is standoffish. Well, you don't really understand what I'm talking about . . ." Scarbach turned silent, contemplating the possibility of serving 30 years.

Uncharacteristically, Petey quieted, too. He would later say, "At that time, I didn't know what he meant. I had never worked with these Phi Bekka Macca Cackas. But I understand real good now."

The next night, Petey sat with Scarbach watching the Irvin Scarbach story on television. "That shit is so far from what happened," Scarbach told Petey. Both of them ignored the other inmates who tried to goad Scarbach. "That's what you did. They got you, man."

Soon after, Scarbach transferred to a federal penitentiary, normally reserved for men charged with White Collar crimes. Taking his place on the list of notable prisoners at D.C. Jail was Pete Generis.

Again, Petey confided in Chinch. "Man, I'm watching this boy Generis. Fuck listening to these black-ass nigguhs. I done heard what they got to say over and over and over. I'm gone make friends with the white guys that come in here, to advance my knowledge and put me a step ahead of these black motherfuckers that is talking pimping. And talking dope. What the fuck I'm gone talk about whores for? I'll talk about that at night with them guys. Right now, I'm gone see what this Greek Generis is all about."

Generis, a local numbers backer, gambler and bookie, immediately liked Petey. He found a way to cement their friendship a few days before the historic championship bout between Cassius Clay and Sonny Liston.

Like most of the population at D.C. Jail, Petey thought Liston could not lose. "Liston's gone kill that little Cassius Clay," Petey commented to Generis as the two watched television one night.

"No chance." Generis spoke with authority.

"Is you crazy?" Petey growled, eyes wide as saucers.

Generis studied his nails, sucked his teeth, then stated flatly, "Let me tell you something. Bet all your cigarettes on this boy Cassius Clay."

Utter disbelief written all over his face, Petey spat back, "Go fuck yourself."

Unfazed, Generis spoke slowly. "I'll tell you what. Bet your cigarettes. If you lose, I will pay all the cigarettes for you."

That clinched it for Petey. With this kind of deal, he couldn't lose AND he could create the biggest buzz of the year at the jail.

As usual, he called to Chinch. "Get a pad and pencil and come with me," Petey said, nearly hopping with eagerness. As they burst into the recreation room together, Petey hollered, "How many of you motherfuckers like Liston?"

Several voices rang out, "I like him." Petey could hardly wait to proclaim, "Well y'all know goddamn well I'm taking that boy Cassius Clay."

Chinch almost dropped the pad. "Are you crazy?"

Petey looked around eagerly for more betters. "Just write these niggers' names down . . . What'dya want? I'm taking two to one!"

Calls rang out for four, for two, for three. Cartons upon cartons faster than Chinch could scribble names, but not as fast as the jailhouse wire sent out the news of Petey's crazy bet.

Muslim inmates, proud that Cassius Clay had stated his desire to become a Muslim, to change his name to Muhammad Ali, rushed up to tell Petey that they, too, thought the young fighter would prevail.

"Man, I don't want to hear that Allah talk," Petey whispered to Chinch. "I just want to get these bets."

Chinch frowned. "We got 100 cartons already. How long do you want to keep this up?"

Realizing he had never worked with Generis before, Petey stopped walking, almost causing Chinch to bump into his back. "Cut them motherfuckers off at 150 cartons," he ordered.

The frown stayed on Chinch's face. "Greene, look at who's betting. This nigguh here alone will crush your jaw. And that's just ONE nigguh. It's some mean mothers on this list. They will kill you if you can't pay the bet."

Chinch was not the only one worried. The prison captain, John Wales, sent for Petey. Captain Wales leaned forward in his swivel chair to be closer to his favorite inmate sitting in a hard chair on the other side of the desk. "They tell me you got 150 cartons of cigarettes betted on Cassius Clay," Captain Wales reported.

"Man! Your snitches work better than anyone I ever seen!"

"Nobody needs to snitch on you. It's all over here and in the women's division, too. Petey, this boy can't beat Liston. And I'm telling you, I'm not gonna let you check into solitary to get away from these guys if you lose." Captain Wales looked searchingly, hoping to see a change in Petey's stubborn posture.

"I don't want to check in. I ain't scared of none of these boys."

No one wanted to see Petey in life-threatening trouble; so next, Sergeant Beach came to Petey's bedside. "Are you out of your mind? I know you don't have 150 cartons of cigarettes because I know everything you are doing. I know how you getting all your cigarettes, and you don't have enough. Petey, I think you're making a bad move. You know anything you do is all right with me, because you make my day the way you keep stuff going in here. But this could get out of hand." The sergeant's grey eyes held no mirth, only stirring fear.

The concern began to wear on Petey, so he sought out Generis. Balancing on the balls of his feet, subconsciously ready to spring, Petey blurted out, "Hey man, I got 150 cartons betted on Cassius Clay."

With an almost imperceptible shrug, Generis trained his onyx eyes on Petey's face, willing a steadying force onto Petey's nerves. "Your money is just like money in the bank."

Petey let out a short laugh. "I want you to take a good look at my T-shirt. You can see my heart beating under this motherfucker."

Generis, bursting out in laughter, clamped Petey's thin shoulders between his solid, hairy hands. "You'll be collecting after the fight."

The television room could not have squeezed in an extra man on fight night. With everyone whooping and hollering, Petey sat in a private battle with anxiety. For a moment, it looked as though the young Clay didn't want to come into the ring after a round that went to Liston.

"He scared. A faggot motherfucker. They throwed him back in the ring," inmates laughed. Their laughter ended abruptly when amazingly, Clay started moving his feet like a dancer and throwing rapid fire punches that knocked Liston flat.

The room seemed more suited to a funeral. Mouths hung open in stunned disbelief. Then one after the other, inmates started groaning, cursing, jumping up, throwing shirts on the floor. Muslims began to cheer, saying Allah helped Clay win.

Petey grabbed Chinch and the list, so he could make a big show of collecting on the bets. But he had never told anyone that Generis was behind his bravado, so he kept his thoughts to himself. "Somebody had to come to visit ol' Pete to tell him the fix was in. Otherwise, how did he know?"

The next time Petey won a similar bet, he relied on his own best guess. That time, already transferred to Lorton, he bet 50 cartons that the Cleveland Browns would beat Johnny Unitis and the Baltimore Colts. When the Browns won 14-10, Petey gathered his booty, ran up on the prison's third tier, and tore the cartons open. As cigarettes rained down on the men beneath, Petey bellowed, "My peasants, pick up these cigarettes."

For Petey, winning was not nearly so important as showing off. Showing off was so important, Petey sometimes risked his safety just to bask in the glow of attention. Ironically, the man who would become a television star used television in prison to keep his fellow inmates off balance and focused on him.

Guards at Lorton had established a routine for selecting what everyone would watch on television in the evenings. Attempting to be fair, they let inmates take turns being in charge for the week. When it was Petey's turn, he'd select shows absolutely no inmate wanted to see. "The Lawrence Welk Show," with its champagne bubbles and big band waltzes, repeatedly showed up on Petey's list. But, it was his turn, so that was that.

To get around Petey, inmates started bribing him. "Hey man, we'll give you five packs of cigarettes. Ten packs of cigarettes if you pass your turn." Often, he would take the bribe, but one time, the power of the choice proved too delicious to forego.

Petey's brother Thad served time in another building. As he and Petey sat outside on a gentle fall afternoon, Thad heard a desperate inmate ask Petey to give up his turn that evening. "Man, why they don't want you in charge?"

"They NEVER want me to pick. No time. 'Cause they know I'm gone pick Lawrence Welk."

"What you do that for, fool?"

"Because this is my way of doing time. Some people fucking sissies. Some guys don't say nothing. Some just walk and talk. Some guys always trying to beat they case. My thing to do time, to release my frustrations, is to keep something going where I am the center of attraction. To keep my adrenaline going," Petey lectured, although he didn't really need to explain to Thad.

"Don't know why I asked you that question. You ain't never been no other way. But this time, they ain't playing." Thad referred to something every inmate at Lorton eagerly anticipated—a Motown and oldies special called "What's Happening Baby," put on by Murray the K. Every dormitory at the prison complex had the special listed for the night's pick. Except one. The dorm Petey controlled.

Late that afternoon, dread began to take up residence in Petey's dorm as inmate after inmate walked over to the posted list of the evening's television viewing. One prisoner, named Bubbie, stared at the list, trying to will "What's Happening, Baby" to appear, then let out a blood-curdling scream. As other inmates groused, scratched their heads, and tried to think of an adequate bribe, Bubbie hustled off to find Petey's favorite guard, who'd come to Lorton from D.C. Jail.

"Mr. Beach, we gonna kill Petey! Look at this mess he's doing!!!" Bubbie's eyes bulged and the list trembled in his hands. Sergeant Beach thought this might be the time, finally, that Petey had gone too far. "Calm down, Bubbie. I'll go talk to Petey."

Upstairs on his bed, Petey could hear the inmates fussing and cussing. When Sergeant Beach walked in, Petey sat on the edge of the bed with a wicked twinkle in his eye.

"Hey, Petey. Can I talk to you a minute?" Sergeant Beach hiked up his pants leg and sat beside Petey. "You know I'm in your corner. Anything you do is all right with me. But, look, go on out there and change that program, 'cause it's gonna cause trouble. I went to four more dormitories, and I see they all got this program. To be fair . . . ."

Petey held up his hand to interrupt. "You know the rules, Mr. Beach, in this place. Last week, it was Smallwood's time because he was in the cell with the pick. This week, it's my time, and next week it's Rudy's time. Y'all set the rules. I didn't make these rules."

Exasperation crept up Sergeant Beach's neck. "Petey, I didn't think you were a damn fool. But now I see you are a goddamn fool. When they kick your ass in here, don't come to me. Are you crazy?"

Petey's expression remained stoic, and he refused to give in to Sergeant Beach's plea. Back downstairs in the rec room, Sergeant Beach reported to Bubbie and a growing crowd of livid inmates. "I tried to talk to him, but he ain't gone take his choice off, and that's his right. Y'all can't change it."

The cherished program was scheduled to air at 9 p.m., which gave the inmates about three hours to work on a plan. Within ten minutes, every inmate in every dormitory had been alerted to the crisis, and anyone perceived to have any clout with Petey Greene enlisted in the cause to save the day. Of course Thad, who held a fighter's reputation, got dragged into the fray. He waited downstairs in Petey's dormitory, watching the anxious eyes of inmates passing by.

"Hey, Dick," Thad called out affectionately when Petey came down for the visit. "Man, I'm tired of these niggers coming over to my barracks telling me that you ain't got that special on the list. You know I don't let nobody do nothing to you, but we don't need this kind of fight. Change that thing, man, change it! 'Cause I do not want to have to kill one of these niggers for fucking with you."

Petey crossed a starched pants leg and took a puff of a cigarette. "I appreciate the facts, Slick, but I can handle myself."

Thad gaped, amazed. "You ain't gone change it? Man, are you crazy? These motherfuckers have come over to my BED, man. Change it, Greene."

Petey rose up, headed back to his bed, and spat back casually to his younger brother, "Fuck you. I ain't changing it."

Right on Thad's heels, three of Petey's friends came calling. Each one imploring harder than the one before. "Look, we'll do anything you want us to do, you know that. You fucking that boy's wife when she come to visit; if he find out, we'll kill that nigguh. Just change the motherfuckin' television. 'Cause these niggers came straight to us. They coming to your back-up. They just gotta see Martha and the Vandellas, the Supremes, all these people!"

Petey looked through the friends he called "my troops . . . my soldiers" as if they were not begging and pleading. He simply repeated, "I can take care of myself. Fuck y'all."

By 8:45 p.m., inmates had showered, tied their towels around their waistlines, stepped into their cutout shoes, grabbed a soda, and parked in their favorite chairs in the rec room, a scene repeated in each dorm of the complex. But in Petey's dorm many of them sat still and slumped, dazed and waiting. Others fidgeted, bit their nails, darted their eyes helplessly seeking a savior.

At 8:50 p.m., an inmate about 50 years old entered Petey's cell. "This is the last time I'm gone say anything to you. I know your father. Me and him was in the jail together. We good friends. I give you anything 'cause you all right with me. But Boy, if you don't change that motherfucking channel, fuck your father, your brother, your mother and every motherfucking body else!"

Petey turned his large eyes up impassively. "You finished?"

The man left, enraged but stumped by Petey's placid immovability.

Finally, at 8:55, Chinch strode over to Petey. "Hey, Slim. One thing I like about you, even though you know it's gone get you killed, you stands on what you believe in. But you believing in the wrong thing, Greene."

Petey sprang off the bed, shoved past Chinch, saying "Get the fuck on out my cell."

At two minutes to 9, Petey swaggered into the rec room. Forty pairs of glazed eyes followed him. Dramatically, he took a seat, then, with 30 seconds before the program would begin, he popped up and turned the channel to "What's Happening, Baby."

Before anyone could react, Petey spoke, sweeping his right arm in an arc encompassing the room. "I told you motherfuckers I hold power over your mind!" Then he dashed back upstairs to his room, leaving the stunned audience to their oldies and Motown hits.

The next day, every inmate whose heart had rested in his throat for the three-plus hours Petey held them in suspense the night before came to razz him. "You ain't got no heart, you faggot motherfucker. You scared motherfucker, you."

Chinch came in, laughing. "Man, I should have known you would change that channel. I should have known you never had no intention of NOT changing. You just always generating attention."

Petey would use that natural-born talent, honed under the tutelage of A'nt Pig, to imprint his name on his hometown as a radio and television talk show host and advocate of "the little people" for more than 17 years.

Chapter 20

Balling Out

THE PROWESS IN sports Petey honed in childhood found an outlet at both DC Jail and Lorton in his adult life. And as usual, Petey took his own special route to recognition, with mixed results.

Petey's voice: Gaming Inside and Out

"I did so many things in the penitentiary with just shrewdness. For instance, I was picking a softball team, 'cause they'd asked me to coach. A lot of the guys there knew I'd coached a team when I was a kid.

"Sergeant Campbell, who was the recreation specialist, would shake dominoes up in a box and dump 'em out. Each coach would pick a domino, and the man with the lowest number would get the first pick for his team. When he throwed the dominoes out, I picked the highest you could pick, double sixes. I say, Goddagg. The guy with the first pick, naturally, gonna pick a pitcher. Barry Ashton was the baddest thing down there, so he got picked first.

"The one with the next lowest number picked a pitcher, too. Now I got to think. I'm always thinking. When it come time for me to pick, it's about four or five more pitchers left. I pick a third baseman. I pick Sonny Flagson. Baddest motherfucker in the penitentiary, but he play third base. Some guy say, 'You should have got yourself a pitcher!' I didn't even say nothing.

"It come back around, they picking pitchers, I picks Mike Torten. Baddest shortstop in the business. 'Man, why you didn't get a pitcher,' another inmate whispered to me. Come back around, three pitchers left. Picked young George Davis, baddest catcher in the business.

"Now, the white man, he see what I'm doing to 'em again. They grabbing up them pitchers and I'm putting a team together with no pitcher. Finally, it's too late, all the good pitchers gone. I got Sonny Thackson, George Davis, Eugene Beverly, big Buddy Fold. I got a team and a half. Other people got a team full of pitchers. So they say, 'Who gone pitch for you?' I say, 'Me.' Now, again, what they don't understand is that it's good to have a fast pitcher that can strike everybody out, but the infield that's gonna play, they don't like a fast pitcher. They want somebody who gone let the batter hit that ball sometimes so they can shine in the field. 'Cause when a motherfucker can pitch, these others don't get a chance to shine.

"Word gets around that Petey Greene has done got out on these nigguhs. Say he's gone pitch and ain't nobody but him got all the good players. The players I got, they happy as a motherfucker. They call me Rabbi.

"Our first game comes and I'm tossing the ball up there, the batters are hitting it but it ain't going nowhere. Acht! We win the first one, we win the second one, we win the third one. Now we got to meet Barry Ashton, and he's a bad motherfucker. He is the baddest thing on the Hill. The whole thing has come down to the wire. This is just the first half of the season. Petey Greene's team ain't lost a game and Barry Ashton ain't lost a game, 'cause he can throw that ball! But I know they got fear in their hearts. I know they got fear, all 12 teams in the league.

"When it come down to it, we beat 'em two to one. They was maaaad! One guy wanted to hit me in the mouth. Wanted to fight. Then I messed around and got me a pitcher. Pittsburgh Stogey. When he started to pitching, we really starting to rolling. He lost some games; I didn't lose no games. But he's a pitcher; I wasn't no pitcher. He wanted to strike people out, crazy motherfucker. But we won the whole thing. Well, they didn't win it with me. I was coaching but in the meantime, I made parole.

And when I made parole, I cut down on all activity. I wouldn't play no sports, wouldn't do nothing.

"When a person makes parole, there's a little while before they can get out. You get a parole date, but it might be two weeks, might be a day, might be about four months before you get out. In my case, it was five months because I refused to take any old job. They came up with a construction job, then a dishwashing job, and I wouldn't take it. I had my plan ready. I had made up my mind that I wasn't going back to Lorton. And I know that if I wasn't comfortable in what I was doing when I got out, that this would be a matter of me breaking parole rules and doing various things, angling, and I would have been back. So I refused those jobs.

"Finally, I saw a guy's picture in the paper on that UPO job, and that's when I took a letter to Ken Hardy and he set it up for me to meet George Holland and Dave Carter, the two head men at UPO. They came down to Lorton to interview me for the neighborhood worker job, as a favor to Mr. Hardy. My Hardy had sold them so much on me.

"When they came down, they said, 'Everybody seems to think you would be a good neighborhood worker. What do you know about poverty?' I said, "I got a PhD in it.' They got back to me in about ten days, and hired me."

*   *   *

Chapter 21

Lessons at Lorton

PETEY NEVER REGISTERED for formal education while he was at Lorton, but he believed he learned more and taught more than any student or teacher could have at a major university. He applied these lessons to help himself and others "jail" and survive Petey Greene style.

Petey's Voice: Jailin' My Way

"I was the one that sent the inmates to school. We had our own academic school and our own vocational school. I was in charge of the academic school, under Mr. McMasters.

"They had put me out of the chapel job. They put us all out and got a new crew in the chapel. With the strength of they started finding things like narcotics in there. And they caught a few guys with sissies in there. So, when they take me out of the chapel, I'm so strong and so over top of everybody, they ain't gone put me in no chain gang squad with no bricks or nothing.

"The civilian in charge of the school asked for me, when he heard about the reorganization. Said, 'Send Petey Greene to me. I want him to come over here.' When I got there, he told me, 'I want you to run this school as well as you ran that chapel. I want you right here on this desk. The guard will be right beside you. When the guys come to school, they have to report to you. You check off who is here, who's not.'

"They had a white boy used to always do that job. I was the first black they ever put on the job. Same thing up to the jail. I was the first black they had ever put in the dentist's office. Again, I'd like to refer to this: White people have always known that I was smart. It's just envious blacks don't figure that with my style and the way I handle myself that I have any kind of sense. But white people sit back and observe me and see what I be doing and say, 'This is the smartest nigguh here.' This is how I was able to get that job, I imagine.

"The first hack on the desk was Sgt. Fawcett. All the black guys liked him. I used to like him, too. Until I got to work with him side by side every day. Then I found out he was one of the most racist white men I have ever seen. He had 90 percent of the blacks in the institution put to sleep, thinking he was concerned about the plight of black people. But I saw him day to day.

"Here's an example. From where we were in the school, the Lorton laundry was right across from us. You had inmates working in the laundry like I was working in the school. On Friday, the inmates in the laundry would come around on the loading dock, which was the back way, and bring out what you called bootleg laundry.

"The reason it was called bootleg was because they were giving it to inmates. They would come 'round there to get it because the regular laundry for the inmates would come back just about one step away from being rough-dried. In order to make money, the guys in the laundry would say, 'Bring that shit on 'round here Wednesday. We got these presses, we'll press it, fold it, crease it. Come back Friday, bring a carton of cigarettes, and pick your bootleg up.'

"When you get it to your dormitory, you save it for Sunday, when your visitors come. The guards ain't gone say nothing 'cause they don't care how many creases you got or how good you look. But if they catch you getting it out the back of that door or on route to your dormitory, then they gone lay you down, put you in solitary confinement, 'cause you ain't supposed to do that. You supposed to wear that shit like it is from the regular laundry.

"I didn't have to go get mine because there's a man called the house man. He know that my cigarettes are good, so when he go over about 2 o'clock to get the sheets and stuff, he pick up all the bootleg for the hustlers and slick nigguhs. It's always a status thing, a in-crowd thing, a different society. You were at the middle-class, bourgeois, whatever, to get that and other fringe benefits.

"He's got a push cart with the sheets and towels. When he comes 'round, he says, 'You got any bootleg? Gimme your cigarettes.' That's the currency. I give him my three packs or five packs or whatever. We got to pay him a price for doing this because he's putting himself in jeopardy. When he push his cart over to get the linen, he give the nigguh there the list of whose bootleg he come after. That nigguh got it all tied up, names on it. In the evening, when I go back, my bootleg is on the bed.

"But the guys that are not affluent enough to get that service got to go 'round to that back way. And it's dangerous around there.

"The guys been doing this for years. So, this Fawcett, who is all right with these nigguhs, he would lay back and look from our school building over to that laundry, pick up the telephone and call the guard over there. 'Hey Jake, they getting that bootleg out the back way. You can catch 'em now. Let me tell you who's over there. Big Tom B . . . .'

"I couldn't believe it. Next thing you'd see the guard back there and guys running all kinds of ways. And this motherfucker done told. He didn't know I was looking at him, because he went to another room. Don't think this man is dumb; he didn't do this in front of me. I happened to stumble up on this man doing this.

"Then one time he saw me see him doing it, and he started to make a joke out of it. I just went along with the joke. But I had him. Because these guys are going to the hole. The guys that was getting laundry are in trouble and the guys that was giving the laundry up might lose them good jobs and go back to them manglers, them washers and dryers. But I kept on laughing, 'cause after all, I am in the penitentiary and I'm working right there beside him.

"A inmate named Jake worked in the school, too. Sergeant Fawcett would give Jake the keys when we line up to go to work.

Jake would go ahead of us and open the building. Sergeant liked
Jake but he played by kicking him in the ass all the time. One day
another inmate named Butler came up. 'Sergeant, you always pluck
us on our heads and kick us in the ass. Why you don't never kick
Petey Greene or pluck him on the head?' I'm thinking, 'Ooooh
no.'

"Sergeant Fawcett got kinda quiet and said, 'Petey Greene don't
play like that. He don't play with me like that and I don't play
with him.' I never know what gave him that indication. I'd never
been a forceful guy or nothing like that. But he was right. He was
definitely right.

"Next day, he kicked Butler in the ass. When he walked away,
I said, 'Butler, you worry 'bout me, and he kick you in your ass
but you ain't said nothing.' Butler gave me a look, then said, 'Don't
even worry 'bout it.'

"Two days later, Sergeant Fawcett bent over to get some pencils.
Right then Butler happened to come in the room where we run off
mimeographed paper, and he came right up behind Sergeant
Fawcett and kicked him in his ass. Sergeant's head went back, he
turned around, and before he could think, he said, 'You black
motherfucker.' Butler said, 'That's right. That's what you want to
call me all the time.' Sarge turned red, but he started laughing.
He had to play it off, because he was kicking Butler all the time.

"Soon as I got a chance to talk to Butler, I say, 'I'm gone bring
you back a pint of ice cream 'cause you kicked that cracker.' I made
sure Fawcett didn't hear me, 'cause I had plans for him."

*   *   *

One of the many lessons Petey learned from his late night
childhood talks with A'nt Pig was never to alienate someone you
might have use for down the line. She also taught him to set goals
and go after them with a shrewd plan. Petey hardly ever set a goal
that didn't include increasing his chances to be at center stage.

He saw Sergeant Fawcett as a means of getting there. It boiled
down to the keys. He wanted them. He detested Sergeant Fawcett

for being a racist and hiding it, but Petey needed to stay on the sergeant's good side, as a means to his end. His chance came when Jake made parole and left the sprawling Lorton complex.

The first morning after Jake's departure, inmates waiting to go to their assignments lined up in the yard as usual. Petey pretended not to know what was coming. When Sergeant Fawcett tossed him the keys, he asked, "What's this," with eyes wide in mock surprise.

"Jake's gone. You gotta open up now."

The first couple of days, Petey performed the task as Jake had done, routinely and quietly. But the temptation to clown always won out with Petey Greene. This time, he had a captive audience of about 1,500 inmates lining here and there to march off to their respective job sites.

On day three with the keys, Petey bopped to the center of the yard, calling out, "I'm the only nigguh in here that carry keys. Y'all see these goddamn keys, don't you? I carry keys. Y'all nigguhs don't carry no keys." Three-fourths of the inmates laughed, while one-fourth groaned. "Aw get on away from here, Greene."

Sergeant Fawcett loved it. In fact, one day Petey skipped the routine. The sergeant pulled him aside with a whisper. "Why you didn't tell 'em 'bout the keys this morning? Tell 'em 'bout the keys every morning."

After that, with the sergeant's blessing, Petey added on to the shtick. "Y'all see these keys? I can let you nigguhs out any time I get ready." Taking it even further, he looked back with a smirk when he set off with the guards before everyone else started walking to their jobs.

"Lock that nigguh up, a black bastard," he'd say to guards in jest as he passed one of his buddies in the line. Some inmates would grumble, others would laugh. Petey didn't care how they reacted. He was just "doing time" in Petey Greene-style.

*   *   *

Time and again, the lessons of compassion he learned from teachers and from A'nt Pig factored into Petey's relationships with

fellow soldiers, prisoners, and his loyal fans. His compassionate
nature usually surfaced when Petey least expected it. In fact, what
started out as a lark often ended up giving Petey a chance to lift a
spirit.

At Lorton, Petey created a series of diversions to keep himself
and other inmates from concentrating on their dire circumstances.
One of his favorite activities revolved around contests, where he
could establish rules, serve as judge, and keep everyone's
expectations turned toward him.

One year into his time at Lorton, Petey called all the homosexual
inmates over to him on the yard. "All y'all like to fix your hair up,
so I'm gone have a contest for best hairstyle. Me and my judges
gone watch y'all for a week, then pick the winner."

For one solid week, Petey had private visits from each of the
contestants and their various boyfriends, all willing to slip him
extra cartons of cigarettes or offer other favors to increase the odds
of winning. Petey made quite a big deal of selecting finalists, then
the winner, a homely inmate nicknamed "The Thriller" from a
horror show popular on tv at the time.

The Thriller's delight at winning paled in Petey's memories in
comparison to another winner, a young man who won Petey's
best dressed contest. In that instance, Petey had sent word around
Lorton that he and his judges would be presenting an award to
the inmate who remained most consistently sharp—creased pants,
starched shirt, shined shoes—for two weeks.

The fervor with which inmates entered the best dressed contest
shocked Petey, who intended the contest to be silly and fun.
Instead, inmates took it as seriously as high school students
preparing for the SAT exam.

Petey realized he had better pull together a panel of judges
and declare a winner on time, once he saw that a quarter of the
population took the contest seriously.

"Goddamn, Chinch, these nigguhs is crazy? What, they ain't
never been in no contest before?" Petey's eyes darted from Chinch
across the t.v. room to one of the young inmates who carefully
placed his highly-polished shoes beside him on a hard chair.

"Sheee-it! That nigguh there gone be the winner. He ain't let a bit of dirt get on them shoes since the contest started."

Once Petey announced the winner, he thought things would settle down. He could hardly believe his ears the next day when the winner approached him.

"Uh, Petey. When I'm gone get my award? I told my mother and them about winning the contest, and they can't wait to get down here to see my award."

Shaping his lips to say, "Aw fuck you man, get on away from here," Petey caught himself when he looked into the eager, shining face of a man he realized had never before had positive reinforcement.

"Well, man, you gotta wait a couple of days because we putting the finishing touches on it. I'll let you know."

"Thanks, Petey. Thanks, man. I'm just so happy I won."

A faint voice inside Petey's head reminded him how important it is not to hurt people's feelings—words A'nt Pig had told him time and again. Petey made a beeline to the wood-working shop.

"Hey, dick," he casually greeted Walter, the inmate in charge. "I need you to do something for me, and I'll cover it with 10 cartons of cigarettes. I gotta have an award for that boy who won the contest, but it's gotta look good. Can you hook it up for me?"

"You ain't said nothing, boy. I'm a master," Walter said. "When you need it?"

Two days later, Petey presented a certificate written in calligraphy and centered in a polished oak frame declaring the winner of the Best Dressed contest. Tears glistened in the eyes of the young man as he spoke softly.

"I never won nothing before. This is beautiful, man. This is the best thing that ever happened to me."

Uncharacteristically, Petey choked on his own words. "!" he thought, "This is the best thing???" He reached out, embraced the winner, patted him on the back, grinned, and simply said, "You deserve it man. You was a sharp motherfucker the last two weeks, boy! You lucky they didn't put you in the hole, 'cause you was the contraband king!"

Although compassion drove many of his life's decisions before, during and after his time in Lorton, Petey's need for laughter more often than not took the lead.

*   *   *

Petey would not trade the spotlight to anyone else on purpose, but throughout his life he encouraged others to take steps to better themselves. At the Lorton school, he took on the mission of urging inmates to get their GED, general equivalency diploma. Most of the prisoners had dropped out of school. Some could not even read and write.

Petey saw a chance to enhance his own profits and at the same time, help inmates get an education. He engaged in a scheme of selling test answers in exchange for 25 packs of cigarettes, and he would register inmates for class whether or not they wanted to attend.

"Who sent this slip over here for me to see 'bout going to school?" A large, nearly illiterate inmate stood before Petey at the school's front desk.

"I sent it," Petey answered flatly. Sergeant Fawcett beside him looked on with mild interest, but the civilian, McMasters listened intently from the next room.

"What the hell you send it to me for, Petey? I ain't coming," the inmate growled, folding his arms across his wide chest.

Petey stood up, thrusting the paper importantly. "Hold it, now. How much time you doing? Fifteen years, right? Let's get down to brass tacks. Your charge is bank robbery. You know what happened? You stuck up that bank, you and that other nigguh, and the bank had a big sign on it saying 'This bank is guarded by cameras.' You couldn't read and write. You went on and stuck that motherfucker up anyway. You home counting the money, your picture came up on the 6 o'clock news. They got your ass.

"So what I'm telling you, fool, when you learn to read and write and get back out and stick up a bank, you'll be able to read the sign and go on down there where they ain't got no sign, right?"

Stifling a chuckle, the inmate reached for the pen. "Put me down for it, Greene. I ain't gone be coming back to Lorton all the time."

With the inmate gone, McMasters came out to where Petey sat tapping a pencil on the desk. "Petey, the Sarge here and I couldn't have said that to him. We couldn't have accused him of not being able to read and write. That's why you are an asset to this place. But I don't understand why you won't take the GED?"

Petey didn't answer. Instead, he changed the subject. "Sergeant Fawcett, I know most of these guys working in the classrooms and library want to go with you when you rotate. You taking 'em?"

Guards rotated every six months. The buzz in the school building centered around the guard coming there, Sergeant Henry Shirley. Sergeant Shirley's reputation as a no-nonsense guard struck fear in inmates who had become used to Sergeant Fawcett's facade of friendliness and laxity.

"Yeah, I'm going to the garage. I'm taking a couple of the guys. The rest have to get ready for Shirley. You wanna come with me?"

Fawcett already knew the answer, knew Petey loved the job at the school.

"No, I'm staying here. Sergeant Shirley already sent me a message that he don't like no jokes. Said he knows I'm a jokester and I'd better find somewhere else, but I sent word back that I am going to try the best I can to work with him," Petey told Sergeant Fawcett.

He wanted to say, "Do you know how good this place is? Visitors coming through here, soft chairs, all we got to do is pick up the paper and get people to sign? Put the blue mark if present, red if absent. Eat before everybody else. Go to the snack lines. And the school in a brand new building. I ain't leaving this sweet motherfucker!"

The morning Fawcett left and Shirley came on, Petey stood in the yard with the other inmates. When he started walking with everyone else, instead of marching to the center of the yard to crow about the keys, four or five inmates couldn't resist ribbing him.

"Shake your keys, Greene."

"You ain't got the key now?"

"Where the keys?"

"Hey, Key Man, shake the keys. You the only inmate carry keys."

Petey knew it wouldn't be long before the tables would turn once more, and he'd find a way to be on top again. Ignoring the taunts, he concentrated on the small Bible he'd tucked in his shirt pocket, based on research of Sergeant Shirley's background. He'd learned that the once enormous sergeant had lost almost 200 pounds in a battle with cancer, and had gone deeply into Christianity.

With zero fanfare, Sergeant Shirley opened the school building and nodded to inmates who scurried toward their assigned rooms. Petey silently repeated passages from the three scriptures he'd memorized, waiting for an appropriate time to use them. He laid his Bible beside his pencils and enrollment forms on the desk, and quietly took his seat.

"All right, everybody line up," Sergeant Shirley called to the inmates before they got to their rooms. "I know you all know me. You know I am not Sergeant Fawcett. I don't condone the bullshit he allowed. I want you to do your work. Don't want any visitors coming, hanging in and out of here. At all times, whatever goes on in here, I will be on top of it. Any questions? You mean to tell me nobody's got no questions?"

He looked around at the silent faces. "Where's the comedian?" No one breathed a word, even though they all knew he referred to Petey. Sergeant Shirley walked directly in front of Petey. "You are the comedian. I saw you on the stage. When I asked for the comedian, you didn't step up."

With all the seriousness he could muster, Petey answered, "Well, I ain't on the stage. This here's my job."

A small smile played at the corner of Sergeant Shirley's thin lips. "You make sure you understand that. This is not where you use any comedy. That's your seat right there beside me? I don't think you gonna last too long."

He was wrong. Before his six-month rotation ended, Sergeant Shirley and Petey Greene had become fast friends. Petey studied the sergeant and prepared for each day the way a college student prepares for final exams. He listened intently to the transistor radio Sergeant Shirley kept on low volume, tuned to a religious station deep in Virginia. Before long, Petey knew the ministers by name, the messages of their texts, and songs of their churches.

Within a week, he found frequent opportunities to quote scripture, hum a line from a hymn, and compliment the sermons from the radio.

"I didn't know you were a Christian. You know that Bible, don't you?" Sergeant Shirley looked wonderingly at Petey. "My grandmother made sure I went to Sunday school and church all the time," Petey smiled, then asked about Sergeant Shirley's church.

He also paid special attention to the methods Sergeant Shirley tried to use to gain absolute control over the minds and spirits of the inmates. The guard still didn't allow inmates to chat freely or have their friends visit in down time, but he started bringing in coffee like Sergeant Fawcett had done. Then, he brought in two boxes of caramel bars with nuts inside.

"I want all of you to know this coffee is your coffee. If you want a cup, it's right here behind me and Petey. Come get it any time you want to." The inmates thanked him and took the coffee, but hatred glared from their eyes.

Sergeant Shirley handed the boxes of candy to Petey mid-day. "Take this candy around to the rooms and give each man two bars."

Each inmate groused about how they wished Sergeant Fawcett could be there instead of Shirley, but they took the candy. That is, until Petey got around to Ike Austin, in the classroom where Ike taught math. "I don't want that candy. To hell with that cracker. I don't want the coffee and I don't want the candy," Ike said stonily.

Ike had been arrested during his senior year at Howard University, charged with check fraud. When Ike arrived at Lorton, he encountered Sergeant Shirley in the bath house where inmates received their clothes and shoes. Ike's feet swam in the shoes the sergeant handed him, so he turned politely to Sergeant Shirley. "Sir, these shoes are too big."

Shirley snapped at him. "You got 'em. Don't stand in front of me and tell me 'bout 'em being too big. You understand that? Move out!" The incident stayed with Ike, cemented as a life-long grudge against Sergeant Shirley. Ike wanted nothing to do with the man or his gifts. Which suited Petey just fine. He pocketed the extra bars of candy, mentally calculating the sale value on the cellblock.

A week later, Petey sat on his bed munching a candy bar he did not sell. He regaled Chinch with his ability to get in good with the guards, even a guard like Sergeant Shirley. "He stopped roaming the halls, going in people's classrooms now. He like to sit and talk to me, because I am a story teller, and I'm good, you understand. I could hold a boa constrictor's attention."

"Aw go 'head, Petey," Chinch laughed.

The next week, on Petey's routine walk handing out candy, he went into Ike's classroom as usual. Petey expected Ike to throw the candy back at him as he had done for the past 10 days. Instead, Ike let it sit on the desk. "Umm, Shirley done worked him. He got to him," Petey thought. Shrugging his shoulders, Petey returned to the front of the building and took his seat beside Sergeant Shirley.

"They take it? Everybody got the candy?" Shirley always asked the question, and Petey always assured him that everyone had accepted the gifts.

Within a minute, Ike's classroom door opened. Wearing anger like a cloak, Ike approached the desk, pointing his index finger at Petey's forehead. "I told you ever since you first brought that candy around that I don't want it. I haven't been taking it and, goddamnit, you stop bringing this candy to me. You understand?" with that, he threw the candy toward Petey's lap.

Before Petey could think of anything to say, Ike returned to his classroom. Sergeant Shirley knew the venom had been directed at him, but he didn't recall the incident with the shoes and was not sure why Ike seethed such anger. "I think we must be rubbing Mr. Austin the wrong way," he said slowly.

"Yes, I guess we did." Petey realized he was off the hook for pocketing the extra candy. By this time, Sergeant Shirley liked him so much, there was no need to explain. The sergeant, however, wanted an explanation from Ike.

Sergeant Shirley let the 15 minutes pass before Ike's class ended, then he called Ike to walk outside with him. Petey could hardly stand the suspense. He wanted to fast forward time so he and Ike could be back in the dormitory, with Ike telling him what happened. He could see the two men outside, but he couldn't hear a thing.

In fact, Sergeant Shirley was giving Ike a chance to explain himself. "Mr. Austin, you brought that candy back this morning. Seemed like you was a little upset."

Ike knew his outburst could cost him his job, so he spoke carefully. "I told Petey I didn't eat candy. I didn't want any, and I've been telling Petey that all the time."

Sergeant Shirley knew better. He put a stick of gum in his mouth and chewed for a few seconds before his next remark. "Yeah, Mr. Austin, I understand that. But the manner in which you brought it back was very hostile. I know you and Petey are personal friends and I know you and nobody else in that school building is gonna talk to Petey like that. So, I kinda think you was directing your comments at me."

Ike felt that he was Sergeant Shirley's intellectual superior, but he knew the sergeant held all the cards in the game. He decided to continue holding back. "Well now, Sergeant, if that's the way you interpreted it, then I have no jurisdiction over how you think about things. I just want you to know I didn't call your name."

The game could have gone on for a while longer, but Sergeant Shirley really wanted the truth. His humanity took over. "I'm just asking you as a man, why are you so hostile toward me. And let's say you are not hostile toward me, then why is it that the candy upset you so much that you had to say those things?"

Ike realized he could finally answer honestly. "I'd like to tell you something. A year ago, when I came in, you were in charge of the bath house and I talked to you like a man about a pair of shoes that were too big for me. You talked to me like I was dirt. Sir, that hurt me, because I hadn't done anything other than ask you for a change of shoes. I guess that was on my mind."

Sergeant Shirley studied his heavily veined hands, steepled his fingers, then cleared his throat before summarizing for Ike. "Well, you'd better get it off your mind. I hope it's off there now. Because I had been intending to not only put you in the hole but to take you out of this good job you have over here. But, being a fair man, I thought I'd better hear your side of it. Now I've heard your side. Let's hope we can bury the hatchet."

Although he knew he might never forgive or forget, Ike thought he could live with the small victory. "Okay, Sergeant Shirley. But Sir, I don't want your coffee and I don't want your candy."

"Mr. Austin, I can't make you eat my candy and I can't make you drink my coffee. Now get on back to work."

In the dorm that night, when Petey raced up to Ike to get the story, Ike admitted to trembling in his shoes. "I was scared to death, man. I thought he was going to throw me in the hole!"

Ike's story bolstered Petey's confidence even more. Since Sergeant Shirley never admonished him for keeping the candy, Petey thought he might push the envelope on the friendship a bit more.

The next morning, in one of the down times between checking students in, Petey spoke casually.

"Sarge, why don't you let me open up in the morning? See, while you getting all the guys counted, you could give me the keys, I could open up and have things set up."

Sergeant Shirley chuckled at Petey's transparency. "You just want to get out there with those keys, don't you."

The next morning, Petey waited expectantly. When Sergeant Shirley tossed him the keys, Petey's face lit up like the lights on the prison's perimeter at night.

Gleefully, he fell back into his old routine. "You nigguhs see these keys? I'm the only inmate in here carrying keys!"

*   *   *

Petey developed relationships with and knowledge of certain guards, and he drew on those experiences time and again in his life in prison and on the outside as a community leader and local star. And Petey proved that sometimes a guard's behavior could come back to haunt him.

Petey's Voice: Contraband Man

"The tailor shop used to make caps. It cost you five packs to get a cap with a lining in it, or it cost you three packs to get a cap with a short bill and four creases. When they issue you a regulation cap, that cap just have a old long bill and didn't nobody want it. When you was into something, you had a cap made.

"It was contraband; you wasn't supposed to have no cap like that. But it was such a teeny order, the guards would never press it unless they wanted to jam you and you kept beating 'em on everything. Then, if you had that cap, they'd take you with the cap.

"When me and Sergeant Shirley got tight, he'd be over on the walk on Sunday. I'd go right up to him and say I need me five caps. He'd say, 'You got 'em.' Next thing you know, a guy would be coming back from visiting. Sergeant Shirley would say, 'Come here, Shorty. What you doing what that cap? I know you don't want to go to the hole, do you? Put the cap in that box.' Next guy come up wearing a hat, he'd say, 'Hey slim, that's a nice looking cap you got on your head. You think that cap is good enough for you to go to solitary confinement? Put it in that box.'

"He'd send somebody over to get me about an hour later. 'You asked for five, I got you eight.' I'd take them on to the school building and sell them nigguhs them same caps back. Me and Sergeant Shirley became real good friends. I talked to Sergeant Shirley one time I went down to Lorton to see somebody. He came to me and told me how proud he was of me. This was right after I got out. He told me to keep up the good work. We just talked.

"Now, Sergeant Fawcett, are you ready for this? Sergeant Fawcett is another story. I'm out, in the street now, I'm Petey Greene, community activist, ex-offender. I'm Petey Greene who has notoriety and popularity, in the vanguard for the little people. I get a call one day asking would I care to be a panelist on Channel 5. They said we got some guards up here from Lorton, part of the union, that are saying Ken Hardy—who was the director—should be ousted because he coddles prisoners. Sergeant Fawcett was in charge of the union, and he was the main one saying prisoners are having too much fun.

"Ken Hardy is telling the station to get some guys who was in Lorton, like Petey Greene, Roach Brown, people like that. I said okay, because I do whatever Ken Hardy wants me to do. We get there and on the panel is a lawyer, me, Sergeant Fawcett, and an assistant superintendent. And people in the audience.

"Sergeant Fawcett come up. 'Hey Petey, how you doing?' I say, 'Sarge! My man.' So he hug me and shit. Then we start the program. After he talks for a while about the inmates, I interrupt. I say, 'Let me tell y'all something right now. Thanks to Sarge right here, we worked together for six whole months. I want you to know he is the no-goodest, dirtiest, racist white man I ever seen in my life. This man hates inmates, especially black inmates. I seen him kick 'em in the tail.' I couldn't say 'ass' on television.

"I kept talking, saying, 'He used to laugh in they face and then go call the guard at the laundry to tell that the inmates was getting bootleg, get 'em put in solitary confinement. He used to get guys to go with sissies, and then tell on them. Six months, I was with this cracker.' He was turning red, so I say, 'Grab me, Sarge. Why don't you hit me? I know it's a thousand names you want to call me right now.' This is on Channel 5. Everybody is shocked.

"So the moderator asked Sergeant Fawcett, 'Do you have anything to say, sir?' First thing he said, damn fool, was, 'I never knew Petey felt like this about me. I never did nothing to Petey. Even though I might have done something to the rest of the guys, I've never done anything to him . . . .'

"I cut in. 'Y'all hear what he said? He done it to the rest of the guys. But he's right. He never ever treated me any other way but like a man. Nice as he could be to me. He let me carry the keys and he told me I should change jobs because he knowed Sergeant Shirley didn't like me. You remember that, Sergeant Fawcett?'

"Boy, the people couldn't believe no shit like this. Finally, the moderator, who was slick, said, 'Well, Petey, since you've changed, don't you think Sergeant Fawcett could change, too?' I said, 'Sure, but I'm just telling you about how he was when I was there.' Man! That was the talk! They had that show on down at Lorton; the inmates saw it. Boy, they told me, 'Petey, that union! You watch yourself. You better not NEVER go to Lorton no more. These guards wanna kill you, boy. They might send some nigguhs up there to kill you!'

"But it was just something that I had to do. Must have been around 1969. I had been out four years. And Ken Hardy was the reason I was doing what I was doing. You had to have a job before you could get out, and I had two or three job offers that I refused while I was in Lorton. First, they wanted me to come out and do dishwashing. I said noooo, I ain't doing no dishwashing job. Then they wanted me to come out and work in a construction job. I said, 'Shiiit, I ain't lifted up nothing heavier than a pencil since I been here. When I leave out of here, I'm gone have me a comfortable job.

"Inmates started the rumor that I didn't want to leave because I was in love with a sissy. I just wasn't going out in that street without the right job. I cut down on all activities when I made parole. I wouldn't play no ball, wouldn't coach no teams. I say, 'You'll never get me in no trouble and stay in this motherfucker.'

"Finally, Mr. Hardy and I was talking. He said, 'Well, I got a guy named George Holland and he's at this organization called UPO, United Planning Organization. Get me a letter to him.' I went to a guy named Welten Powell and got him to write me a beautiful letter. He had beautiful penmanship. I took Mr. Hardy the letter and got the job, making $3,900 a year.

"I got out on August 6, 1965. It was a Tuesday, and them dumb motherfuckers was having a talent show down there that coming Saturday and had the nerve to ask me to stay or come back to moderate. I couldn't believe that! I was the best emcee and the best comic there, but I did not go back that Saturday."

Chapter 22

Winners and Losers

PETEY MAY NEVER have served time in Lorton in the first place, had it not been for the actions and reactions of another guard, and Petey's inability to keep his mouth shut.

Petey's Voice: Doing Myself In

"I got sent to Lorton from the D.C. Jail because they said I was inciting a riot. It was in 1963. I wasn't trying to incite a riot. One of the police just didn't like me, because, again, I was the center of attraction.

"What happened, we had ball teams over at the District Jail. I'm coaching a ball team and it's down to the championship. My team was playing for the championship, and I got the best pitchers, the best catchers, I got all the best. We beating the other team, but we have to play in a time frame. There's a certain time you have to go back in. You can't stay out like you do in the street.

"This officer, a big fat officer named Shuman, big ol' wall-gut officer, blows the whistle, even though we winning and he know if he blow his whistle you got to revert back to the first inning and start all over the next day. But he ain't got to blow the whistle. So, I'm madder than a motherfucker.

"That night, we sitting watching television. He come in and he knows I'm the center of attraction, and he don't like that. All the nigguhs is sitting around. He's an officer. He walks right up to me and starts in a sing-song voice, 'I blowed the whistle on Petey

Greene. I blowed the whistle on Petey Greene. You got to play tomorrow.'

"All the motherfuckers is laughing. It's crackers like that in the street today, and it's nigguhs like that. Just don't like to see me get out on nothing. I bring that on myself, because when I get out on motherfuckers, I just goes off, too. I looked at him, but I ain't gone let him provoke me into saying, 'Fuck you,' or hit him in the mouth like a lot of guys would have done. I'm too smart for this cracker here. I'm ten times smarter than this cracker.

"I'm just looking at him, everybody laughing. The next day, we got to replay the game. We get so far in front of the other team, even the whistle can't help 'em. We got to win. Shuman up there wherever he was the next day, watching. There's a inmate named Dotson out there with us. He big and fat. I say, 'Dotson, you big, fat motherfucker, blow your saxophone. I know you's a saxophone blowing big funky ass motherfucker. I hate all fat, black motherfuckers.'

"Everybody in there know that I ain't talking to Dotson. They know I'm talking to Shuman. And Shuman know I'm talking to Shuman. I say, 'Roll your belly, you big hog-head motherfucker. Blow your saxophone, bitch-ass. Just go head.' Everybody just laughing like a motherfucker. Dotson is aware that I'm talking to Shuman.

"When we came in, took a shower, I'm the champion now. Sitting there watching television. I see the police when they come in. They take me to see the captain. 'Petey, I want you to go back to your cell and get your stuff because you're going to be transferred from here to Lorton in the morning. You tried to start a riot out on the yard today, and called Officer Shuman . . .' I said, 'Who?' Shuman come in, 'Yeah, he tried to start a riot and was calling me all kinds of names.'

"I said, 'Captain, can I have something to say?' He said, 'No, you don't have nothing to say, Petey. You don't have nothing to say.' I said, 'Yeah, okay.' Now, my father or my brother Thad would have hit that man in his mouth. They woulda hit Shuman in his mouth, right there in front of the captain. And then they woulda got beat. That never entered my mind. But it showed me what white motherfuckers will do to you. The day before, he had come into the room where we were watching television, and he had showed his ass on me. And then he couldn't take it.

"So, I went on and pulled my shit. Then a whole gloom come over the jail. Everybody's fucked up. 'Man, motherfuckin' Shuman! Why he do that to Petey?' Of course there were a lot of old inmates wanted me to go, too. They wanted me to leave, just because they know I run the place.

"The next morning, they got me on a bus, took me on down to Lorton. I knew I was going to take that over. When I got to Lorton, they put me in solitary confinement on the strength that my father was bad. That's why they left me at the D.C. Jail at first, because my father was bad. I got the same name as my father, 'cause I'm a junior. When the man at Lorton ask me, 'Ralph Greene your father?' I say, 'If my name is Ralph W. Greene Jr., what you think my father's name is?' He say, 'Uhp, put him in solitary.' My father had served time in Alcatraz, 1800 miles from there.

"He might not have been in jail right then. Just me and my brother Thad was in jail at that time. But he had been in Alcatraz for a helluva crime—21 robberies. He was in Alcatraz when I went to Korea. He fucked up a whole lot of penitentiaries. He broke a guard's jaw at Lorton, messed up a hack in Atlanta. He was just an incorrigible motherfucker. They just kept shipping him and Alcatraz was where you went when they couldn't handle you. He spent 14 years of a 21-year sentence there. He got that 21 years when I was about 9 years old.

"In the short time that he was home, we knew he loved us. And he could write with both hands. His penmanship was excellent. He was one of the best Chess players I've ever met. He was a good guitarist, and he was a helluva athlete. But, put all that aside. My father took money. He said the white man was never supposed to be his boss, but they stayed his boss because he was always incarcerated."

∗   ∗   ∗

Walking With Humor

Whereas Petey's father, Ralph W. Greene Sr., carried his anger with him into the penitentiary and fought his way through each day, Petey walked always with humor at the top of his agenda. He especially found delight when he could put the joke on himself. That way, he accomplished two goals—making people laugh and making people look at him, not remember something funny about someone else.

One of Petey's classic examples of self-effacing humor won him the heart of a fellow inmate's wife during a talent show inmates were allowed to put on for their families. Of course Petey served as emcee for the show—a natural role that complemented his other starring role as prison radio deejay.

About seven or eight months after he arrived at Lorton, Petey's ever-shrewd mind cooked up the deejay position. On Saturdays after breakfast, there was a lull in activities that Petey convinced officials he should fill by spinning records, taking requests and talking much trash in between.

"It went over like wildfire. They want me to play at night, but I don't want to. Just give me my four hours. I call it The Petey Greene Show, and my theme song is by the Marques, "The Morning After," Petey told his mother, Jackie, on one of her rare visits to Lorton.

"Some nigguhs put the cover over they heads. They hate it, especially on the mornings I just play nothing but Hillbilly. But most of the guys just love it. They get their people to bring the latest records down here."

By the time Petey was less than a year from being released from Lorton, his reputation as a radio deejay and an emcee for the prison talent shows added to the name he'd already made for himself as a stand-up comic before his arrest. Many inmates knew Petey from his days as a comedian in Brandywine, MD, at Wilmer's

Park, where he traded jokes for wine. Petey served as the warm-up act for stars such as Sam Cooke, who once paid Petey's way out of jail when he was arrested for public drunkenness.

On the evening of the last talent show he would emcee at Lorton, Petey stepped onto the stage. His mother sat in the audience with his half-brothers. Almost every inmate had family and friends either sitting with him or applauding his stage act.

Halfway through the program, Petey walked out before the capacity crowd and lifted a hand for the band to lower the music. "Well I'm gone take a little break in the pace. Just being here with you makes me want to do a number, 'cause we're all in this together . . ."

With the microphone held at the proper distance, Petey took up the words of a famous Brook Benton song, "It's Just a Matter of Time," and deep, melodious tones drifted over the heads of the enraptured crowd.

Women screamed and swooned, inmates stared in awe, and one of Petey's brothers leaned over to their mother. "Dag. I didn't know Petey could sing like that." Jackie whispered in his ear, "I don't know who that is singing, but that ain't your brother Petey singing. I do know that."

Sitting in the next row over, an inmate who had taken on the task of getting men to sign up for the Lorton band confided in his girlfriend: "Damn, that sumbitch been here all this time and we been looking for a vocalist for the band. I never knew he could sing!"

Before she could respond, the stage curtain started moving back slowly. Just as Toto uncovered Oz's wizard, the inmate pulling the cord revealed another inmate ghosting for Petey in a serious croon.

People started laughing and throwing cans at Petey, who stayed in form, eyes closed, mike held lovingly. Then, in mock surprise, he whirled around to see the curtain exposing his cohort in the act. Of course he'd planned every detail, rehearsing the song's timing with the silky voiced Joe Echols, and pinpointing the exact time the curtain would interrupt his "scam."

Mrs. Wheatley, the warden's wife, chuckled with the officers near the front row. Placing her lips near her husband's shoulder, she spoke softly. "I told you Petey is the best thing that ever happened to the penitentiary."

Petey, Echols, and the band took a smiling low bow—which was Petey's way of ensuring that everyone knew he had "got out on them once again."

Mrs. Wheatly by far was not the only woman in the audience impressed with Petey Greene. One of them, a pretty woman named Joyce, determined that night that she would get to know Petey and get to know him well.

The following Sunday, after families visited, then waited at the prison chapel for the bus that would take them away, Joyce lingered near the inmates who served as ushers. Petey was among them, dapper in his contraband.

"Hi. My name is Joyce. You're Petey Greene. That was really a funny thing you did down at the show."

"Thank you," Petey responded respectfully. He had seen Joyce a time or two when she brought her children down to Lorton to visit their father. He'd also seen her husband entertaining another woman on alternate Sundays.

Joyce smiled sweetly, studying Petey. "You're a lonely person, ain't you?"

"No, I'm not lonely."

"Don't nobody come to see you. Anybody write you?"

Petey decided to be honest. "Uh uh."

"Well, then, you're lonely. Could I write you?"

It occurred to Petey that a friendship with this woman could cause friction, since her husband slept a few beds down from his in the prison dormitory.

"You can write if you want to, but what about your husband?"

Joyce smoothed a non-existent wrinkle from her dress above her knee and tried not to frown. "I just bring the kids down to see him. I know his girlfriend comes down here other times."

Petey nodded slightly, knowing she was telling the truth but not wanting to embarrass her by acknowledging it. Joyce didn't wait for any more encouragement.

"Look, I'm gone write you. It'll be all right?"

Petey's wide, toothy grin took all Joyce's nervousness away. She took a slip of paper out from her purse, asked for his detail number, and promised to be in touch as she walked to the bus.

*   *   *

It should come as no surprise that Petey's need to be center stage would not allow him to keep a romance a secret for long. A chance to stir trouble and sit amidst a swirl of gossip proved too aluring, even when part of Petey wanted to carry on a private affair. Then too, the old mental tape of Ralph Greene senior's voice telling his sons, "A dick is for fucking," made cuckolding a fellow inmate in fact a prideful thing to do.

Petey's voice: The Infidel

"Me and Joyce's husband slept 'bout three beds apart. I used to ask him, 'Hey, dick, what's happening? How your children?' He say, 'Man, my children all right. But that goddamn wife of mine, she ought to just go 'head.'

"So, she was writing to me and didn't nobody know it. We were corresponding. She sent me a pair of $125 shoes down there, lizard skin shoes. Sent me a big sweater. Now nigguhs in the penitentiary, when they see me getting this shit in there . . . I love the way I come up and I love my constituents. Them motherfuckers see them shoes coming in and see that sweater, they said, 'This nigguh got a 'ho in the street.' I said, 'Shit no.' But my man Chinch knew it; I told Chinch. Chinch said, 'Well, man, just be cool.'

"Then one day we had a fair. I'll never forget. A September fair. She told me she was coming down and bringing the children. She's got to bring the children. Her husband's mother also coming down. We having another show that day, and I'm gone be with that.

"When she came down that day, it was pretty cool until she just left the children and spent the majority of the day sitting on the wall with me. We just talked. Then nigguhs started putting shit together. After we got back in the dormitory that night, her husband came to my bed and said, 'Hey man, you know, I don't appreciate what went down with my wife.' I said, 'What went down?' He was mad. 'You know I know my wife was coming down to see you.' I stared right back at him, and said, 'Let me tell you something. That's your wife, then you write her a letter and you tell her. Don't you come to me with no shit like that.'

"So he went on. Now the shit gets wide open. She gets on my mail and visitors list. She starts to coming down there to see me and I get to going up to the visiting hall and we hugging and kissing and shit like that. In the visiting hall, we become the center of attraction, because another nigguh's old lady come down to see him and the first thing this nigguh tell his old lady is, 'You see that woman right there hugging Petey Greene, you know that's her husband sitting right over there with another woman.'

"The whole scenario is getting fucked up down there. The penitentiary goes into two factions. Half of 'em were on that boy's side and half of 'em were on my side. Didn't matter to the ones on his side that he had another woman. That ain't the point. Here you in the penitentiary, this is a motherfucker's wife. That other bitch didn't mean nothing. But my brother and his mob say 'Fuck that nigguh, little sissy-ass. Take that woman!'

"Now it gets all the way up to the front office, to our counselor, Mr. Jessie Jones. Me and Mr. Jones laughed about that since I been in the street. So Jesse call me up there, say, 'Petey, what I'm getting ready to ask you, I'm not gone believe but one answer.' I say, 'What you talking about?' He said, 'Have you got Tolsen's wife coming down here to see you?' I said, 'That's the truth.' Boy, he couldn't believe it. 'Are you crazy?' I told him about the other woman, Mildred, coming to see Tolsen, but he said, 'So what?'

"I told him, 'If his woman coming down here to see him, then his wife is my woman and she come down here to see me.' He shook his head and told me, 'Petey, I cannot put you in the hole for no shit like that and I cannot make that woman get off your list, but it's gonna be dangerous.'

"So now it's a hub-dub-rubbing and everybody is mumbling. My man Chinch told me to not even discuss the situation. 'Them little nigguhs is gone press this boy into doing something to you, so don't even say anything about this.' But I can't help it. One day I'm bragging, 'Shit, I pimp 'hos, I take nigguhs' bitches,' and on and on like that. We all sitting down on the diamond and he walked up to me. 'I want to speak to you, man.' I said, 'What you want, boy?' He looked off a little bit, then said, 'I want my wife to stop coming down here.' I stood up and said, 'What I tell you, boy, about that?'

"When I said that, he hit me right on my motherfucking jaw. So I grabbed him and pulled him to me. I don't want to go to no solitary confinement, and I saw the guard coming. You can't be fighting. I talked right into his face. 'You little motherfucker. Now you see what you done done? You getting ready to get us both put in the hole. Don't you say a word when them guards get here. You let me do all the talking.'

"When the guards get there and ask us what's going on, I say, "It's my fault. I went over there to try to give Juanita some cigarettes.' Juanita is a faggot. I say, 'I didn't know this boy had already set something up.' The guard say, 'You two motherfuckers down here fighting over a faggot. Go on away from here.'

"After the guards walked away, the boy threatened to have me killed. Chinch said, 'See, I told you don't brag. I told you that boy was gone hit you on your jaw.' But didn't nothing else happen because we fucked around and both of us got out on parole at the same time. We was both in for armed robbery. Everybody in for trying to take money.

"When we get out, I go and start living with Joyce in Parkland. They call me down to the parole board one day. I had worked about five months at UPO, and I had made a mark then. I was rolling. Mr. Avery called me in when I got there, and that boy is sitting there. Mr. Avery say, 'Petey, Tolsen here says you are living with his wife.' I say, 'I do, but he don't live with her. He living with his girlfriend.'

"Mr. Avery told Tolsen, say, 'Look here, let me say this to you. Petey is working for the United Planning Organization, and he's doing a goddamn good job. Do you want your wife?' He say, 'No sir.' Mr. Avery stood up. 'Well, if you don't want her, stop fucking with this man. You understand that? Don't be calling talking about sending him back. Get on out of here before I send You back.'

"After the boy left, Mr. Avery turned to me. 'Sit down! If I was that boy, I would kick your ass. Out here taking somebody's wife like you some Rudolph Valentino. I should send you back anyway. You just as bad as that goddamn boy. Don't think I'm on your side. You got them people fooled at UPO. Get your ass on out of here.' I went out and went right on back to Joyce's place."

Chapter 23

On the Radio

AMONG THE MANY inmates at Lorton who admired Petey for treating life as one big con game was a man named Sam Hughes. Sam—in prison on a rape charge—would unknowingly alter the course of Petey's life, setting him on a path to success he'd never even imagined. Sam did it by merely introducing Petey to his older brother, Dewey Hughes. Petey did the rest.

In the late 1960s, Dewey himself was stepping into a career unimaginable when he was a boy growing up in the all-black section of D.C.'s Southwest quadrant. His neighborhood had long since given way to what was known as Urban Renewal—a euphemism, as it turned out, for pushing the poor folks away to make room for government buildings.

With polished good looks, innate intelligence and drive, Dewey had worked his way from floor sweeper to program director at D.C.'s popular, white-owned WOL radio station. Dewey visited his brother at Lorton out of obligation. He did not feel comfortable there. Sam, of course, bragged to fellow inmates about his brother Dewey's professional prominence. And to Dewey, he bragged about being friends with Lorton's star, Petey Greene.

*　　*　　*

Petey's voice: The Dewey Days

"How I met Dewey Hughes, well I was in Lorton and Dewey's brother, Sam Hughes, was in Lorton, too. We were in the same dormitory and he used to always talk about his brother who was in the army, his brother Dewey. Dewey at that time was stationed in Camp Pope, Louisiana. Then he told me when Dewey got a job at WOL radio. So by me and Sam becoming such good friends, when I was released, I went by WOL where Dewey was working to tell him a few things for Sam.

"When I met Dewey at the station on Wisconsin Avenue, he wasn't even a jockey or nothing. He was more or less of a handy man around WOL. But he was a ambitious cat, so in turn he used to work for days and nights, sometimes without even going home, and learning all he could about the machinery, the mechanics of radio.

"When I went over to see him, it was at a time when wasn't nobody in the station but him. And we talked about his brother and then I told him about the radio show I had in the reformatory. And I did some rhymes and he put them on a tape and he was impressed, you know. After Dewey cut the tapes of me, he played the tapes around in the station for the Vice President and General Manager, John Pace, a white man. And he played it for the black guys, Sonny Jim, Carroll Henson, Bob Nighthawk Terry, and them who were disc jockeys and they were known as the Soul Brothers.

"Dewey wasn't a big man at the station but he got a chance to get involved in radio when a white boy left, called Sherwood Ross, who was public affairs director. Dewey got that job. At that time, the station was trying to go all-black. It was in the 60s and blacks were beginning to move.

"When they gave Dewey that job, Dewey started doing a lot of innovative things, as opposed to just bringing on big people to be talking about the problems. It was the right time to bring on the little people, the welfare recipients and things like that. And I had started an organization called EFEC, Efforts from Ex-Convicts. And money was being allocated for the help of ex-offenders, welfare recipients and so on.

"Dewey knew I could rap, so he, at that particular time, didn't give me a show, but he would get me to bring on five or six ex-offenders. In fact, Dewey was doing a show of his own then. It was called 'Speak Up.' And he would bring us on and we would talk about the ex-offender problems and what was needed. Came on at 6 on Sunday evenings.

"Every week, he would have on a different low-income program. But he was more concerned about me, because I could deal with all the issues. I was rolling pretty good with the EFEC program and I was working for UPO. Then I became a household word. It was 'Whatever Petey Greene says, let's go along with that,' at rallies and those types of things.

"Around that same time, a guy named Charlie Puckheimer got me an engagement at the Cellar Door, which was a club in Georgetown. Dewey saw the crowd there and the people in town leaning toward Petey Greene. I was on the speaking circuit, too, talking about problems poor people have.

"In late '67, I started on the radio. Looking back on Dewey, Dewey was a very cunning guy. And he saw that I was very talented, and that I liked him. He saw I really, really liked him. And Dewey wanted to be a star himself. I can understand. He was a handsome fellow, young, talk like a white boy. People who had never seen Dewey used to think he was white. They used to call him on the radio and think he was a white boy.

"So, Dewey saw me as an asset. He started letting me come and sit with him on Sunday, so it would be him and me. He named the program, "Rappin' with Petey Greene." Dewey and I would be there and he would push the buttons and we would both talk. People started saying, 'You don't need that white boy on there with you, Petey. Why don't you get that white guy off there?"

"I was rolling. So everytime Dewey would have to go out of town, he would say, 'Well, man, we got to cut a tape,' and we would cut a tape and then he would go out of town and they would play the tape. We wouldn't be there. One time, though, he had to go out of town and couldn't get to me in time. I went on the radio by myself. I had been sitting there with him about eight or nine months, and it wasn't nothing but to press the telephone. That was his demise. I did the program by myself and the next

Sunday, people started calling saying, 'Why don't you come on by yourself all the time? You don't need that white man.'

"I'd say, 'He's not white.' But I had my confidence up and I knew I didn't need Dewey there with me. And so he phased hisself out. The show got hot. Sometimes Dewey would try to tell me to say something, but I would always deviate from that. He even tried to get me to stop saying, 'I'll tell it to the hot, I'll tell it to the cold . . .' And that's a thing I've been saying over the years.

"Looking back on it, he did that because he didn't want to be identified so much in the black community. He was always trying to be professional, but he couldn't change me because I told him one thing I wanted to always be was honest. He said, 'Okay. Solid.'

"I used to bring guests in, but them people in the community, just like now on television, they always used to say, 'You don't need no guests. We like to talk to you by ourself.' See, when I first started out, they used to call me up with they problems. 'I got a boyfriend, Petey Greene, and my boyfriend, you know, he goes with my best girlfriend, Petey, what should I do?'

"I say, 'Do you love him?' If she say, 'I really do love him,' I'd tell her, 'Ain't nothing I can tell you to do.' Bam, and gone. So people liked that. One that I'll never forget, this little kid called me, said, 'Hey Petey Greene, every day I go to school and I have to cut 'round through this back way. This dog always out there chasing me. And make me late for school.' I said, 'Get yourself a iron pipe, rap it up in a piece of paper, and when that dog come after you again, you bust him in the head.'

"The next Sunday, he called back. 'Hey Petey Greene. That dog don't chase me no more. I got the pipe and piece of paper and did what you told me, but the lady, his master, saw me getting ready to hit him and she told me don't hit him, so now she keeps him tied up. Thank you, Petey Greene.'

"One time I almost got in some trouble. A guy called me and said, 'Hey man, this broad I got, everytime I look around she's over there with another dude, and he act like he disrespect me.' I said, 'Well, man, just get a gun and go kill that nigguh.' Boy, I got in serious trouble. People at the station told me, 'Petey, you got power. These people don't just call you and ask you these questions just to be calling. These people believe in you, man. Somebody called and told us that you told a man to get a shotgun and kill another man.'

"I didn't say nothing like that again. Cortez Thompson was Public Affairs Director. Then what happened, a guy named Ralph Matthews hooked up with a guy named Dick McCormick to do a television show on Channel 26, and they came and asked me to host. Neither one of us, me or Dewey, had been in television. They took me over to Channel 26 where the white boy, Dick McCormick, was the co-host, and we began to do a show called Jobs 26, which had been the show of a guy named Harland Randolph who later became the president of the University of the District of Columbia.

"When me and the white boy took over, the white boy was the producer and he was the co-host with me. We used to talk about low-income jobs and where to go, and it was really entertaining because I used to just talk. Dewey would come over every day, standing around. He is a cunning guy. He would stand around just like a little lost sheep. You know, that was Dewey.

"One day they came up and said they need a producer, a black producer. Now I know Dewey had never been in no television, but I went to Dewey and said, 'I'ma tell 'em that you's a black t.v. producer.' We messed around and got Dewey the job. He brought me in radio; I brought him in t.v.

"Dewey is a very shrewd person and he will listen. This was in the 60s, when a black man didn't have to do much, just be black. Dewey caught on very quickly. He stayed up in that t.v. room. In fact, that's how Dewey got most of his training, at Channel 26. I was still the host, and he was the producer. We did a lot of things. He even changed the show from Jobs 26 to a show called 'Where It's At.' We did issues with guests, me and the white boy. And we also did certain segments with entertainment, local bands and national acts, too. The show ran from '69 to '70, from 7 to 7:30 each night, 'til the grant ran out from HEW. Then we didn't get refunded.

"Me and the white boy used to really go at it on television. People would be amazed, because we would really get hot at each other. And in the dressing room, we would cool out, you know. We'd be arguing about race issues. I'd say, 'Man, don't you be calling nobody a 'bama. You don't know what a 'bama is.' Then we did a whole half an hour on what was a 'bama. He was really a good guy, Dick McCormick. He was from Boston, had a job with Labor. Lived on Capitol Hill.

"That was really my start. I won an Emmy for that. But around the time after the grant ran out, Dewey and I became unbeneficial. We weren't friends for a short span. I don't know what it was, except he wanted to be a perfectionist and I didn't. I had got drunk, and we were supposed to go somewhere or something, and I was drunk and didn't go. He got mad and I didn't care.

"I was still doing the radio show and he was producing a television show for Carroll Henson. This was in '69 when me and Dewey had that falling out. Another guy in radio, Sam Johnson, who they called Sammy Jay, got me to be a keynote speaker for the convention for black radio and t.v. broadcasters. That's where Capital Records heard me speak and gave me a contract. And like I say, liking Dewey, I got his mother to give me the phone number where he was down in Acapulco with Sandra Butler, and I called him to tell him what had happened.

"He flew back the first day of his vacation. I introduced him to the people as my agent, and we started working on the album. I worked on the album and Dewey was flying out to California to check on the album. I went out a couple of times and we did the album here at Ed Murphy's Supper Club and at Eastern High School.

"When I thought Dewey was out in California doing things for me, he was setting up hisself to get on 'The Dating Game' and all this type of stuff. I was doing shows at the Howard Theater. When the album was produced, the record company, Capital, got in some kind of financial bind, and they didn't keep nobody but Lou Rawls and Nancy Wilson, people like that. They had paid me, but the album didn't get released.

"That didn't even bother me, because, I had, again from my grandmother, a thing that she taught me, 'You can't let one failure worry you the least bit because if you do, what you might have going for you down the road, you might blow.' In other words, if I'da went into a moping thing and kept concentrating on Capital Records, I wouldn't be here today. I knew from my grandmother that I'm a very talented, very versatile person.

"But I still drank. I could go six or seven months without drinking, then I'd get drunk for six or seven days. I loved liquor. I had a buddy tell me one time, 'Petey, I've never seen a man get more chances than you, then you get drunk. Now that makes me think you are scared of success.'

"Maybe he was right. We was in kindergarten together, so he knows me, but I never looked at it that way. I just thought I had some bad breaks. Missed some appointments that would have been advantageous for me. And I went on the Howard stage drunk and fell off the stage in the middle of the performance. Dewey had to come out and do the rest of the show, to bring out the acts, but he didn't have no jokes or nothing. All his relatives was there, and it was one of my biggest shows.

"I got drunk during intermission, and just busted my chin open when I fell off in the orchestra pit. I went on 'cross the street to Cecelia's and continued to get drunk.

"Dewey and I were just on two ends of the spectrum. I cannot take this from him: me and him have went to a lot of places and he would never take my money. We went to the Poconos, they had me as a speaker up there at a big YMCA convention. And he took me to Clemson University. I was hot then, but Dewey could see that liquor was gone mess me up. When I was drunk, I'd tell him, 'Fuck you, man. You don't run my life.'

"But we done some helluva nice things together. It got me exposure and I got paid. I cut a Census album with the Temptations, James Brown, and some more entertainers. 'I'm James Brown, you better get on the good foot and get counted,' that kind of thing. 'I'm Petey Greene, ex-offender, television and radio talk show host, and I want you to know the Census really means a lot. Being an offender, I wasn't counted . . .' They put it on an album with the stars.

"Then Sears recorded information about me along with all the big people for a radio campaign. They'd say the person's history then ended it with, 'Dr. Ralph Bunch, a black man.' They said Petey Greene, Washington, D.C. ex-offender, came out of jail, blah blah, United Planning Organization, helps people, EFEC, Petey Greene has really worked hard to change his life and now he is blah blah. Then they said, dundaduhn, 'Petey Greene, a black man.' They ran it all 'cross the country on all stations, as a Sears promotion, around '69 or '70. Around the same time, Ebony did my life story. That's when my first daughter found out who I was.

"I was at WOL for I guess 10 or 11 years. After I left Channel 26, I was off television for about two years, then I went to Channel 20. I have never solicited a radio or television job. Milt Grant came after me for television. Sanders and them solicited me for radio.

"After they didn't want me on WOL, a guy told Dewey and Cathy, 'How could y'all have a all-talk format and get rid of Petey Greene?' They told him something like, 'He didn't fit into.' The guy said, "I know y'all crazy.'

*   *   *

Petey's meteoric rise to prominence as a radio talk show host rested not only on his gift of gab but on his instinctive knowledge of how to generate attention. Like a dog sniffs the wind for friend and foe, Petey kept his nose open for whiffs of subject matter that would get people riled up. If no subject matter presented itself, he'd throw out one of his own lines to see what it hooked.

"The Redskins ain't nothing," he blurted out on the radio one night. Rewarding Petey instantly, the phone lines lit up like a Christmas tree. Not a one failed to blink. Caller after caller complained, "That's our team. Don't say nothing bad about our team."

"Uhoh, this is a goldmine," Petey thought, clamping down on the sentiment like a Pitbull whose jaw cannot be pried open—no matter the danger. And in the case of the Redskins and their die-hard supporters, the danger was real.

A month into Petey's trumped up anti-Redskins campaign, he sat in his car at a redlight one afternoon. Another motorist pulled up beside him, recognized the face of Petey Greene, and lost it. "Man, let me tell you one thing, stop talking about them Redskins," he yelled. Petey turned placidly to utter his characteristic, profane response. "Aw man, fuck you."

The other driver opened his door with a jackhammer in his hand just as the light turned green. Petey sped off, realizing, "Aw shit! These people is serious!"

Naturally, the incident convinced him to always talk about the Redskins and to look for ways to take the issue to greater heights. In late 1971, he found a way. He announced to his fans and to the people who hated him but listened nonetheless:

"If the Redskins *go* to the Superbowl, they ain't even got to win it, I'll do anything you people say. We got six weeks for y'all to decide."

The lines stayed hot at WOL, and they practically melted when the Redskins started winning games and ended up securing their spot to play in the Superbowl in Los Angeles. After unprecedented ribbing on and off the air, Petey and his audience agreed that he would ride a tricycle from 15th and U streets to 8th and Florida Avenue.

For his memoirs, Petey recalled the challenge:

"I stepped on that corner Sunday at 5 o'clock. I had to be on the radio at 6 p.m. Wasn't nobody out there yet and I was 'bout to get back in my car. Five minutes after 5, a Cadillac pulled up. Two nigguhs set that tricycle in front of me, and in three seconds, the streets was black with nigguhs. Cameras flashing and stuff. And Petey Greene, the center of attraction.

"A little girl came to me as I was trying to crawl with that tricycle. I got to 14th and U, and the little girl say, 'Mr. Greene, my

mommie and daddy are over in the car. They say do you want me
to ride it for you?' I say, 'No, that's all right, sweetheart.'

"I couldn't ride it, so the adults hollered out, 'Pick it up and
put it on your shoulder.' They all wearing Redskins caps. One
nigger was walking beside me with a big jar of coffee, 'cause it
was cold. I got to 8th and Florida Avenue, at the end of my journey.
Everybody was hollering and screaming. Then a man roared up
in a big Cadillac, said, 'Excuse me, Mr. Greene. My name is Mr.
Johnson. I'm George Allen's chauffeur.' George Allen was then the
coach of the Redskins.

"He said, 'Mr. Allen told me to pick you up and carry you to
the radio station.' I got right on the air at 6 o'clock. My phones lit
up. First thing they say, 'One thing we can say about you, Petey,
you fair. You shore is fair.'

"Some other nigguhs saying 'Aw, Petey is a goddamn fool.'
My friends say, 'Why he's a fool? He didn't do a thing but have
10,000 people talking about his ass.' And when I do that, it's
clean, it's fun, and suckers think I'm the goat. Number one, I'm
the hero, and number two, I'm in complete control of everything
around me. That has enabled me to become what I am today—a
personality on and off the air. Because I want to just make people
happy in my way, and people become more happy when they are
on what they think is the other side, laughing at somebody.

"So that has just been one of my ways of helping people, and
it do a lot of things for me. It stopped me from using drugs. It
stopped me from getting high. It keeps me a different kind of
high. It stopped me from drinking. And it makes me a controversial
person. It's just a mechanism that works."

Friends in Fame

Petey's childhood contemporaries in his Georgetown
neighborhood and on the football field included Walter Fauntroy,
who played for the LeDroit Park team and would become the
District of Columbia's first non-voting delegate to Capitol Hill

under partial Home Rule in the 1970s; and Robert Hooks, who attended Stevens Elementary and Francis Junior High with Petey. Robert hit fame in the 1960s with his television role as a policeman on the popular drama "NYPD."

These kinds of people readily answered Petey's call to be guests on his radio and television shows, or to salute him in numerous tributes throughout his life.

Another Georgetown friend of Petey who became an actor was Max Julian, who gained attention for his movie role as "The Mac." In Georgetown in the 30s and 40s, he was Maxwell Banks, younger brother of Petey's classmate Tazwell Banks.

While Max played basketball, thrilling the girls by flinging his hair back from his face, Petey recalled that Tazwell concentrated on his studies.

In the 1980s, Tazwell surprised Petey by coming to a Francis Junior High School reunion. By that time a noted physician, Tazwell felt stunned when the man collecting the money at the door refused to take his check.

"It's a white man trying to give a check," one of the alums whispered to Petey not far from the entrance. Petey looked up and broke into his classic grin. "Naw man, that's Tazwell. Take that check. That's Tazwell Banks."

Tazwell arched his eyebrows and delivered a stage whisper of his own. "What's wrong with these people, Petey?"

Petey put his hand on his long-time friend's back, and teased in typical Petey Greene fashion: "You's a Imitation of Life-ass nigguh, that's what." Tazwell just shook his head at Petey's reference to the classic movie of a light-skinned black woman passing as white.

Nearly a thousand Francis graduates and guests crammed into the auditorium. Robert Hooks, who friends referred to as Bobby, called Petey on the phone earlier in the day to rib him. "What are you doing giving a junior high school reunion and Maxwell and I aren't there?"

They reminisced about the singing group Bobby formed, called the Spoons, and about the Georgetown neighborhood reunion 15 years before when Bobby was able to make it.

"Man, you walked in that door wearing a tux and all the people ran to you for your autograph," Petey recalled. "And you came right back at 'em, saying 'Goddamn if I'm signing autographs. Y'all know my name. I come here to party!' And remember the testimonial dinner they had for me in '69?"

"Yeah, yeah, at the Shoreham Hotel," Bobby threw in.

In preparation for the testimonial, planners racked their brains to come up with a star to host the evening. Petey's manager Dewey Hughes and his friend Barksdale, along with an organizer named Marilyn McCarol, kept throwing names on the table. Dick Gregory. Dean Martin. Finally, Petey said, "What about Bobby Hooks?"

"You know him?" Dewey asked, surprised by the constantly growing list of names Petey could rattle off as personal acquaintances if not actual friends.

"Just call him and tell him it's for me." Petey sat back confidently, handing a personal phone number for Dewey to dial. As soon as Dewey hung up, Petey asked calmly, "What did he say?"

"He's on his way."

Bobby came and gave the keynote address. The Rev. David Eaton, who'd grown up in D.C. in Petey's generation, served as master of ceremony. Walter Fauntroy also came to the event. Years later, Petey would invite Fauntroy as a guest on WDCA-TV's "Petey Greene's Washington."

In his introduction of the esteemed congressman, Petey said, "I've known Walter Fauntroy ever since he was a little acorn-headed boy living on Westminster Street." Fauntroy had to catch himself from doubling over with laughter. "Boy, Petey Greene! You'll never change," Fauntroy managed to say.

Chapter 24

God's Stormy Weather

PETEY'S HUMOR, HIS material for his shows, came more from inner reflections than from external information. Toward the end of his life, his ruminations and his life experiences reflected his growing appreciation for his relationship with his God.

Petey's Voice: I Know Who Has Control

"I know I don't have control over anything, not even my life. And I know again that man is working hard at transplanting that heart and all that. But I believe it's by the grace of God that Lena Horne looks as good as she looks right now.

"I'm a strange person because of my beliefs. I don't discuss it with nobody. I'm telling you this, Lurma, because we're into this project here, but this type of conversation, I don't have with nobody.

"For instance, take how I feel about the weather. I have a radio show and they ask all the radio commentators to give the weather report. Other commentators say the weather report is 65 outdoors and so forth. I go on the radio, I say, 'Raise up your window and you'll tell what it is outdoors. I ain't got time to tell y'all the weather. Go outdoors.' Because I think they just say 'The relative humidity is . . .' to give people better jobs. That's employment. 'Cause do you know what 38 celsius is? And you went to college!

"I got tricked one time. The weather man said it's no rain, no precipitation and so forth. And I got out and it's raining. I called the weather station, the weather bureau, and said, 'Man, why don't

y'all just take that man off. He don't know what he be doing, see?'
They got big charts where they show you all where the moon go
down over here. I don't even know why they waste time with the
weather.

"Let me tell you what they did on ABC Nightline. I watch
that. When all that snow came before Easter, Ted Koppel had who
was supposed to be the highest paid, best weather man in the
country on ABC Nightline. He asked him what's going on. The
man said, 'It's beyond me. We're working on it right now.' To me,
that's God. That's my interpretation of God. This man couldn't
say nothing but 'Ted, we working on it right now. We don't know
what happened.' All you college people sitting up listening to it,
waiting for this man and his crew to come up with some computer
status and, heh, I just looked at him. I said, 'You told the right
truth, cracker. You don't know. And you and a staff can be working
on it, and I say you making all that overtime money and everything
when people out of jobs, they got y'all trying to figure out the
Lord.'

"If I'd a been drunk, I wouldn't have even paid that any mind.
But being here sober, laying back there on my bed, looking at
ABC Nightline, just had watched them digging snow out knee
deep three days before Easter, and they bring on the weather man.
I say, 'Uh oh, just let me see what he gone say. Now, I'm ready for
him to tell a outright lie about 'Well a small compression of hot air
came in from the Florida Keys and when it came through the
Mississippi Gulf . . .' I was gone say, 'You lying bastard.' But the
man tricked me. He say, 'It's beyond me.'

"And that made me have three times stronger belief that there
is God, you understand? That's what the old people say, that you
can't tell God what to do. You can't do his work. Christians can
give the reason, and when they explain it to you, if you ain't into
it, you ain't gone pay it no mind. You turn and you say, 'Well if it's
a God, why he didn't do this and why he do that?' Then they tell
you, 'God don't come when you want him, but remember one
thing, he's always on time.' You see, that's the old thing. In other
words, you say, 'If God is so good, then why I get 20 years for

doing this little thing?' That's when they'll tell you, 'You know God just don't move when you want him to move. At least you got 20; you didn't get the electric chair.'

"Before I really got heavy into this, I wouldn't pay it no mind. I used to tell my grandmother when she be putting money in the church, 'Why you give that man that money for the church? This man driving Cadillacs and all this stuff. And here we can't eat and you giving him money?'

"She say, 'Because I ain't giving it to him. I'm paying my tithes for the Lord. When he meets God up in heaven or wherever, he got to answer to that.' So I say, 'But he got a Cadillac and he drives around all the time.' She say, 'Well, if you got a problem with the preacher's Cadillac, boy, then go to where they make 'em at in Detroit. Is it the Cadillac that you mad with? If you mad with the Cadillac, then go to Detroit. If you mad with the preacher, then change churches.'

"And I could not go for that until my life changed. Now I know that all some people have to hold onto is they religion. I have a crew of people that I call my Twilight Family, because I'm on from 7 to 9 and my show is called Twilight Time. They have become my extended, adopted family. At the end of each show, I pray. Just before I wind up my prayer, I ask all my Twilight Family to touch the radio and let's pray together. And as we pray, let's just don't pray for the food stamp recipients, let's pray for the people that issue the food stamps. Let's just don't pray for the poor. Let's pray for the rich. Let's just don't pray for the convict. Let's pray for the correctional officer.

"So many people call me and tell me that, Petey, I waits for your prayer and I touches the radio with you and I feel so good just touching the radio because I feel as though God has changed your life and your message comes through that radio. I even have chumps to walk up to me in the street and say, 'Man, I had to leave out my house cuz my mother was mad with me because I wouldn't come over and touch that radio. And nigger, I know you ain't nothing.' I wink and him and say, 'Praise the Lord and thank you, Jesus.'

"Then he'll say, 'But one thing about it, I ain't gone disrespect my mother. 'Cause if I'd a stayed there, I would have touched that radio because I love my mother.'

"I think the most touching thing that ever happened to me was about six or seven months ago. I went in to Ben's Chili Bowl—that's a lunchroom up on U Street and at some times the drug traffic guys come in there 'cause they hungry, drinking sodas and things. So I'm in there one day and it's crowded. Naturally when I go in, I'm the center of attraction. Half of it's positive and half of it's negative. Half of it is 'That's Petey Greene, he's come a long way.' And half is 'Aw fuck Petey Greene.' You understand what I'm saying?

"While I was standing there waiting to get my chili dog half smoke, a nigguh walked up to me with a baby in his hands and he said, 'Man, I want you to pray over this baby right now.' I said, 'Man, I ain't praying over that baby.' he said, 'Niggah, it ain't my baby. It's that girl's baby back there and as soon as she walked in the door, she said, That's Petey Greene, do you know him? I told her yeah, I know him, and she said get him to pray over my baby. This woman begged me to bring this baby. Man, I personally could care less about you praying over this baby.'

"So he called the girl up and three more of them came up and then I could see that they were drug users. The girl was, too. And she had a pretty baby. She said, 'Mr. Greene, this is my baby. I listen to you on the radio, along with my mother and everybody. Would you pray over my baby, please, that he won't have no bad luck?'

"Now when the conversation gets like this, a complete silence falls. The junkies start to looking. And something in me just seemed like it guided my hand and I put my hand on the baby's head and I began what I thought was going to be a short prayer. I was going to try to pray as low as I possibly could, but when I looked around, I was praying and I was praying loud. I was saying things like, 'Father if it's in your power like I know it is, bless this child through me if I'm working for you. Not only bless this child, bless his mother for having confidence in me as being one of your workers.'

"And as I began to pray, everybody got quiet and a funny feeling came over me. It seems as though the prayer was the right prayer and the length of the prayer was long enough for it to be a prayer. Everybody was just at a complete standstill and when I finished, the silence broke when the nigguh turned to the girl and say, 'Is you satisfied now?' She said, 'Thank you, Mr. Greene.' She had tears in her eyes and two or three of them nigguhs look like they was about to cry. I was sweating.

"Now that didn't make me step out of Ben's Chili Bowl and say I am one of God's workers, follow me. But after I got into my car, I just rode and said, 'Thank you, Jesus, for preparing me to be able to give that child something to hold onto, and God, many people holding onto your hand 'cause your hand don't never change. You got a unchanging hand.' I prayed to myself and I guess just the same way it came to me, it just went on away. In the next 15 or 20 minutes, if I saw the same nigguh at another corner, I'd probably cuss him out.

"But I believe it was God, and I believe that if I ever become a preacher, a minister, that God is gone call me to preach. With God's work, everything is possible, but I'm not gone go on no trial sermon. If he calls me, I will answer. I'm not gonna go to no Robert E. Webster Biblical Institute or no School of Divinity. I read the Bible every now and then. I don't cite scriptures. I hear guys when they be saying 'Matthew 25 says the least of these come unto me saith the Father.' I don't do that.

"When I pray in the evening, I pray to the point of deep down in me, and I pray from my experiences, because I know that people once thought that I was nothing, because of my drug addiction and a host of other things. **I think God has just taken me from a chunk of black coal and just smoothed me into a diamond. And pretty soon there ain't gone be no flaws in this diamond.**

"I hope there is somebody somewhere out there that'll say, 'Man, look at that nigger up there. I can remember when this nigger was right out here with us. This nigger was pushing a supermarket basket.' I used to have a supermarket basket to collect soda bottles and trash and stuff that I could sell, to get wine. I would go round in trash cans, just be picking up paper. And I hope somebody will say, 'Man, I remember when Greene used to do that. If he can stop drinking, I can, too.' I hope that I give somebody some incentive."

CHAPTER 25

When Drinking Ruled

ONLY A WOMAN of A'nt Pig's faithfulness and foresight could have seen the potential in Petey back in the days when nothing mattered to him but drinking. His resolve to give up heroin may have fueled his alcoholism, but the ember had flickered for as long as he could remember. He had watched alcohol nearly destroy his mother, his father, his uncle. And when Petey gave up his cowboy boots at age 12, he took on as a favorite pastime pouring the corners from discarded bottles to make enough for one shot.

Before 1960, he'd spent all his Army earnings, worked an occasional temporary job, then settled into doing only what was necessary to buy a bottle.

"Why you spending your life as a bum, boy?" Petey's mother asked him one day, as he sauntered toward her with the stench of liquor and unwashed skin billowing around him.

Petey stared coldly at her. "Because when you's a bum, this is what you do: You don't have to work. You sell newspapers and rags. People give you little odds and ends jobs. You just lay around, sleep in old cars, you ain't got to work. Evidently, I do not want to be a part of the workforce."

Jackie Greene shook her head in disgust. By this time, she was turning her life around, and she couldn't tolerate the reflection of her past mistakes. "If A'nt Pig didn't let you come home anytime you ready, you'd be singing a different tune. You ought to do better," Jackie offered as her parting shot before pulling out a coin for the bus-ride across town.

Although A'nt Pig never dreamed of kicking him out, she let Petey know how much she disapproved. Occasionally, she would stop him on his way up the stairs to ask, "Why don't you just try to straighten up sometimes, boy?" After these times, Petey would find work. He would go out to a golf course to carry golf bags. Or he'd get a stint with a moving company hiring men to ride long distances to deliver households, with their pianos, refrigerators, beds.

"They call me the lampshade man, 'cause I never lift nothing but lampshades and a few little hats. Fuck them deep freezers and all that," Petey reported to Freddy Coles one afternoon when he'd returned from a trip.

Another of his hustles was visiting housewives in the neighborhood who drank. They used Petey as their runner, because they didn't want their neighbors or their husbands to discover their liquor habits. When they got ready to send off for what they called their "nip," they'd turn to Petey. "Get me that Scotch and pick up a fifth of wine for yo'self, Petey," the women would say. "And bring my cigarettes."

In his reflections of the past, Petey talked about the payment for his errands. "Every now and then, I'd luck up and fuck one of them women. But sometimes I'd be so drunk, I didn't want no pussy. I just settled for the 50 cent they give me for a half smoke or a bag of fries."

Besides, Petey had a girlfriend, a pretty woman who loved wine as much as Petey did. To get money, she often dated older men, then she would spend the money they gave her on wine or gifts for Petey. But she finally got tired of that life and married a soldier. On her wedding night, once her groom fell asleep, she climbed out of the bedroom window to go find Petey.

She found him in a crap joint, where Petey had gone to drink away his sadness about losing the first woman he really fell in love with. When he looked up and saw her, Petey grabbed her arm and shoved her outside. "Why you do that? Why?" Drunk and angry, Petey slapped her face repeatedly. The next day, she took her bruises with her to Germany with her new husband.

Petey resumed his life of being a bum, working on trucks, laying in alleys, sitting around fires. He kept eating sardines and potted meat out of cans, cheese and crackers, french fries, half smokes with mayonnaise spread over them. He had seen how the other side lived, but at that time, he didn't care.

Later, he would offer an assessment of why he allowed himself to hit such a low. "I didn't want no restrictions. It wasn't nowhere for me to go. I couldn't discuss no Socrates, no Plato. I wasn't sitting around eating sardines by myself. There was 10 or 12 others, and I figure, looking back over it now, that was just like a cabinet. We were Phi Beta Kappa brothers. We were fraternity brothers. We was Q's in our own little bailiwick. There were Rhodes Scholars, 8th grade dropouts, 3rd grade dropouts. But we all had one thing in common, and the least common denominator was that we all liked wine.

"A white boy, he's drinking and smoking, he's a hippie. I was a bum; he's a hippie. Naw, we was hippies. Material shit didn't mean a thing to us. We didn't want to be programmed, or no guidelines. We could play golf, go to the movies. We could talk sports. And we could tell a motherfucker to kiss our ass. And we consumed gallons of wine. It's like being a kid again, messing up. Either you get lucky and come out of that, or either you go on and die being a wino bum."

A'nt Pig saw it at the time. "You are drinking because you don't want to do nothing. You's a lazy sucker," she'd tell Petey. "I'm not gone let you bring them other drunks in my house. If you want to be with them drunks, you stay out there wit' 'em. But when you come 'cross that door where I pay rent, Mr. Greene, your buddies ain't coming in.

"And don't you set in none of these soft chairs. Set on a box or something, boy, 'cause you stinkin'. And you probably lousey."

Following his visits to A'nt Pig's house, Petey would be called in as he walked past the barber shop. "Come here and get a haircut. Your grandmother called 'round here. We'll cut it, she'll pay," the barber, Mr. Yates, would explain.

Every now and then, A'nt Pig's prayers would be answered when Petey came up with a job. Once he got a job with a crew laying asphalt in the neighborhood. A'nt Pig would pack his lunch every day, and Petey would walk three blocks to the worksite. The next worksite was in Northeast, and Petey felt comfortable in the job. He made $125 a week, which was great money at the time, and he could get an advance on Friday's paycheck on Tuesdays.

This time, Petey took himself to the barber shop, paid his own bill, bought a $20 Panama straw hat, a pair of black and white Footjoys, and grey slacks. He still hung with his crew of wine-drinking friends, who had moved into a buddy's house once the man's wife left, unable to stand the drinking.

Then winter approached, and Petey knew he wouldn't want the outside work that remained. As usual, fate stepped in for him. On the site one day, a foreman called out, "Anybody know anything about how to fix flowers?" Rubbing his hands in the chill October air, Petey—who knew nothing about flowers— answered yes, he did.

They drove out Military Road to the house of the man who owned the construction company Petey worked for, where the Mrs. waited for someone to help plant her garden for the winter. A'nt Pig could hardly catch her breath from laughter that night as Petey told her the story. "The flower was called a Pachysandra or something. You put it in the ground in the winter and it blossoms in the spring. I didn't know nothing about it, you know. When the woman told me we were going to the nursery, I thought she was going to pick up some children. We get to the nursery and it's about flowers."

They picked up peat moss and plant food, and a pick for Petey to use to soften the ground. Back at the house, Petey met the butler and the maid, both black and both with their noses in the air to look at him. But Petey's gift of gab won their employer, Mrs. Spears, over right away. He regaled her with stories about the Army, once he found out her son was overseas in the service. At the end of the day, Petey had been invited back to rake the leaves and tend the grounds.

"We starting a friendship," Petey recounted later. "She got me raking the leaves and cleaning the porch. The butler and the handyman put them flowers down. That ground was too hard for me."

The black people in the Spears's employ resented Petey greatly, especially when they'd notice him down in the basement shooting pool whenever Mrs. Spears left to attend her social club meetings. Mrs. Spears didn't care; she found Petey to be funny and charming, and that was all that mattered.

Never one to let well enough alone, Petey approached Mrs. Spears one day. "Miss Spears, I can't come back out here no more."

"Why not, Petey?"

"'Cause I can't get a chance to work on Saturday, to get the overtime, unless I'm laying asphalt in the week," Petey said, adding a touch of sadness to his voice.

Mrs. Spears smiled softly, pushing a wayward strand of silver hair from her high forehead. "Who's your boss. Scotty? And who's Scotty's boss. Mr. Spears? And who's Mr. Spears's boss? I am. So, you come out here on Saturday, stay for a little while, and you can get the overtime."

Delighted, Petey came every Saturday, filling the days with looking through Mrs. Spears's scrapbooks of her daughter and son, drinking buttermilk that he pretended to like for Mrs. Spears's sake, and occasionally doing a little yard work. The fellows on the crew started calling Petey "Little Spears," acknowledging that he could call the shots about the kind of work he wanted to do.

Petey might have settled into being a "gardener," had it not been for hitting the number. On a dollar, he won $540, and, feeling rich and invincible, went to Mrs. Spears to tell her he was quitting the company. She felt heavy hearted, but gamely assured him he could have the job back if he ever wanted it.

"Man, them people is rich! The way that lady like you, she would have left you something in her will," one of Petey's friends on the crew chided. "You crazy to give up that job. Had the butler giving you a ride downtown in them people's Packard and all!"

Far from a ride in a luxury car, Petey got a ride to the drunk tank days later. That time, the judge gave him a substantial sentence.

"You've been in front of me too many times, Mr. Greene, for being drunk and disorderly. I'm going to make sure you don't come back next Saturday. I'm going to give you six months to clean yourself out."

Chronic drunks spent their sentences at a facility outside of Washington, D.C., in Occoquan, Virginia, known as the DC Workhouse for drunks and misdemeanor cases. Petey's job there was to make up beds, which he finished in record time so he could spend the bulk of the day roaming around the complex. Additionally, Petey got tapped to work with the Jail's recreation program, coaching baseball and basketball.

For some drunks, the Occoquan facility replaced family because of the caring attitude of a white man, Mr. Flemming, who was in charge. Not only would he refuse to release drunks in inclement or cold weather, he would send someone to DC to look for them if he knew they'd left with government checks and were likely to be drunk out in freezing temperatures.

Petey's destiny kept him out of the drunk tank long enough to befriend a group of teens who gave him wine and, ultimately, would take him along for the ride that would lead to their arrest in a liquor store stick-up.

The teens loved Petey's company because he could talk trash. In fact, they put him up to a contest with the most famous local deejay of the day, Lord Fauntleroy Bandie.

Bandie, in his double breasted jackets, ascots, straight-legged pants, and British accent, attended Howard University and worked as a disc jockey for WUST radio station, in its studio on U Street. He made a name for himself by sitting in the studio window, in the Republic Theater, calling out the scene in front of him.

The things he said sounded as though Petey Greene made the rhyme. Off the top of his head statements like, "As I sit here looking near and far, I see Pamella Shivers in Rob Marvin's car." Petey's teen admirers came to him one day with a challenge.

"We know somebody you can't beat talking. Lord Fauntleroy Bandie."

Petey propped himself up on one elbow, as the boys seated themselves on the stoop by his feet. "Fuck y'all. I'll eat him up, spit him out."

"No you can't," they insisted.

Petey rubbed his thick mustache. "Tell you what, y'all go get me a gallon of wine and we'll go right where he at."

The boys gathered up $4 and within ten minutes, were back with the wine. On route to Bandie's U Street window, the parade of winos, teens and curious onlookers grew to nearly 500 people—all drawn by the knowledge that Petey Greene had been challenged to out-talk Bandie. Cars slowed, horns honked, and one emissary went in to tell Bandie the gauntlet had been thrown.

"Well, it looks like the crowd is full of glee. Who is the gentleman who wants to out-talk me?" Bandie asked, as he stepped outside the studio. He looked over to see a man with untended mutton-chop sideburns, wearing a torn, dirty army jacket, untied and scuffed army boots, and soiled jeans.

Petey's mind buzzed. "Well, I'm a bum and you're mighty clean, but the man who's gonna talk with you is Ralph Petey Greene."

The crowd roared, bets flowed, and everyone strained to hear. The banter ran back and forth for about 30 minutes, with each man scoring points but Petey maintaining a strong lead. Feeling his rating slipping and Petey's gaining, Bandie glanced at his watch then delivered the final blow.

"Well, the sun is gone, I got to get out the shade. You talk for wine, but Bandie gets paid."

The teens whooped and hollered. "Aw, Petey, he knocked your shit out!"

The stage was set, though, for a great friendship between the two rhymers. Bandie would get into his promo car, with WUST written on the side, and drive the local streets looking for Petey.

Like others before him, he puzzled over the waste. "As talented as you are, why d'you drink this wine?" He'd even offer Petey jobs with him spinning records at the Y. Petey would spin a couple, then say, "Bandie, give me 2 dollars," that would immediately go toward a bottle of cheap wine.

Bandie went on to marry an heiress, while Petey took one ride too many with his teen pals. The next time he landed in D.C. Jail, he did not go to Occoquan. He checked in for the long haul on a robbery beef that he couldn't escape, even though the teenagers testified that they had taken their older pal along just for the laughs, just to hear him talk.

Petey went into jail for the final time in late 1960, was released in 1965, and left all criminal intent behind. But for the next 15 years, his love affair with alcohol would threaten all that mattered to him.

*   *   *

Petey's voice: On the Wagon

"I had never thanked God for the things that happened in my life. I was always begging him. Whenever I was in trouble, I would call on him. So, I had to make up my mind that it was time for me to thank him. I made up my mind about that in 1981. It was after I'd stopped drinking.

"The last time I was drunk, I was begging him, again. I begged him to help me stop drinking, because drinking was becoming detrimental to me physically, mentally, morally. I asked him one night, as I was laying back there in the bed with a hangover, that if he would for one more time get me through this crisis of sickness and nausea, that if he would do that for me, I would never take another drink. And it seems as though after I had finished praying and begging him, that my hangover began to go away.

"The next morning, I woke up and I felt as though I hadn't been drinking. That was about three years ago, in April. Wasn't nobody here but me, by myself. And at the same time, I had been hitting that pipe. One compensated for the other. When I stopped messing with that oil, I stopped hitting that pipe. I knew I could be much better, perform much better with a sober mind.

"I know my limitations. I know how shrewd I am and I know that God has blessed me with a mind to deal with all types of situations, and I knew that the only time I was at a disadvantage was either when I was high or when I was drunk.

"I had conditioned myself to believe I needed alcohol to give me courage, and I know that was a lie because I been holding people's attention from my formative years of living, not my teenage years, but 7 or 8 years old. I could talk and I know that I didn't need to drink to be humorous.

"And I know the only times I would actually make a spectacle of myself was when I was drinking. People who didn't like me but pretended to like me would buy me drinks. The people who cared something about me would always get into arguments with those other people about giving me liquor. The people who were concerned about me had problems with me drinking because they had seen my accomplishments after I had become a productive citizen of society.

"People would catch me sober after seeing me drunk and they would show me in detail the good things I was doing for people in the community. How young people and old alike looked up to me, both white and black. Vice President Hubert Humphrey listened to my show and was ON the show one time. My friends would tell me how much good I could do for people, but when I went on a binge, I'm giving people a chance to shake their head and say, 'Petey's not for real.'

"One time when I was on WOL, Herman Washington was public affairs manager then, and he pulled me aside to tell me I was ruining my image showing up drunk out in the community. I really appreciated him for that. And I stayed sober for a while after we talked.

"I think what finally got to me, my doctor told me, 'I listen to you all the time. You're always talking about you like your car, your big house and all that. But you're lying, 'cause every time I look up, you're coming here to me to get over these hangovers or you got the shakes. You are going through all the changes of an alcoholic. Eventually, your drinking is going to mean you won't have the house and car and everything you say you like.'

"Sometimes I used to vomit blood because I wouldn't eat. I know I was killing myself, physically. I'm not a damn fool. But I would always stay down for about six months, stop drinking for about six months. Then go back. One of my best buddies said, 'You're not an alcoholic, 'cause there's no way in the world you could stop drinking like you do for six or seven months then all of a sudden go on a drunk for about ten days.' But it was because I liked liquor. I still like it. I really like drinking liquor. Burn so good, and it makes you have such a good feeling.

"I don't touch it, though, I guess because I'm living alone and by myself and all the income I'm making and got to make for Petrie and Pine . . . and again, it's back to God. God has been good to me. As much as I used to drink and all of the things that I done, I never got to a point where everything crashed in on me.

"And I have enough sense from my hustling mentality to know that you can't keep getting away all the time.

"When I was a bum and a drunk, people used to stop and talk to me and start crying because they knew me as I grew up. They would say, 'Man, how can you let your life go like this, as smart as you are?' I mean, these were guys.

"One friend of mine, he's dead and gone now, he used to promote shows. He was bringing in a big show on a boat. Dewey Hughes was working with me then. One day I was going down the street—I was drinking then, heavy, wasn't paying no mind and wasn't thinking 'bout no shows. And somebody told me, "Man, see you down on the boat.'

"I say, 'What you talking about?' He said, 'I see your name on the poster with Peaches and Herb and all.' I finally went over and saw my name on the poster. I called the guy and he said, 'I ain't had time to get to you, so you gone do it. I'ma pay you. I just went on and used your name. Sue me.'

"We went on and I done the show, and we had a talk. He said, 'Nigger, you were the best in the business. Who else I'ma get?' Gene Chandler didn't show up that night on the boat and I kept the whole crowd at bay. They was hollering for Gene Chandler and hollering 'bout getting they money back. I was the MC and I kept 'em entertained. My man told me, 'You see, that's one of the reasons I got you. When I see Gene Chandler, I'm gone knock his head off. But nobody could handle them people like you did.'

"He gave me a piece of money and he gave Dewey a piece of money. Dewey wouldn't take the money. Dewey said, 'Give it to Petey.' So he gave me all of it. When we started out the door, he called me back. Dewey was gone. He said, 'Watch him.' I said, 'What you mean?' He said, 'Watch Dewey. He's dangerous.' I said, 'Man, you don't know nothing 'bout that man. How can you say that?' He said, 'He refused money. Any nigger that refuses money don't mean you no good.'

"Jack Tinker told me that. That's just a hustling mentality. Professionals have idiosyncracies. Hustlers have it. Hustlers know that money is where it's at. That's their thing. He said, 'You know, Dewey all right with me. I know Sam. I know 'em all. But that nigger refused money. Anytime a nigger refuse money, he's dangerous.'

"You know I didn't pay that no mind, 'cause I know me and this man's all right. I told Dewey what Jack said. Dewey said, 'Aw, don't pay that no mind.' But I lay back sometimes thinking 'bout that. So, you see, Lurma, I get lessons from all walks of life. I listen to politicians, I listen to hustlers, but most of all, I always have to go back to my grandmother, with the basics."

*   *   *

The time Jack Tinker pulled Petey from the bottle to emcee a show was not the first time he'd been given a chance to end a binge for the stage. Before his arrest for robbery, when he was living as what he called "a winehead bum sleeping in alleys," an old friend started looking for him.

Taking long strides, Petey loped down one of his favorite blocks toward a group of kids who loved to talk with him when they got out of school. This day, though, instead of asking him to tell them stories, they had a message.

"Hey Petey. There's been a man come 'round here two or three times looking for you. We told him we didn't know you. He had a big brand new automobile and he say he was your friend, so he shoulda knowed where you at. He just left. He should be back pretty soon. He got a big bottle.'

As the wide-eyed children continued to describe the man, Petey looked up to see his old friend "Hawk" Chase coming his way.

"You little motherfuckers! Thought y'all told me you didn't know this man?" Hawk's friendly exasperation failed to ruffle the kids. They shrugged their shoulders and headed on down the street when Petey assured them the man they took as a stranger was really a friend.

"Goddamn, hey Hawk! How you doing?" Petey reached out to grab his buddy with a hug and handshake, using his childhood nickname.

Chase looked at the backs of the retreating children. "Man, I asked these little black bastards did they know your motherfucking ass. They told me they don't even know you." Petey grinned, scratched his stubble, and waved toward the children who were turning the corner toward their houses. "This is my crew. What's up man?"

Chase steered Petey to his new Bonneville. "Look at you, you bum ass motherfucker. Reach down there and get yourself a drink." Petey picked up the fifth of Scotch and took a long swallow. Wiping his mouth on his sleeve, he asked Hawk, "What you want, man?" Pulling out into traffic, Chase explained, "My son just bought a nightclub over in Baltimore. We getting ready to put live acts in there. Can't have but one emcee. That's you. We waiting for you."

Petey nodded his assent and Chase continued on route to his son's house. "Man we want you to emcee, and don't worry about a thing." Assessing Petey's disheveled state, Chase and his son determined that step one would be a trip downtown to buy clothes. They bought three outfits, but as Petey tried the clothes on, Chase and his son realized step one should have been the bathhouse.

They took Petey to their house and gave him two baths before putting him into the new clothes and heading on over to the Comedy Club on Pennsylvania Avenue in Baltimore where he worked as emcee for nearly a year. He spent many nights in a hotel above the club, and other nights, he returned to D.C. to give A'nt Pig some money and hang out with his ne'er do well friends.

"Everything was going along all right until I found out something I shouldn'ta found out. I found out that if you was a entertainer or worked in the club, your check to get liquor was always open. You could get it without money, and then when it come time to be paid, they would pull all your checks. When I found out you could drink without money, sheee-it. They sometimes wouldn't be able to pay me. Sometimes they would have to loan me money, 'cause I be done drank up all the money," Petey recalled in talking about his life.

"I fell off the stage one night, drunk, and they thought it was part of the act. I fell back into the drums. The thing that was so beautiful, when nigguhs in Washington heard I was over there, they started bringing their business to The Comedy Club."

Ironically, drinking and falling off the stage didn't end Petey's stint at the club. Instead, he stopped going nearly a year into the job when a big snowfall grounded him in DC one night. After that, he just stopped commuting to Baltimore. Eventually, Chase and his son lost The Comedy Club, and years later, Chase became a minister in suburban Maryland.

Even a reputation of getting too drunk to perform well didn't end Petey's opportunities for stand-up comedy. His friend Ed Murphy, a well known entrepreneur, made sure of that.

*   *   *

Petey's voice: Murph's Supper Club

"Ed Murphy was the first one of the guys my age to make progress in black nightclub life here. And he handled it real well because, by him coming up hustling, he had enough suaveness with him to maintain a club with an atmosphere that would attract the doctor, lawyer, the Howard University crew. And then he had the ability to attract a certain segment of hustlers, too.

"We used to call him 8-Ball, because he could play that pool real good. He was a helluva gambler and a ladies man, at all times. I liked his club, Ed Murphy's Supper Club. You had to wear a necktie or a turtle-neck when you went in there. Wasn't no rowdy shit in there.

"But he allowed me to do things he just wouldn't let other people do. I used to go in there drunk with tennis shoes on and everything. People would run and get Ed, and he would come out and he would stand back and fold his arms. I'd be up on the stage, took the microphone from somebody.

"I remember the first time I got up on the stage at Murph's, Donnie Hathaway was performing. I got the mike and went on and on. Everybody was laughing. A few mackacukalackies got mad, you know. Ed would tell the people, 'Leave him alone," so people would pass me a drink and I'd talk, though I'd be all fucked up. Then he would come, walk right up, wouldn't touch me, say, 'All right, dick, come down off that stage. Come on here, dick.'

"I'd come on down. He'd say, 'Goddamn, that's my man, he can tell that toast. Give this nigger another drink.' Then he'd take me on in the back to his office and say, 'Goddammit, boy, you're still sharp as a motherfucker, telling them jokes.'

"And I never abused that, you understand. Like you wouldn't see me in there two or three months at a time. You wouldn't see me in there 'til I go on a drunk.

"One time he sent for me, asked me did I want to make some money. He said 'It's a bus load of doctors from Detroit or somewhere and they're having a whole weekend to theyself away from their wives. I'm going to have a smoker. I want you up there talking shit and telling toasts.' So I went up there that Saturday morning at 10 o'clock. He had all them old doctors in there and had two broads dancing. I'm telling them goddamn toasts. I was sober when I went in. I was drunk as a motherfucker when I come out. The thing was over at 1 o'clock in the day! Can you imagine, 1 o'clock in the day, stiff drunk.

"Ed gave me my $50. He always did like my toasts and rhymes. His favorite was one called The Thin Thin Dime, about a guy who was rich and had plenty money and fell in love with a whore. The whore turned him around. After he had been so good to her, she told him, 'Here's a thin thin dime . . . I wouldn't give you nothing but a thin thin dime . . .' It all rhymes, and Ed used to love it."

"Ed Murphy's club was a bad motherfucker! He brought in the type of entertainment that people wasn't ready for almost. Wasn't nobody ready for Donnie Hathaway. See Donnie Hathaway was going to Howard, and coming down to Murphy's fucking around. That boy was way ahead of his time."

Chapter 26

Missing A'nt Pig

Petey lived his life exactly as he wanted to, and he had only a few regrets. Chief among them were allowing his alcoholism to drive his wife and kids away, and not having his grandmother with him to enjoy his success. He rarely gave a speech or talked of his past without bringing his grandmother's memory alive.

Petey's Voice: My grandmother's wisdom
  "If my grandmother was alive, she'd be sitting right in that chair while you over there recording or we be in the other room. She'd be sitting right there now, smoking a pipe, 100-some years old with a nurse washing her and taking care of her. Because I wouldn't put her in an institution. She didn't put me in one. My grandmother never ever wanted me to be confined nowhere.
  "And I'm so sorry that she's not here to enjoy this good living. I told her from a little boy when she used to have me with my head laying down in her lap, and I used to look up at her ... we was poor, too ... and I would tell her, 'When I get big, I'ma get you a big car, I'mone take you to the Lincoln Colonnade. We just gone have a good time.' The Lincoln Colonnade was one of our elite dance halls. All the muckety mucks used to go. 'And I'mone have you an evening gown, with big rings and everything.'
  "She would say, 'I know you is, Rabbit. But you know you so lazy, you got to work.' And I'd say, "I'ma work, Grandma, 'cause I'ma have to take care of you.'
  "That's why I didn't have no problem when I was overseas sending her all that money. I used to just send it and send it. She

believed in me so much. I must have sent her about $25,000. I was stealing good, I was black-marketing. I was doing everything. Could have bought the Lincoln Colonnade.

"My grandmother taught me, 'Boy, you ain't got to keep reaching for the moon. Just snatch one of them stars and you'll be all right. Let the rest of them nigguhs reach for that moon. You got to go past the stars to get to the moon. Just take one of them stars and keep on stepping.' Her philosophy was good. And she could smoke that pipe, that stinking-ass pipe. Union Leader was her favorite tobacco, so if a nigguh bring her Prince Albert, she'd take that back and change it and get Union Leader. She used to dip that snuff, chew that tobacco. But whatever she was doing, whether it was smoking a pipe, dipping snuff or chewing tobacco, she could philosophize so good and so easy.

"When I was a kid, I was sure of my grandmother's love at all times. When I got in trouble, fuck a lawyer. When I look out in the courtroom, I wasn't looking for no lawyer. I would see if A'nt Pig was out there. If she was out there, solid. And she couldn't tell you one law from another, but I know she could put people to sleep. 'Just get my boy out this time.'

"She say, 'If you get into trouble, I ain't coming a step to get you. I mean every word of it.' I ain't pay it no mind. I didn't go try to get in no trouble, but if I get in trouble, she gone kick the door down. I know this. She did not want to see me institutionalized."

"My grandmother could make a good story out of anything, and she had something sharp to say about everything that was going on. Take Alex Haley's 'Roots,' for example. I know my grandmother would have looked at it and perceived it like this: Now you see that nigguh done made all that money with 'Roots,' and going back finding his folks. He lying anyway, but now watch all these nigguhs start to going back looking for they roots, and while they going backwards, watch that white man go straight ahead while these nigguhs are looking for they roots. And when them nigguhs look back, this white man gonna be kicking 'em in the ass while they bent over looking for they roots.

"She would have said that, I know she would have. And it seems like that is really what happened. We had come so far in the 60s, opening doors, the civil rights laws signed and everything. We rolling, you understand? All of a sudden everybody gets into looking for they roots and heritage. And we looked around again here in the 80s, the Voting Rights bill is in jeopardy, they talking 'bout giving money to private schools for segregation. If my grandmother was still living, she'd say: See, now that never woulda happened if you nigguhs had kept looking straight ahead like that cracker.

"And that is the truth. All of a sudden finding your heritage was a main factor, when nigguhs like my grandmother been trying to find a dollar."

Yet, Petey always kept the balance. A slap at the race, then praise.

"You know, people who come up through that era and before her were kinda wise. I guess that's why Frederick Douglass, Harriett Tubman, and all them people was able to gain and beat the white man so good. Don't care how bad it was, them people back then musta could handle 'em for us to get as far as we got.

"So, we had lynchings, but some of them nigguhs had to be sho' nuff sharp, shrewd and intelligent to come out from all of that, the deprivations of the south." Still, Petey never strayed long from humor, and found a way to lighten even the deepest of reflections.

"When I was coming up, though, we didn't follow nobody 'til a motherfucker got to talking 'bout integration. When Rosa Parks and all them people got to talking they was tired, they was tired of taking that shit, you understand? She wasn't the one that was supposed to be the leader, you understand, but she was the one that God had picked to open up the eyes. Here comes Martin, who had the know-how and the heart.

"See, we wasn't following nobody. We would follow a *parade*. If the Elks parade come ... *diddywhop, diddywhop* ...get tired, stop, go on back home or some motherfucking where, or follow it to the end of the line. That's all you follow was a goddamn parade.

Or follow them nigguhs when they getting out of a crap joint and somebody say 'POLICE,' you follow the first nigguh out that window.

"But it's just a matter of time, another Martin gone come, somewhere. Everybody says we'll never get another Martin Luther King. Goddamnit, they said we'd never get another Paul Robeson, another Malcom X. There's always gonna be somebody. God is gone always put somebody.

"You know, they keep trying to tell me that it's me. The Lord KNOW it ain't me; he done told me that it ain't me. Said 'It ain't you, Petey, so don't even pay no 'tention 'bout what the rest of these people say. I'm God and I control you. What I want you to do, I'ma send you to do, then I'ma snatch you back.'

"Thank you, Lord, don't send me too far out there. 'Cause He know I ain't got no heart, you understand? You can laugh if you want to, but I'm being very serious. I can make a move at times and expound on a point and get it over and establish the fact that I know what I'm talking 'bout, and I'm concerned. But I be looking widely around for people with blunt instruments in they hand or daggers or some motherfucking shit ... So I'm going to stay at a running distance at all times.

"But, there will eventually come a person who these nigguhs are going to have to follow."

CHAPTER 27

Loving the Children

PETEY'S PHILOSOPHY OF life precluded too much crying over spilt milk. But not having his children around numbered among his chief regrets. In fact, he envied his good friend and co-worker Charles "Chuck" Ramsey's family life and actually felt a low, heavy sadness at times when he saw Chuck interact with his daughter, Kenya, and son, Kofi, who were near in age to Petey's children Petra and Pine.

"I can't go to Chuck's house too much, 'cause it gets to me when the children run up to hug him, saying 'Daddy this and Daddy that.' It just makes me miss my magpies," Petey would say a year before his death.

He wanted to do so much for the children and believed he could. "Materialistic things mean a lot to me in my life and keeps me away from drinking and makes it possible for me to keep a sober mind and a clear mind. And that enables me to be the father that my children would like for me to be, and to know that they won't have to reach the age of 20 or 21 and be broke like I was," Petey continued.

But for too many years, his love for the children—though genuine and strong from the moments of their births in 1968 and 1969—did not keep him from drinking. And, finally, the drinking drove their mother to take the children and leave. Judy—who began her love affair with Petey Greene a little over a year after he started working for UPO—left for brief stretches several times, but in the final break, she took the children to California, then later to Miami.

Devastated and heartbroken, Petey lived for the times he would speak with the children or have them for visits. When they came, he generously bought them whatever they wanted. When they were little, however, the generosity came with a caveat typical of Petey Greene.

"I ain't buying y'all no two of nothing. Y'all got to share," he admonished when Petra and Pine each wanted a slinky toy.

"But I might want to play with it at the same time he wants it," Petra pouted.

"You go buy your own then," Petey tossed over his shoulder on the way to the check-out counter of Toys 'R Us.

When the children got older, he relaxed that rule. What he retained was An't Pig's advice on spankings.

He explained the philosophy to Judy: "An't Pig didn't believe in punishment; she believed just whip a nigguh's ass. Don't cut off his recreation, nothing. Whip him. And beat his ass good enough so when you get through, he won't do it no more. She said if you cut a child's shit off, you gone make him sneaky. You'll make him sly, because when you turn your back, he'll do something. He'll go out when he know he ain't supposed to go out."

Judy needed the explanation because Petey lit into Pine over a broken rule, alarming her with the intensity of the spanking. She agreed, however, that their 6-year-old son had a lesson to learn.

An hour before the spanking, Petey could not find his namesake, nicknamed Pine. Summer darkness had begun to fall in Petey's suburban Maryland neighborhood of split-level and two-story houses. Children's voices could be heard ringing out to mothers calling them in for dinner. Petey stepped onto the sidewalk that divided his well-manicured lawn, and saw only Petra coming toward the house on her bicycle. Both children knew the rule: Get home before dark.

"Where Pine," Petey asked, looking down the curved road.

"I don't know."

"Well, go out there and find him," Petey demanded of his 7-year-old daughter. About 10 minutes later, Petra returned to the house unable to locate Pine. With a discomfort edging near fear,

Petey jumped into his blue Cadillac. "Come on, let's go," he said to Petra, who climbed in the passenger side as Petey backed out into the street. In less than a block, they saw one of Pine's friends heading to his own house.

"You seen Pine?" Petra shouted.

"Yeah, he over at James's house."

Relief flooded Petey's clenched guts, only to be replaced by anger. Aware of what awaited her brother, Petra picked up the brass knocker on James's door with the ready warning for her sheepish brother who stood across the threshold: "You gone get it, Pine."

Pine's legs could hardly carry him to the luxury automobile. While he stepped in cautiously, he started pleading, "Daddy, I didn't know how late it was."

Petey shook his head, "Noooo, Pine," and closed his ears to the sobs that started wracking Pine's perfectly formed frame. "Daddy, I'm not gone do it again. Daddy, I'm sorry."

Back at the house, Judy had dinner on the table. "Petra, wash your hands and go in the kitchen," Petey commanded through clenched teeth. He grabbed Pine and headed for the master bedroom. There, Petey picked up his belt and lashed it across Pine's bottom. Pine screamed so loudly after the first four licks, his sister dashed in the room wild-eyed.

"Daddy, don't hit him no more!"

"Get the hell out of here before I hit you, too!" Petey's threatening voice belied his own hurt. Seeing his beautiful son sobbing, welts rising on his cinnamon-brown legs, Petey dropped the belt and went into the bathroom and cried. It was the last time he spanked Pine.

Petra got her last spanking from Petey a few years later when the children came to visit. Proud as a peacock, Petey walked downtown with the children on either side. Coming out of a watch-repair store, they ran into one of Petey's fans and casual acquaintances.

"Hey Petey, I didn't know you had these pretty children. Let me take they picture."

Deep into her pre-adolescent posture, Petra looked coldly at Petey. "I don't want no picture taken." Surprised and a bit embarrassed, Petey looked down at the child he called his favorite. "Come on, Petrie, take the picture."

"I don't want no picture taken, Daddy," she retorted, folding her arms across her chest, convinced that it wasn't her best-looking day and believing she could have her way.

Petey's face began to flush. "Petrie, I ain't gone tell you no more."

She heard the rumble under his words, turned and stood next to him while the man who was a stranger to her made his day. "Wow, I got a picture of Petey Greene and his two children. They so pretty, look like movie stars," the man gushed.

As soon as the man moved out of earshot, Petey steered the children toward their parked car, then spoke low and slowly. "We still going to the movies. But before I start the car, let me tell you something: Petrie, when we get home, I'm gone beat your ass. What you did today was not right. How many little children you know can be walking down the street and people stop to take they picture? So, I'm gonna beat your ass."

Following the two-hour matinee show, Petey stopped on several errands, giving the children cause to believe his anger may have dissipated. Toward evening on the ride out Oxon Hill Road, as the car turned onto Fort Foote Road, Pine leaned over to Petey's ear from the back seat. "You ain't gone beat her, right?"

"You know I got to do it, son. I don't want you to interfere," Petey stated calmly. Pine tried once more. "Daddy . . . ."

"Shut up."

The children hopped out of the car, stepped onto the hardwood floor of Petey's foyer, looked into the blue-carpeted living room, and tried to scamper on toward the den to play a board game. But Petey put his hand on Petra's shoulder.

"All right. Let's get ready, Petrie." Making her bare her rear end, Petey took off his belt and landed it hard 10 times. Leaving her sobbing on her bed, Petey returned to the den to watch television with Pine. About 15 minutes later, he called to her, but she refused to answer.

Her stubbornness reminded Petey of a time when Petra was less than 8 years old, angry with him and Judy. She slammed her room door, locked it, and refused to answer his calls from the other side. Unruffled, Petey went to his garage toolbox, picked up a screwdriver, and took the hinges off Petra's bedroom door.

"Get mad if you want to, now. Just go on, but you don't lock no doors around here. You ain't the boss. You ain't paying no rent, and you don't need no privacy. You don't need no door on your room, Petrie, I'll just take the whole door," he lectured while he lifted the door from its frame, his face showing no trace of the amusement tickling his heart.

*   *   *

For a man who cherished his children and once loved their mother, Petey talked very little about his life with Judy. His hurt ran deeply, but he adamantly refused to paint his ex-wife in a negative light or to cast her in any role other than victim of his mistakes.

Petey's voice: A Love Lost

"Judy is very pretty, extremely beautiful. We were at the Howard Theater one time when I was the emcee and Walter Jackson was singing. He met Judy and said she was the most gorgeous woman he had ever seen.

"She didn't have to work after I got the job at Channel 26 and was still working at UPO, but she said the walls was closing in on her. She couldn't stand to be a housewife.

"But this marriage situation is my fault, 'cause goddamn if Judy wasn't good to my motherfucking ass. I take all the weight. I fucked the marriage up. It wasn't Judy. One of her friends had a hand in it—telling her I was messing with another broad. But I fucked it up. I was just a dog-ass motherfucker like most men are. I was a no-good trifling motherfucker.

"Judy was beautiful, good to me, and represented me all shapes, forms and fashion, and didn't fuck around on me or nothing. I just wanted all the pussy in the world, and messed up what would have been the most beautiful marriage in the world.

"We will never ever go back together. I don't want to do it no more, but she was the best wife any man could have ever wanted. You know she had a bad side, she did some few little things to me, but everything Judy did, I deserved. I was a no-good husband, it was just as simple as that.

"One time Judy took me to court, but she dropped the charges. I would have probably gotten a 30-day probation or something like that if she hadn't dropped it. I had been asking her every day if she was gonna drop the charges, telling her 'My career will be messed up . . .' She said, 'Well, you shoulda thought about that when you was getting drunk and jumping on me.'

"The way I knew she was gonna drop it was this: I was laying in bed and my little boy Pine crawled into the room. He was about 6 or 7; he was a young boy. He eased in there and whispered. 'Hey Daddy, Mama gone drop them charges. She already told me and Petrie, but don't tell her I said it,' and he crawled on back out of the room. I know he wasn't lying and I know she had discussed this with them, and that's the type of thing that you see in a family. Good wife, good children, and liquor don't let you see that.

"If Judy and the children was to come back now, her and the children could stay here and I would stay in the house I have in Washington. Her name is on this house. But Judy don't know nothing about finances. I'm gone have to keep some money for my magpies, 'cause she'll just spend it.

"When Petrie and Pine come visit, I take 'em everywhere they supposed to go. They spent summer before last with me and we had a excellent time. In fact, I thought I was reborn, again. We went to the museums and all down to the Capitol, and I was explaining different things. I'm a very educated person about geography, history and all that. I teach 'em everything but black history. I let they mother teach them that.

"Comfortable is a word that I try to put in my vocabulary for my children. Another word, because it's two or 'em, is share. When they come to stay with me, they say, 'Daddy, it's a different ballgame when we get up here with you.' I say, 'It's no question about it. Get that vacuum, let's roll.' They jive work at home, you know, but not like I make 'em work. I make 'em work unusually hard. Judy makes 'em work 'cause she has to go to work. Judy shows them the luxurious part of life. They travel and get to see everything.

"Everytime they come, it's 'Daddy, you seen Richard Pryor Sunset Live? We saw it. Daddy, you don't never go nowhere.' If I can work a social trip into a business trip, I'll go. Anytime I leave here, I want to be working."

CHAPTER 28

Balling Out of Control

THE DRAWBACKS TO a failed marriage went beyond mental and emotional anguish and into physical danger for Petey. But only on rare occasions did he pull himself back from the edge.

Petey's Voice: One Warning Sign

"When me and my wife wasn't together, I had too many women in and out of the apartment I was in. I was living in the Massachusetts House and I used to have different broads over every night. I had this broad in there one night and we was jammin' and the broad got high. Well, we got in an argument and she ran out in the hall naked and rang the fire alarm. Oh buddy, when the police came, I'm in there holding my door shut and she in the hall naked.

"They knocked on the door and when I didn't open it, they said they would knock the door down. I'm thinking, 'Oh my God, I got all this glass furniture in here.' I opened the door with my robe on. The police came in with the woman. 'Hey man, was this woman in here?' I said, 'Yeah, she was in here, but this woman is crazy.' They said, 'Where her clothes?'

"They were looking around, getting her clothes. So the black roller, he was hip. He took me to the side, told me, 'Man, let me tell you something. You a bachelor, right? Man, you can't fuck all the women you see. This gone cost you $25 for a false alarm.'

"So they got all her clothes but couldn't find her coat. Could not find that coat for anything. I said, 'I don't care, just get her outta here.' They let the broad go and took me down to the precinct to pay the $25. I wouldn't even go back to my apartment. I went over to a broad's house that I was going with. I stayed over there for three days. As soon as we finally decided to come back to my apartment, she walked right in and found the coat. Everybody had looked for that coat, she found the coat.

"I say, 'I'ma stop letting nigguhs use my apartment.'

"Then another time I was fucking a different broad, and when we got through, I looked down and I say, 'What's wrong? You didn't tell me your period was on.' She said, 'Shoot, my period is not on. What do you mean?' I say, 'Look at all this blood!' She say, 'It's coming from you.' I said, 'Shit!'

"Blood was coming out my dick. I grabbed my pants and started to running, trying to catch a cab with my pants halfway on. I ran in to the Washington Hospital Center. The cab driver was saying, 'You owe me . . .' I said, 'Fuck that shit.' When I got inside, the nurse was telling me, 'You got to get behind . . .' I said, 'I ain't got to get behind no motherfucking body! My dick is bleeding!'

"Another nurse came up and said, 'Let him see the doctor. That's Petey Greene.' I was sober as a motherfucker. I went in and saw the doctor, a young doctor. He started laughing. He say, 'How old are you?' I was 38 or 39 or something. He said, 'You know why that blood is coming out of there? Because you don't have any cum in there. You're probably having sex two or three times a day. You've got to slow down. If you keep this up, this thing won't get hard. It will be on your mind, but nothing will happen down there.'

"He said I had fucked out. He gave me some medicine and said, 'You can't have intercourse for about six months.' He gave me some medicine and a prescription for some blue or purple shit I was supposed to put my dick in every morning. I must have went for 'bout three and a half months without fucking, 'cause my dick was hard as a motherfucker and I know I was well. Ain't nothing happen to me no more. I was just running and running, you know, and it was God's way of slowing me down and saving me.

"See, God has kept me here for something. Ninety percent of my wine-drinking buddies are dead. People are still amazed at the life I've lived, that I look like I look and act like I act. And I'm not a bit more amazed than the man in the moon. It's because God has something for me to do. I talk to him a lot.

"I say, 'Well, Lord, you know I got to go speak at this Georgetown University banquet and it's one of the greatest banquets of all time. They've had such great people there as Al McGuire, Frank Herzog, George Michaels. First of all, Lord, I want to thank you for putting me in a position to be offered this type of job. Now I just want you to carry me on through it tonight, Lord, and make me good as you always do. Don't let me say the wrong things, and Lord, will you make me funny?'

"At that event, I really laid 'em out."

CHAPTER 29

Stationed With The Gospel

PETEY ALWAYS FELT A'nt Pig's hand in the sea changes of his life. The switch from WOL, a secular station, to WYCB and WUST, gospel stations counted among those times. Joining stations where religion permeated the staff and audience moved Petey closer and closer to his own reunion with God.

His first three months at WYCB presented a test for the station's general manager, Herbert Sanders. Staff and some listeners complained vocally and through letters, even threatening to shut the station down because Petey hosted an evening show.

"Look at these letters," Sanders said, sitting in his small office, holding a stack of mail out to Petey, taking off his reading glasses, rubbing his hand over tired eyes. "But I want you to stay."

Of that trying time, Petey would later reflect, "At no time did I feel threatened. I know Mr. Sanders believed in me. At no time did I feel like turning back. The whole time they was abusing me, I never even thought about running, never thought about telling them to take me off. I just laid right there with 'em, and I saw the whole transition."

The transition meant winning people over one by one, two by two, congregation by congregation, to the point of reaching the station's highest rating within a year of being there. He did it by talking, innovation, and by baring his soul. He established a sort of club, called the Twilight Family, for the elders who listened to his evening show that began with the theme song, "I Got a Feeling, Everything Is Gone Be All Right." And he developed a loyal following for his philosophical monologue on current events—or whatever hit his mind—wrapped up in 60-second commentaries and short interviews on a five-minute spot called The Second Cup of Coffee that aired every morning.

He even got the station to agree to a beer commercial, bringing much-needed revenue to the small business. "Why is it that you on a gospel station with a beer commercial," an irate caller asked one night. "Uh, where you live," Petey asked. Hearing the name of the apartment complex, Petey continued down his pre-planned path. "Do they let you live rent free?"

"No, I pay rent . . ."

"We don't get this station free either. We got bills. It's only a commercial. If you don't drink it, then don't drink it now. And I want you to know that all my Twilight Family out there know I don't drink it," Petey said, before moving to the next call.

When the beer company official complimented him on his professional handling of the calls, Petey told them he did it for the station, and for the older people. "It's a lot of old people setting in homes isolated that ain't got nothing but a radio, and they waits for the Twilight Time to hear Petey Greene, because they saying to theyself that he's just like my son. I tell old people as they set and listen to me, 'Jesus gone make everything all right.' So, I'm doing this for them."

But when he told Sanders he was thinking of bringing a Johnny Walker Red commercial on, Sanders slowly shook his head, telling Petey, "You're going crazy."

Many listeners followed Petey from WOL, turning their radios to WYCB from 7 p.m. to 9 p.m. and in the mornings to hear his Second Cup of Coffee advice. It didn't matter to them whether Petey was on WOL, WYCB, WUST, or on television, they relished the chance to listen to his outrageous assessment of current events.

Once he started working at WYCB and moving closer to the day he would be baptized, Petey established an enviable routine for successful living.

"I get up at 5:30 in the morning, I pray, and I read the paper and eat. I get to my office at 9 a.m., at 2929 Martin Luther King Avenue, and I'm dealing with problems all day long," he explained.

At this time in the early 1980s, Petey worked at one of UPO's satellite centers, "helping senior citizens, helping little children, taking people on tours, getting people clothes, and trying to show people about housing."

Throughout his professional life at the United Planning Organization, he remained engaged with helping people get jobs, get day care, get their lives together. Only Petey Greene could inspire people with insults like, "Stop eating them donuts and get some job training." He would say he could talk to "the little people" in their language because he was one of them.

At about 6 o'clock on Fridays, Petey would arrive at the radio station to cut a week's worth of monologues for The Second Cup of Coffee. But if anything hot came up in the interim, he'd pull the plug and record a new one.

"Sometimes my Second Cup of Coffee is humorous. I did one last week about Nursery Rhymes. I got a lot of babies listening to me and they don't never get no groove out of nothing. So, let me talk with my Second Cup of Milk, I said. And Mr. Sanders gives me this type of flexibility, because he says I'm a creative person," Petey explained.

On Tuesdays from noon to 1, Petey taped his radio show for Thursday evening, because Thursday night, he went on television with "Petey Greene's Washington," which was growing in popularity and catching the attention of Bob Johnson of Black Entertainment Television. By the time of his death, Petey was seen across the nation on BET.

"Both of my shows, television and radio, is an asset to my job. I'm a community worker. I give out all kinds of information about UPO programs on my radio show and t.v. show. God, again, put me in a position where all three of my jobs are in conjunction," Petey said, in 1982, talking about the high points of his life.

"I can pick up the phone and say, 'I need 10 turkeys right now,' or 'I need a ham' and business people I know will get it to me for the poor people we service through UPO. Or I'll tell Melvin, who owns Melvin's Crab House, 'I need five bushels of crabs,' or

Morgan at Morgan's Seafood. And this is because of the radio and television."

Petey's connections to the restaurateurs resulted in a commercial spot for one of the elderly women in his Twilight Family. One night after Petey ran the Melvin's Crab House commercial, Mama Barnes called in. "Petey, as I set here listening to you, guess where I been? I been over to Melvin's to get some of them crabs. They ain't steaming hot, jumping out the pot, but they steaming hot, jumping out the bag. These crabs is good!"

The next day, Melvin called Petey. "Petey, get me Mama Barnes's number and tell her I got a $150 check for her. She got to sign on the dotted line. I'm gone use that as a commercial! I taped what she said last night."

"She's 80-some years old, and loves it every time they play her commercial in the summer," Petey said, genuinely happy to have brightened the life of one of his elderly listeners. He also felt blessed to be able to assist the poor through his job at UPO; however, the frustration of intractable problems sometimes got him down.

"At UPO, we have a food bank and a clothes bank. When it comes to generating proposal money and grant money, that has become increasingly scarce, but that's not my job. I'm an organizer. My pet peeve this year has been people not being registered voters. And I gives myself two or three hours a week on that, on radio and television.

"But what's the use of registering when we have an inefficient voter registration board, breaking down the machines, bringing a new man in. So you see, sweetheart, I'm caught between a rock and a hard place. I'm concerned, I'm dedicated, but I will never ever take a leadership role because that's nowhere I can take my people . . . but to God, and I'm not a minister.

"I tell people a lot of you cause that stuff to happen to yourself. You set around eating donuts, watching soap operas, and won't go register. I don't just get on the establishment and don't get on the people in the low income community, too.

"They keep worrying about me and how good I'm doing, but I tell 'em, 'You know where I come from and y'all know how I came up, and if I was to sit back and just let a nigguh with an education make me think that I was inferior, then I woulda been still where I was at.'

"People think I got a hangup about people with education. I ain't got no hangup. I just want educated nigguhs to know that half of y'all ain't doing as good as me. That's all my thing is, you understand?"

Petey drove that point home often with humor. When people he considered to be snooty criticized his manner of speaking or a topic he chose for television, he would retort, "If you don't like it, get your own t.v. show."

Less than a year before he learned of the cancer that would take his life, Petey spoofed health food on his television show. His invited guest, a noted cook, stood in front of about 10 pans of soul food—chit'lins, ham hocks, ham, pigs' feet, black-eyed peas, collard greens, mashed potatoes, sweet potatoes, potato salad, string beans, fried chicken, corn bread.

Before strolling with the microphone over to the display to proclaim each dish more succulent than the one before, Petey talked off the top of his head about hoity-toity rich people who claimed to be into eating healthy foods but still indulged in habits such as snorting cocaine at parties.

Then he shocked one of his old friends who'd been invited to sit in the audience by calling him to come on stage, and flabbergasted his biographer when he pulled her up, too.

"I want all y'all sitting out there to look at this man. You eat po'k, don't you?" Petey's friend, speechless with amazement, nodded and smiled. "You darn right, you eat po'k. This man eats po'k morning, noon and night. Been eating po'k all his life. His wife makes him a po'k sammich for lunch every day, with the grease just running all down. He carrying a lot of weight, too.

"Now, I want y'all to look at this little lady standing here. She don't eat no po'k. She just eat sprouts and cottage cheese and all that health food stuff. I told her boyfriend, 'man, don't never hit her. If you hit her, you'll break her half into.'

"Y'all stand here beside each other," he instructed. Pointing to his friend first, then to his biographer, he concluded through a wide-mouthed grin, "This is po'k and this is a joke!"

While the guests roared, the po'k and the joke took their seats, knowing Petey's intent was to make people laugh, not to hurt anyone's feelings. While the credits rolled and the audience mounted the set's stage to enjoy a hearty meal, Petey told his biographer, "I know the mackacuckielackies will be calling the station saying, 'How can you let this man have that food up there, licking his fingers, acting like a nigger? But I don't care. They gonna keep watching me to see what I'm gone do next."

Chapter 30

The Commencement Address

PETEY OFTEN FELT that formally educated people considered themselves smarter than he, and in fact, thought of him as ignorant. Nothing rankled him more. And nothing pleased him more than having transcended his meager beginnings, being recognized or awarded above the "mackacuckalackies" with their various degrees and their monied backgrounds.

He glowed with pride when recounting his successes for his memoirs.

"I spoke at Harvard. Here's a nigger with a 8th grade education speaking at Harvard. They fly me all 'round the country to speak. I just get in my hotel and laugh and say, 'Thank you, Jesus, because I know he made this possible. And when I step out to go to speak, I be so clean. I just put all kinds of clothes on because I'm the one that had cardboard in his shoes.

"My grandmother made me wear some girl shoes to school one time, and I was the leader of the gang. I said, 'Grandma, them is girl's shoes.' She say, 'They anybody's shoes that wear 'em, boy. Just put 'em on and go on to school.' They had big ol' buckles on 'em, like Little Abner's mother used to wear.

"When my friends came in class, they said, 'Why you wasn't out on the basketball court this morning?' I got my shoes up under my desk. Finally one of my buddies saw them shoes. 'Oh my God! Dance ballerina, dance.' I said, 'I'll kill you.' The teacher said, 'What's wrong back there?' I said, 'He talking 'bout my shoes.' Then everybody got to looking.

"I know my grandmother didn't make me wear those shoes because she thought my friends would make fun of me. She wanted me to get a proper education. That was all she had at the time."

Petey could hardly believe the twist of fate when he was invited to deliver the keynote address at the DAR Constitution Hall to the graduating class of suburban Maryland's Walt Whitman High School on June 7, 1982. Whitman's student body president, John Bourgeois, loved Petey's radio and t.v. talk shows, and submitted his name as featured speaker for the predominantly white graduating class.

In the face of criticism from parents, teachers and faculty, the students banded together, gathered petitions and overwhelmingly elected to have Petey as their speaker. The adults relented, under an agreement that Maryland Congressman Mike Barnes would share the stage, speaking first.

For Petey, the engagement was the ultimate chance to prove himself more than equal to the typical commencement-day guest of honor. And he delighted in the fact that Mike Barnes would be there. Mike, too, knew Petey and liked his show.

True to himself, Petey delivered a speech full of homespun wisdom, raucous humor, and classic rhymes. He approached the podium with an icebreaker, tacitly acknowledging the controversy surrounding his invitation: "I know you're nervous because you don't know what I'm gone say. And I'm nervous because I ain't never spoke in front of this many white people." After the anticipated laughter, he added, " . . . so y'all might as well relax, 'cause I'm gone be all right."

He told the students of his childhood memory of the Daughters of the American Revolution barring singer Marian Anderson from performing at Constitution Hall. He went on to explain that with the blessing of First Lady Eleanor Roosevelt, Ms. Anderson sang before a crowd of 75,000 people on the grounds of the Lincoln Memorial. The next week, Mrs. Roosevelt canceled her membership in the DAR.

"I ain't no ignorant nigger; I know my history," he declared, before delivering the meat of his remarks, which encouraged the students to "get a game plan," stay away from white collar crime ("Don't take short money."), lead with compassion, and stick to their areas of expertise.

In explaining that his own area of expertise involved verbal skills, Petey elicited another rousing applause and sustained laughter when he rattled off the intro he used for his three-card game hustle during his Army days and young adult life:

> "This is the game from Newport News,
> the red you win, the black you lose.
> It's a mile and a quarter from the Mexican border
> when three broads got to scuffling over a dollar and a
>   quarter.
> The first one looked up and the second one said,
> you lose with the black but you win with the red.
> Your pick sir."

In an eerily prescient moment tinged with both sadness and optimism about his future, he told the audience, "I been out in the street now 17 years. I came out in 1965. I'm a member of DON'T, Efforts for Ex-convicts, and I got another organization called VOTE, Voice of the Ex-offender. I don't think I'm going back.

"I'm 54 years old, and I ain't got too much longer. I've got two beautiful babies, one 13, one 14, and one day, I'm going to be in the audience while them two chumps is gone have on a cap and a gown."

Again, wild applause interrupted Petey's flow. As he moved toward his finale, Petey told the crowd.

"Take this from the bottom of my heart: I'm so glad that you had me. And to the parents and to all of you that don't like me, it don't make no difference; you got to come because the babies wanted me."

As soon as the laughter, applause, and cheers ended, Petey lobbed his final off-the-cuff rhyme that caused the room to erupt.

"As I stand before you this evening, on the stage of Constitution Hall, I really enjoyed rapping to you, and I done had myself a

ball. Now the most important thing that I want to tell you, may
you jump and shout, one day you gone be in the field somewhere,
and you gone hang a shingle out. Now you might be a
Huckleberry Finn reader or call you Tom Sawyer; maybe you're a
doctor, physician, or some of you gone be a lawyer. Sometime
you'll jump around and sometimes you'll think it's sweet; even
with your education, try to get something from the street. When
you put it all together, whether you go near or far, I owe all this
speaking tonight to my main man, John Bourgeois. Thank you."

Petey returned to his chair but the students still stood cheering,
whistling, whooping and hollering. The moderator called out,
"Settle down for the benediction," and several minutes later, order
returned to the room. Quietly, students congratulated each other
for selecting one of the most memorable graduation speakers of
all time.

CHAPTER 31

A Working Philosophy

LONG BEFORE PETEY received his invitation to address Walt Whitman's graduating class, he had determined that his two favorite groups of people were kids and old folks. He treated the old folks as if they could be a substitute for his grandmother, and the world's children as if they could fill the chasm left by his own. He filled several tapes with advice he'd like to leave for children, much of it based on the way his grandmother reared him.

Petey's voice: Money Talks

"I would never ever tell young people that material things don't mean nothing. And I would never ever tell young people they got to pay some dues. I will tell them to get a education. If you are a dumb motherfucker and can't think and are not concerned about school, then come out. Quick. If you ain't got school on your mind, get where you think you can be successful. Do whatever it is to be successful.

"But if it's something illegal, be able to understand that there is a price you have to pay, and that price might be your life. It might be a long-time incarceration, or whatever. But if that's what you want to do, and you think you can handle it, then go 'head and do it. I'm not gone say, 'See, I got to be a star on this television because I paid dues, or on the radio because I paid dues.' Fuck that bullshit. I ain't paid no goddamn dues.

"Somebody might say, 'Well all the time you was drunk, you was paying dues.' I was drunk because I was a drunk-ass motherfucker. Or 'All the time you was in jail, you was paying dues.' Paying my ass. I was serving time for a crime that I committed. That dues-paying shit ain't about a goddamn thing.

"It gets on my nerves to hear people always telling children you got to pay some dues. I'm serious about that. If you gonna guide young people, and I'm speaking personal, let young people understand that you can achieve things, you can accomplish things, and education is a good thing for you to have. But you have also got to understand that you got to have some cash.

"Because it's people out here with three degrees and can't pay the check. But there's another cat can't read and write and he own the club where the check is, 'cause he got money. I also believe to tell a youngster, 'Well, boy, if you just gone have to have that, you better try to get yourself 6 or 7 dollars and put it in lay-away, and then try to scuffle and get that motherfucker out.

"Don't tell a kid he can't have no $90 shoes. You want a pair of $90 shoes? Okay, how much you got? 'I got 8 dollars.' Put 'em in the will-call and scuffle and get 'em. Now if you don't get that money, you gone lose them shoes. Try to serve yourself some papers and try to wash some windows and try to do something.

"How you gone tell him those shoes don't mean nothing when every time he look up in the window, there is something sitting in the store?

"And I don't tell children I had it hard as a child. I was a happy child. I was just a poor child with a million other poor children. We went all down the creek, we rode stick horses, and once we found a dead baby in the woods.

"I knew some other children had more money than me. Sometimes one of 'em would take me in his house and say, 'Mother, can me and Petey have some cookies?' 'Yes,' and I get a glass of milk and he get a glass of milk and his mother put some cookies on the table and we eat them motherfuckers. I know when I be eating them cookies, this is a rich motherfucker here 'cause when we go by my house, you ain't getting no cookies or no milk either. I wish I would take somebody in asking for something! You might not even get a drink of water.

"I could say, 'Calvin wants some water,' and my grandmother wouldn't even look up. 'Well, let Calvin go back home and get the water 'cause I'm doing something.'

"But I know that one day I'm going to be a senior citizen and I want to smile, if I'm fortunate enough to get a rocking chair, to have good memories. I'm not going to just eradicate all my good memories to try to sell a story to some people and tell them I was a poor motherfucker. I wants to remember how I burnt that tree down. George Washington cut one down, they made him the president of the United States. I burned one down, they put me in jail.

"And then there were things like May Day exercises, when I had to do minuets in school. I remember, with my little white clothes on, 'toe, toe, toe and step. And bend and face your partner and bow.' Those were good years. Marching in the school boy patrol parade, and seeing my grandmother on the side and people saying, 'There go Petey Greene.' And to come back here in the parade with the 3rd Armored Regiment Calvary, riding the jeep down Pennsylvania Avenue to Arlington Cemetery, getting ready to bury General Blackjack Pershing. I was in the honor guard, and people saying, 'Petey Greene!'

"So, I ain't going to eradicate all my life to just keep talking about dope and all the bad things. I was a dope fiend. I was a winehead. I slept in trucks and alleys. I messed with people. But I also had good times."

CHAPTER 32

Baptism

PETEY STOPPED DRINKING in 1979 and began to attend church regularly. Two years later, he received an invitation to sit with dignitaries for the installation of the Royal Guards for the United House of Prayer. The United House of Prayer's spiritual leader, Bishop "Sweet Daddy" McCullough reigned as one of the most important bishops in the country.

VIPs attending the service at 601 M Street included then police chief Bertell Jefferson, community leaders Frank Hollis and Pat Shannon, and city councilmembers John Ray and Betty Anne Kane. Bishop McCullough, tall with long hair, presided from a high throne as dignitaries came to the foot of the altar to pay respects and make brief remarks.

After the city officials each spoke, Bishop McCullough raised one hand and in his mellifluous voice, intoned, "Somebody else in here has something to say. I can just feel that somebody else in here wants to talk. If he wants to say something, I want him to stand up and say it."

Never one to fear center stage, Petey stood.

Bishop McCullough's wise face beamed. "Brother Greene, I figured it was you. I catch your show when I'm in town. Come on and say what you got to say."

Petey, delighted to have the eye of such a powerful religious leader whose returns to his D.C. base were rare, talked about how God was moving in his life; how glad he was to be there. He mentioned that he'd been in the church on many occasions to buy food in the basement, but was in the sanctuary for the first time."

At the end of Petey's remarks, Bishop McCullough surprised everyone. "Brother Greene, this is June. In August, I'm going to install a new Paradise and I'm putting a brand new pool in it, and I'm saying this before my congregation that I'd like for you to be the first person that I baptize in August. Would you accept the offer?"

Without missing a beat, Petey answered, "Yes sir," and was immediately surrounded by the faithful, embracing, encouraging, and congratulating him on his decision.

But for all his sure-footedness that day, over the next three months, Petey had many doubt-filled days. He was thinking, "I want to pick up my stuff and run, 'cause my grandmother always told me, 'You don't play with the Lord.' This is very serious."

As fear circled his heart, Petey headed toward the baptismal pool with a group of people, at the front of the line. Parishioners known as "saints" stood nearby in white robes, watching Bishop McCullough walk toward his appointed spot, preparing to receive the sinners.

Wondering if he could feign illness, Petey's face held none of its usual mirth. Just as he had worked his nerves to the point of really getting sick, Petey saw one of the church elders coming toward him. Sensing Petey's conflict, Elder Abertha grabbed Petey by the shoulders, whispering close to Petey's right ear.

"I know just how you feel, son. I felt like that myself years ago. But don't worry 'bout it. That ain't nothing but the devil."

Awestruck over the elder's ability to read his soul's anguish, Petey stood rooted. The elder continued, "Stand fast, Brother Greene, stand fast. I'll be right here with you. Don't even think about doing anything different. That's the devil working in your life."

Fortified, Petey began his slow path toward the water, a journey that had been publicized for weeks. People from all walks of life attended this service, just to see Petey baptized. Petey later described his fans who came as "narcotic dealers, bank robbers, priests, preachers, co-workers, and six or seven women I was messing with at the time," sitting, standing, leaning over the balcony to witness Petey's transformation.

He wore white pants, a white shirt and white shoes. Bishop McCullough beamed, reached out for Petey and embraced him. "Son, you don't know what this means. I'm just so happy for you."

Right then, Petey would recall, "Something just run through me, and he just picked me up and took me under the water. He was standing in the water when I walked down, and when he brought me up, I just felt good. I felt good. I just wanted to shout. It was a different kind of feeling.

"When I got out of the water, my friends had a towel waiting for me. I asked them to let me kneel and pray, and thank Jesus. Thank Jesus for bringing a dope fiend nothing bum who people said would never live to get 21, who had a good grandmother who raised him. And somewhere in that room she was watching me, and she had tears in her eyes, 'cause she was looking down on me, and here was her Petey Greene.

"I said, 'Thank you, Jesus. Thank you, Jesus. Hallelujah.

"One lady said when they put me under the water, steam came out of the water. She said all the devil was just coming out. She said, 'Boy, you ain't never seen so much smoke come out of that water!' It was her way of saying, 'You look like a different man.'

"And then when I went to working for the Lord, he stopped me from staggering and stumbling and started me to strutting. You know, when you strut, you shake your shoulders and you smile. When you staggering and stumbling, you're falling and you're vomiting. It's different when you're strutting. I struts now. He took the frown from my face and gave me a smile. It's so easy to smile, and when you smile and you're strutting at the same time, that's gonna start you to singing. When you start singing, you begin to know that you're moving spiritually.

"God can do anything. God can change your life."

Epilogue

The Grand Finale

Petey's voice: Consequences

"I don't believe I've got a stomach. I don't think I've got no liver. I don't think I got nothing. I'm probably not healthy. But God has really taken good care of me, because I didn't use no chasers. I didn't have no cut card, when it come to drinking liquor. I just drank it all.

"Liquor takes over your brain, and you a abnormal motherfucker, but you just feel good. All in your dick, everywhere. I just dug liquor. Acting crazy, drunk, I probably made lasting enemies until I took this life that I have now, 'til I turned my life around to become a Christian."

*　　*　　*

Petey was right. His organs indeed suffered from the years of abuse, and they finally gave in to a rapid and virulent cancer that took his life in 1984, on a Tuesday in early January, the month he would have turned 53 on the 23rd. Ever since he boosted his age to enter the Army, he had claimed to be two or three years older; so, many people were surprised by news accounts of his age at death.

As for enemies, if they existed, they were patently outnumbered by the people who loved and respected Petey, who flooded Union Wesley AME Church on Sunday, January 15, and lined up in the snow for blocks and blocks outside his funeral service. The rich and famous, the poor and unknown, the young, the old, black, white, powerful and powerless all mourned the loss of a man who dedicated his life to uplifting "the little people" he bonded with and loved.

Two thousand mourners packed the church on that frigid January afternoon, five days after his death, to say farewell. Outside, thousands more stood quietly with their own memories and broken hearts. For the wake the night before, police estimated that as many as 20,000 people lined up, waiting their turns to file into the church between 3 p.m. and midnight, despite the below-freezing temperatures.

Earl Byrd, then a reporter for The Washington Times, covered the wake and funeral. He quoted the wife of Ken Hardy, former head of the DC Department of Corrections, as she talked about the sheer number of people who turned out for Petey's final tribute.

"I haven't seen anything like this since President Kennedy's funeral," Mrs. Hardy told Earl.

Petey's childhood friend and then Congressman Walter Fauntroy spoke at the funeral and also was quoted in Earl Byrd's article. "If Martin Luther King was a dreamer of impossible dreams, Petey Greene was the epitome of a dream becoming a living reality. He rose from a prison cell to become the champion of the last, the lost and the little people."

City Councilwoman Charlene Drew Jarvis confirmed Petey's lifelong habit of jabbing at people who might hold themselves above others when she took her turn among the eulogizers. "With no training, he had his own TV show, won two Emmys, and stayed irreverent. He verbally removed the layers of pretension and hypocrisy of the middle-class, upwardly mobile blacks. He ridiculed us and challenged us. To say he loved Washington is an understatement. To say that Washington loved him is evident."

As the voices of children in Petey's WUST Radio ABC Family rang out, "Lift Every Voice and Sing," it seemed as though I could hear Petey talking to me.

"Rackley, why you crying? I see ol' Clayton sitting there crying, too. I'm glad I introduced y'all. Clayton can give you all the pictures for the book. Why you crying? Don't you know I'm at peace? My body was wore out, baby, and soon as I left it, don't you know A'nt Pig put her arms out to me.

"She's right here, looking at everybody, telling me, 'Rabbit, I knew you was gone be famous. Knew your mouth was gone get you kilt or get you rich, 'cause you was the talkingest boy I ever seen.' We just talking and laughing. I can't believe how many people out there in the cold! Boy! Tell me I'm not the greatest nigguh ever born and died in D.C.! Them hustlers and them politicians and everybody coming up in them limos and Jaguars and Cadillacs and Mercedes. All for Petey Greene.

"Well, Rackley, I'll miss my magpies, but I know they know I love 'em, throughout eternity, like A'nt Pig love me. And you write my story, baby. You tell everybody the lessons An't Pig taught me. And stop crying. I don't want to make nobody cry. I just want to make people laugh."

A procession of hundreds of cars followed the hearse carrying Petey's body to Lincoln Memorial Cemetery. The previous day's paper rested on the seat beside the hearse's driver, folded to Washington Post columnist Dorothy Gilliam's lengthy tribute, which read in part:

"In this capital city, Official Washington with its power and headlines overwhelms the Other Washington—that 70 percent black city of neighborhoods, traditions, struggling families, kids, and a touch of the seamy side. Petey Greene . . . reminded us constantly that the Other Washington was just as important . . . . They'll bury a bit of the Other Washington's heart and soul with Petey."

*   *   *

I miss Petey deeply and I look for his advice in my dreams. But I am blessed to have known him. Finally, I have no fear of reaching the beyond, because I have finished this book. If I hadn't finished it, I feel sure he would have accosted me the way he always did when I didn't understand one of his references or a point he was trying to make. He'd tease: "What college you say you went to, Rackley? Clark? Is that a black school? Oh, well, that explains it."

Over the years, I've imagined time and again what Petey would say about current events, what irreverent way he would spin the news about presidents and mayors, about illnesses and wars. He's not here to comment, but from reading "Laugh If You Like . . . ," we can pretty much figure how he'd "go off on these mackacuckalackies." We know it would be hilarious, and he'd sign off with his signature rhyme:

"I'll tell it to the hot, I'll tell it to the cold, I'll tell it to the young, I'll tell it to the old, I don't want no laughin', I don't want no cryin', and most of all, no signifyin'. Acht! This is Petey Greene's Washington."

Printed in the United States
84095LV00002B/151/A

9 781413 432886